About Island Press

Since 1984, the nonprofit organization Island Press has been stimulating, shaping, and communicating ideas that are essential for solving environmental problems worldwide. With more than 1,000 titles in print and some 30 new releases each year, we are the nation's leading publisher on environmental issues. We identify innovative thinkers and emerging trends in the environmental field. We work with world-renowned experts and authors to develop cross-disciplinary solutions to environmental challenges.

Island Press designs and executes educational campaigns, in conjunction with our authors, to communicate their critical messages in print, in person, and online using the latest technologies, innovative programs, and the media. Our goal is to reach targeted audiences—scientists, policy makers, environmental advocates, urban planners, the media, and concerned citizens—with information that can be used to create the framework for long-term ecological health and human well-being.

Island Press gratefully acknowledges major support from The Bobolink Foundation, Caldera Foundation, The Curtis and Edith Munson Foundation, The Forrest C. and Frances H. Lattner Foundation, The JPB Foundation, The Kresge Foundation, The Summit Charitable Foundation, Inc., and many other generous organizations and individuals.

The opinions expressed in this book are those of the author(s) and do not necessarily reflect the views of our supporters.

Rewilding Agricultural Landscapes

Rewilding Agricultural Landscapes

A California Study in Rebalancing the Needs of People and Nature

Edited by
H. Scott Butterfield, T. Rodd Kelsey,
and Abigail K. Hart

ISLANDPRESS | Washington | Covelo

Library of Congress Control Number: 2020942999

All Island Press books are printed on environmentally responsible materials.

Manufactured in the United States of America
10 9 8 7 6 5 4 3 2 1

Keywords: Island Press, habitat restoration, San Joaquin Valley, San Joaquin Desert, drylands, agricultural sustainability, water scarcity, rewilding, deserts, farmland retirement, fallowing, people and nature, Sustainable Groundwater Management Act, groundwater sustainability, water for nature, water for agriculture, endangered species recovery, diversified agriculture, multibenefit land use planning

Contents

Acknowledgments

The editors of this book thank the California chapter of The Nature Conservancy for its generous support of this work. We thank Scott Morrison, Sandi Matsumoto, and Dick Cameron for early discussions about this vision for rewilding the San Joaquin Valley. We thank all the authors of the individual chapters of this book and many others who contributed foundational science and policy pieces that we used in the development of this book.

The authors of chapter 3 are grateful to Brian Cypher for helping frame the chapter, contributing to early drafts, and reviewing all iterations; to the members of the Land Retirement Team for their leadership on the project, particularly Bea Olsen of the U.S. Fish and Wildlife Service and Stephen Lee of the U.S. Bureau of Reclamation; and to the many individuals in the U.S. Bureau of Land Management, the California State University–Stanislaus Endangered Species Recovery Program, and the farming community who performed the arduous tasks that made the Land Retirement Demonstration Project a reality.

The authors of chapter 4 thank Piper Bean for her illustration and Alyssa Semerdjian, Abigail Rutrough, and Ivy Widick for sharing data and thoughts about modeling kangaroo rat distributions.

Chris Lortie, the lead author of chapter 5, was funded by a Natural Sciences and Engineering Research Council of Canada Discovery Grant.

The authors of chapter 7 thank Landon Peppel for information on elk reintroductions, and thank D. Clendenen and Melissa Dabulamanzi for providing photographs.

The authors of chapter 9 thank the California chapter of The Nature Conservancy for the Science Catalyst Fund grant that made that analysis and work possible.

The authors of chapter 11 thank Nathaniel Seavy and the other co-authors of *Water and the Future of the San Joaquin Valley* (Hanak et al., 2019), which lays the foundation for this chapter.

The author of chapter 12 thanks Samantha Arthur for agreeing to be interviewed and providing notes from Audubon's experience in developing the tricolored blackbird Voluntary Local Program, as well as Anna Schiller and Ann Hayden for their insight and helpful notes on the Regional Conservation Investment Strategy being developed in the Kaweah Subbasin.

The author of chapter 13, thanks Andrew Plantinga, Eric Edwards, Henry McCann, Ellen Hanak, Ryan Abman, and this volume's editors for helpful exchanges that improved the chapter. All remaining errors are his own.

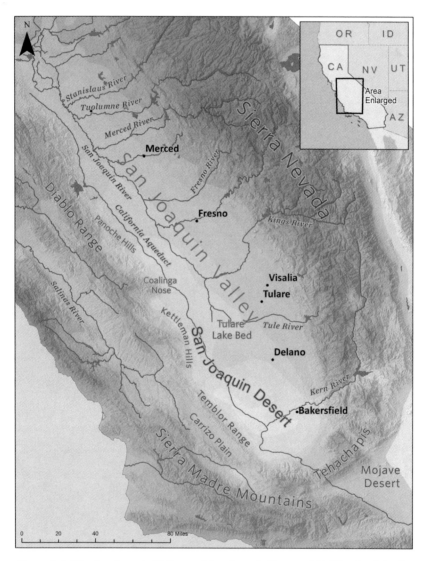

Figure 0-1. The San Joaquin Valley and San Joaquin Desert of California. (Map by Connor Shank)

Chapter 1

Opportunity Knocks: Water Scarcity and the Potential for Rewilding Agricultural Landscapes in Desert and Dryland Ecosystems Globally

T. Rodd Kelsey, H. Scott Butterfield, and Abigail K. Hart

Two hundred years ago, if you were walking across the Carrizo Plain of California in the spring of a very good rain year, you would have witnessed a vast, isolated valley beaming with a rainbow kaleidoscope of desert wildflowers (Mayfield 1993). Desert shrubs including saltbush and ephedra dotted the hills and lined the edges of the mirror-like Soda Lake (see chapter 2). You would have heard the buzzing of hundreds of species of native bees and may have also glimpsed herds of tule elk or pronghorn antelope bounding across the open plain. Along the way, you would probably stumble on the open burrow of a giant kangaroo rat in the midst of an island of similar burrows that make up the precincts they create as communities (see chapter 4). Living among these precincts and benefiting from the kangaroo rats' engineering of the landscape would have been blunt-nosed leopard lizards and burrowing owls, both keeping their eyes out for abundant insect prey on which they could pounce. It was a wild place where it would not have been unheard of to see a grizzly wander through.

By the 1970s, as you drove across the Carrizo Plain you would have been hard pressed to find a single pronghorn. It would take more effort to find a kangaroo rat precinct, lizard, or owl. And by that time grizzlies were long gone. Rapid expansion of agriculture—mostly cattle ranching at first after World War II, then transitioning into dry farmed wheat and, ultimately, back to cattle ranching—had transformed the landscape. The Carrizo Plain was dominated by crops and weedy nonnative grasses.

Leap ahead another thirty years and you would once again have a good chance of watching pronghorn sprint across seas of native wildflowers (figure 1-1). Kangaroo rats are again abundant enough that we can see their precincts from space. Although agriculture remains and there has been expansion of solar farms to the north, the Carrizo Plain itself is now once again fairly wild and even has been referred to as California's Serengeti.

What happened? Local landowners recognized that this was a tough landscape for agriculture because the average annual precipitation is less than 10 inches. Indeed, Carrizo Plain and much of the western side of the San Joaquin Valley are in a true desert climate, now recognized as the San Joaquin Desert (Germano et al. 2011). And now, climate change projections predict that the entire San Joaquin Valley will be in a desert climate within the next fifty years. Without adequate annual rainfall and little surface water naturally available, irrigated agriculture at an industrial scale has never been sustainable. This fact set the stage for more than thirty years of land protection in the Carrizo that has resulted in more than 300,000 acres of land permanently protected for conservation and managed collaboratively as the Carrizo Plain National Monument (by the U.S. Bureau of Land Management [BLM]) and Carrizo Plain Ecological Reserve (by the California Department of Fish and Wildlife [CDFW]). Starting in the 1980s The Nature Conservancy, BLM, CDFW, and others identified this landscape as unique, not just in California but in the world. A movement was begun to protect it from further development and

Figure 1-1. The Carrizo Plain National Monument, looking down on Soda Lake from Temblor Mountains. (Photo by Sue Pollock)

to restore large parts of this landscape to its former self, a collection of annual forblands, alkali sink scrub, saltbush scrub, and San Joaquin desert scrub (see chapter 2).

The first purchase was the Oppenheimer property, an 82,000-acre ranch, in 1988. This was the foundation on which land managers from The Nature Conservancy, BLM, and CDFW began removing large tracts of dry farmed wheat and restoring them to natural vegetation so that giant kangaroo rats, blunt-nosed leopard lizards, and many other endemic plant and animal species of the Carrizo Plain could reclaim the area. This restoration of the Carrizo Plain has not only helped restore native communities and begun rebuilding populations of imperiled San Joaquin Desert endemic species, it has also created recreational opportunities for people who now flock to the super blooms that occur every few years and hike, bike, and drive through the region. In forty short years we have witnessed the rewilding of the Carrizo Plain.

Rewilding

Rewilding is a hot topic these days, getting a lot of attention in both the popular press (Monbiot 2014) and scientific community (Fernández et al. 2017). There has even been debate about whether the idea is a good one, ecologically and financially speaking (Rubenstein and Rubenstein 2016). It can mean different things to different people. The term *rewilding* was originally coined by Soulé and Noss in the 1990s to raise awareness of the value in restoring large areas of wilderness and reintroducing top predators as critical regulators of whole ecosystems (Soulé and Noss 1998). More recently, it has been expanded to include such ideas as introducing nonnative top predators and large herbivores (megafauna) based on their potential to act as top-down engineers of whole ecosystems where the native megafauna are long gone (Cromsigt et al. 2018). There is certainly evidence that "ecosystem engineers" can play an important role in creating and maintaining diversity and ecosystem function, a topic we examine more closely for the San Joaquin Valley in chapter 4. For example, wolves are credited with a significant transformation of the Yellowstone ecosystem by moderating the population size and behavior of elk, which trickled down to affect riverine forests and the species within. Beavers serve a similar engineering role by holding back and slowing down water, thus maintaining stream-flows and groundwater, purifying water by filtering out sediment and pollutants, supporting large wetland complexes, and shaping the habitat for countless plant and animal species that depend on these wetland systems.

The term *rewilding* is being used more broadly these days to refer to restoring diversity, variability, and function so that ecosystems can once again support the full diversity of species and become self-regulating and resilient to climate change (Perino et al. 2019). Aside from the more dramatic and controversial proposals for rewilding based on reintroducing top predators, we can take advantage of obvious and less controversial opportunities for simply restoring native systems to places where they have been lost (see chapter 3). The idea of restoring intensively farmed landscapes back into natural habitat and wild communities is gaining traction because of ongoing or imminent shifts in land use and water availability (see chapter 11). This is an important opportunity to rewild these highly altered landscapes and, by doing so, to increase their sustainability and improve human well-being of the communities in and around these areas (see chapters 12–14). Already our most picturesque and vibrant agricultural regions are those where there is abundant diversity. Imagine the most attractive agricultural regions of Mediterranean Europe that have been cultivated for thousands of years but still retain native forest along the rivers, wild farm edges, and a diversity of crops, an idea we examine in greater detail for the San Joaquin Valley in chapter 10. Some of these more diverse agricultural systems are the result of deliberate use of traditional agricultural management systems that provide habitat for endangered species, such as the *dehesa* agroforestry system, which supports the Iberian lynx in Spain (Halada et al. 2011). By rewilding intensively farmed landscapes in small and large ways we have the opportunity not only to restore wild species that have been pushed to the brink but also to increase the sustainability of agriculture and create tangible benefits for human well-being.

The "Unwilding" of the San Joaquin Valley

The San Joaquin Valley of California is one of the most remarkable examples of modern agricultural intensification and the challenges this can create. It is also an important emerging opportunity to rebalance food production with other needs and values through rewilding.

Since 1945, more than 2 million acres of native annual forblands, scrubland, wetland, and riverine forest have been converted to highly intensive, irrigated agriculture (figure 1-2). As you travel south along Interstate 5, your primary view will be seemingly endless orchards of almonds and pistachios. Because of its Mediterranean climate and fertile, deep soils, the San Joaquin Valley is

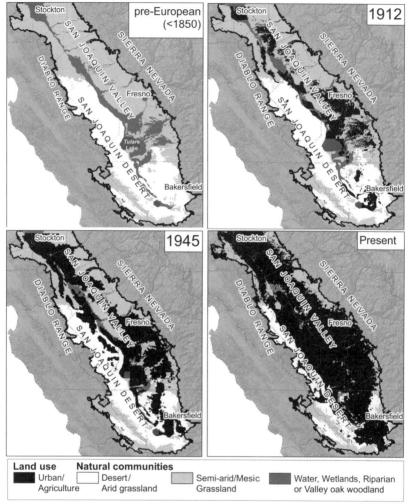

Figure 1-2. Land use change due to agricultural expansion and urbanization in the San Joaquin Valley over the past 150 years. (Map by Scott Phillips)

one of the most productive agricultural regions in the world. The San Joaquin Valley produces more than 80 percent of the world's almond supply and 24 percent of the pistachios. Now, more than 4 million acres in the San Joaquin Valley produce one quarter of the fruits, nuts, and vegetables consumed in the United States along

Figure 1-3. The California Aqueduct, which supplies water to the San Joaquin Valley and Southern California.

with important exports all over the world, supporting an economy of $30 billion per year.

Not surprisingly, such impressive levels of agricultural production have required the use of large quantities of water in what is naturally a water-scarce environment. The valley is characterized by an arid climate with large fluctuations in rainfall across years, typical of deserts. As a result, there is more farmland than local surface water or groundwater supplies can support. Two of the largest surface water infrastructure projects ever built have been developed and managed by state and federal governments in order to provide sufficient water to farm the San Joaquin Valley and also to supply the major urban areas of Southern California. Water is pumped uphill via a network of human-made channels such as the California Aqueduct, paralleling Interstate 5 (figure 1-3), to bring water to the San Joaquin Valley and Los Angeles. However, the large water supply projects have not been adequate, especially in drought years. So San Joaquin Valley agriculture has also relied on intensive groundwater extraction.

Annually, the valley uses about 4.3 trillion gallons of water for all water uses, 89 percent of which goes to growing crops (Hanak et al. 2017). A little over half of this comes from local surface water, including streams and rivers. About one third is imported from the Sacramento Valley watershed through aqueducts and canals. The rest, about 650 billion gallons, is pumped out of underground aquifers each year; this is essentially fossil water by percolation that occurred in much wetter times thousands of years ago. This rate of extraction is now much faster than these aquifers can be replenished through natural percolation of rain and floodwaters. To put this in perspective, only one hundred years ago, real estate developers attracted buyers to new communities in the valley by advertising developments based on the abundance of water. Parts of the valley were known for their abundance of artesian wells, where water was bubbling up out of the ground. Now, average groundwater depths are around 150–200 feet. Since 2014, more than three thousand drinking water wells have gone dry, leaving residents with no water other than what they can buy elsewhere.

Creating an agricultural economy dependent on extracting so much water out of the ground has also caused land subsidence, meaning the land is actually sinking over time. More than 5,100 square miles (3 million acres) of the valley have been affected by subsidence since 1950. Parts of the valley have subsided by more than 20 feet, causing what has been described as the single largest human alteration of the earth's surface. Large-scale intensive agriculture in this arid climate has also resulted in severe air and water quality problems that are contributing to chronic human health problems (Almaraz et al. 2018). More than half a million people in the valley suffer from asthma, many of them children, making life challenging and costing hundreds of millions of dollars in emergency room visits each year.

It is not only people who are suffering. This happens to be a unique region, with several wildlife and plant species that occur nowhere else on Earth. These include the giant kangaroo rat and blunt-nosed leopard lizard, as well as Tipton's kangaroo rat, San Joaquin kit fox, Bakersfield cactus, and San Joaquin woolly-threads. All these species, and more than two dozen others, have become extremely rare through loss of their natural habitat and connectivity between the patches that remain.

The Sustainable Groundwater Management Act and Rebalancing the San Joaquin Valley

These challenges in the San Joaquin Valley are inspiring and forcing local and regional governments, as well as the farmers themselves, to reconsider the fate and future of land use in the valley. The tipping point was California's 2012–2015 drought. As human water demand in the valley has increased, meeting both those needs and those of the environment has become increasingly difficult. This problem has been made worse with severe and prolonged droughts driven by climate change. Farmers have made up for decreased surface water supplies by pumping more groundwater. Over the last couple of decades, groundwater withdrawal has exceeded nature's ability to replenish it from scarce rainfall in this arid climate. The most recent drought resulted in more severe restrictions on surface water use, with many farms not receiving any surface water at all for years. Farmers once again turned to pumping groundwater, this time even more rapidly across large areas of the valley in order to maintain their crops and protect the investments they had made in their farming operations. This need to keep the water flowing was made even more necessary by the dramatic expansion of nut orchards in recent years. This rapid and expansive conversion to perennial crops such as pistachios and almonds has hardened the water needs of the valley because trees cannot go without water during drought years. This has increased dependence on groundwater and during the drought led to an alarming acceleration of land subsidence, with land sinking a foot per year in some areas. Orchard owners without reliable surface water supplies or access to groundwater have relied on buying extremely expensive water on the open market or have simply removed some or all of their trees.

These events were a wakeup call and final straw. They led to the passage of the Sustainable Groundwater Management Act (SGMA) in 2014. SGMA requires valley communities to achieve sustainable use of groundwater by 2040 in order to stabilize groundwater levels, decrease water quality degradation, and halt land subsidence. Implementation of SGMA in California is going to have a profound impact on land use and farming, especially for farmers in the southern San Joaquin Valley, where they are highly dependent on groundwater for irrigation. Groundwater sustainability will not be possible in some parts of the region without permanently taking some lands out of agricultural production (Kelsey et al. 2018; Hanak et al. 2019). Recent estimates suggest that more than 200,000 acres of agricultural land will need to permanently come out of production (Bryant et al. 2020). The key questions now are which lands should come out of production (see chapter 9), what are the best alternative future uses of these lands, and how do we make that transition in a way that creates the best outcome given the challenges the valley and state face (see chapters 11–13). How do we as a society do this in ways that are equitable for farmers and communities who will pay the heaviest price? There are a variety of options (Kelsey et al. 2018). One is expanding sources of renewable energy on former agricultural lands to help the state meet its important goals to reduce greenhouse gas emissions (Pearce et al. 2016; Wu et al. 2019). This transition has already begun, with dozens of solar projects being planned for the valley.

Most transformative, though, is the potential for this crisis to catalyze the rewilding of the San Joaquin Valley in thoughtful, strategic ways that create a new balance between people and nature. We can do this by deliberately using some of the land that will need to come out of agricultural production to restore San Joaquin Desert ecosystems. This also creates an opportunity for the valley to be a world leader, demonstrating how to collaboratively design and reconfigure agricultural landscapes in ways that help protect biodiversity and human well-being.

Doing so will require proactive planning for retiring consolidated areas of the least productive lands and restoring them to natural habitat that can recover biodiversity, ecosystem function, and landscape resilience. Rewilding this landscape by thoughtfully restoring some agricultural lands to natural habitats, including San Joaquin Desert landscapes, can achieve many benefits. By reducing overall water demand in the valley, it will be a key part of making groundwater a renewable resource again. By restoring these lands rather than just letting them lay fallow and weedy or be converted to big box stores and houses, we can revive the unique natural communities in the valley. By having more nature embedded in what will remain a vital agricultural region, residents will reap the benefits of cleaner air and water. Natural spaces will provide recreational opportunities for people with few options for outdoor activities in nature (see chapter 14). Finally, more nature in and around the many remaining farms can provide practical benefits by restoring ecosystem function. This includes increasing natural pollination services for crops and natural pest control by the wild creatures that begin to repopulate the landscape (see chapter 10).

In California, there is growing recognition of this opportunity, and many public and private partners are coming together to formulate a plan for what will be a very different San Joaquin Valley in 2040. It can be a future in which we reap the benefits of rewilding while minimizing the negative impacts to agriculture and local communities. To take advantage of this opportunity in a smart and equitable way, it is essential that we understand the ecological, social, and political challenges so that we can maximize the benefits for nature and people and minimize the costs. Getting the best outcomes for nature and people will not happen automatically. In fact, without careful consideration of where and how to achieve the many benefits (see chapter 9), the outcomes will at best fall short of what is possible. At worst, the results will be harmful to people and nature. Therefore, it is important to learn from the past (see chapters 3 and 5). We also need to bring the best new ideas and science together to have a chance of realizing the kind of transformation witnessed on the Carrizo Plain over the last forty years, where kangaroo rats, pronghorn, kit foxes, and native bees once again flourish. This is not just a technical problem about how to restore these lands effectively. We also need to understand and address the social and economic barriers and opportunities for making this kind of shift equitable and successful.

That is what this book is about: revealing the lessons learned from projects on the ground in the San Joaquin Valley, synthesizing the best available science from around the world that can guide rewilding of this region, and understanding the social and economic opportunities and obstacles to success. In part I, "Lessons Learned from the San Joaquin Valley," regional experts reveal what is understood about how these natural systems work and can recover after restoration of former agricultural lands. They share the hard lessons learned from implementing restoration, as well as what the best available science tells us. In part II, "Principles of Farmland Rewilding from the San Joaquin Valley," leading thinkers on water management and spatial planning provide examples and guidelines for how to plan for strategic restoration of retired agricultural lands across the valley in order to get the best return on that investment. In this section, the authors also lay out how locals, policymakers, and implementers should integrate the restoration we propose with other land use changes that will also be part of the new mosaic that can create a more resilient San Joaquin Valley. In part III, "Socioeconomic and Political Dimensions of Rewilding the San Joaquin Valley," a group of practitioners and economists examine the social, regulatory, and economic implications of such a major land use change. In these chapters, the authors provide decision makers with principles about how to structure and incentivize the change so that restoration can be a socially and economically viable part of the solutions. Part IV, "A Rewilding Vision," explores a path forward for rewilding the San Joaquin Valley and similar desert and dryland ecosystems.

Conclusions

Changing land use over hundreds of thousands of acres in a socially, economically, and ecologically diverse landscape may seem like an impossible task, especially if rewilding is a core part of that change. However, large landscapes can change dramatically in short periods of time. The Carrizo Plain went from mostly wild to wheat farming then back to mostly wild over the span of one hundred years. And there was nothing like the pressures now driving the San Joaquin Valley toward a different future. One hundred years ago, there were very few dairies in the San Joaquin Valley. Now it produces most of California's and much of the United States' milk. In less than twenty years, we have seen the San Joaquin Valley go from mostly row crops and dairies to a landscape that produces 80 percent of the world's almonds. In this moment, we need the vision and will to support these communities in making a transition that allows nature and people to thrive in this amazing valley. This can be done with collaboration, major investment, and political will. And it can be done in ways that ultimately secure a sustainable future for agriculture in the San Joaquin Valley and a higher quality of life for its residents.

If we succeed, rebalancing land use in the San Joaquin Valley will also provide a vital example for other regions around the world of how to maintain productive agriculture in a sustainable way while recovering natural systems and ecosystem services and improving other aspects of human health and well-being.

References

Almaraz, Maya, Edith Bai, Chao Wang, Justin Trousdell, Stephen Conley, Ian Faloona, and Benjamin Z. Houlton. 2018. "Agriculture is a major source of NOx pollution in California." *Science Advances* 4, no. 1: eaao3477.

Bryant, Benjamin P., T. Rodd Kelsey, Adrian L. Vogl, Stacie A. Wolny, Duncan MacEwan, Paul C. Selmants, Tanushree Biswas, and H. Scott Butterfield. 2020. "Shaping land use change and ecosystem restoration in a water-stressed agricultural landscape to achieve multiple benefits." *Frontiers in Sustainable Food Systems* 4: 138.

Cromsigt, Joris P. G. M., Mariska te Beest, Graham I. H. Kerley, Marietjie Landman, Elizabeth le Roux, and Felisa A. Smith. 2018. "Trophic rewilding as a climate change mitigation strategy?" *Philosophical Transactions of the Royal Society B: Biological Sciences* 373, no. 1761: 20170440.

Fernández, Néstor, Laetitia M. Navarro, and Henrique M. Pereira. 2017. "Rewilding: a call for boosting ecological complexity in conservation." *Conservation Letters* 10, no. 3: 276–78.

Germano, David J., Galen B. Rathbun, Lawrence R. Saslaw, Brian L. Cypher, Ellen A. Cypher, and Larry M. Vredenburgh. 2011. "The San Joaquin Desert of California: ecologically misunderstood and overlooked." *Natural Areas Journal* 31, no. 2: 138–47.

Halada, Lubos, Doug Evans, Carlos Romão, and Jan-Erik Petersen. 2011. "Which habitats of European importance depend on agricultural practices?" *Biodiversity and Conservation* 20, no. 11: 2365–78.

Hanak, Ellen, Alvar Escriva-Bou, Brian Gray, Sarge Green, Thomas Harter, Jelena Jezdimirovic, Jay Lund, Josué Medellín-Azuara, Peter Moyle, and Nathaniel Seavy. 2019. *Water and the Future of the San Joaquin Valley*. San Francisco: Public Policy Institute of California.

Hanak, Ellen, Jay Lund, Brad Arnold, Alvar Escriva-Bou, Brian Gray, Sarge Green, Thomas Harter, Richard Howitt, Duncan MacEwan, and Josue Medellin-Azuara. 2017. *Water Stress and a Changing San Joaquin Valley*. Public Policy Institute of California.

Kelsey, Rodd, Abby Hart, H. Scott Butterfield, and Dan Vink. 2018. "Groundwater sustainability in the San Joaquin Valley: multiple benefits if agricultural lands are retired and restored strategically." *California Agriculture* 72, no. 3: 151–54.

Mayfield, Thomas Jefferson. 1993. *Indian Summer: Traditional Life among the Choinumne Indians of California's San Joaquin Valley*. Berkeley, Calif.: Heyday Books.

Monbiot, George. 2014. *Feral: Rewilding the Land, the Sea, and Human Life*. Chicago: University of Chicago Press.

Pearce, Dustin, James Strittholt, Terry Watt, and Ethan Elkind. 2016. "A path forward: identifying least-conflict solar PV development in California's San Joaquin Valley." University of California, Berkeley, Center for Law.

Perino, Andrea, Henrique M. Pereira, Laetitia M. Navarro, Néstor Fernández, James M. Bullock, Silvia Ceauşu, Ainara Cortés-Avizanda, et al. 2019. "Rewilding complex ecosystems." *Science* 364, no. 6438: eaav5570.

Rubenstein, Dustin R., and Daniel I. Rubenstein. 2016. "From Pleistocene to trophic rewilding: a wolf in sheep's clothing." *Proceedings of the National Academy of Sciences* 113, no. 1: E1.

Soulé, Michael, and Reed Noss. 1998. "Rewilding and biodiversity: complementary goals for continental conservation." *Wild Earth* 8: 18–28.

Wu, Grace C., Emily Leslie, Oluwafemi Sawyerr, D. Richard Cameron, Erica Brand, Brian Cohen, Douglas Allen, Marcela Ochoa, and Arne Olson. 2019. *Power of Place: Land Conservation and Clean Energy Pathways for California*. Arlington County, Va.: The Nature Conservancy.

Part I

Lessons Learned from the San Joaquin Valley

Chapter 2

Painting the Scene: Natural Plant Communities as Palettes for Restoration on Retired Farmlands

Jennifer Buck-Diaz, Ryan E. O'Dell, Mitchell Coleman, and Christopher J. Lortie

IMAGINE YOURSELF SOARING OVER THE San Joaquin Valley long ago, perhaps taking part in a great migratory journey of birds along the Pacific flyway. As you depart from the Sacramento–San Joaquin Delta, "a shining thread of light mark[s] El Rio de San Joaquin" and guides you south (Mayfield 1993, p. 32). These are the wild lands that the young John Thomas Mayfield, John Muir (Badè 1924), and other early California settlers witnessed more than 150 years ago.

In a plentiful rain year, the San Joaquin River and its tributaries are swollen and overflow their banks onto extensive floodplains. You spot fall-run Chinook salmon leaping in the river under majestic valley oaks and towering sycamores that spread thick branches in riparian forests along creeks and channels. In some areas, the forest is open with a thick understory of creeping wild-rye or sedges, in other places choked with shrubby willows, poison oak, and lianas of wild grape roping around branches reaching for light. You stretch your wings over hundreds of thousands of acres of open land clothed with native grasses and broad-leaved herbs, studded with vernal pools and larger playas that extend to the horizon.

As you continue flying south, the oaks and sycamores of the northern San Joaquin Valley rapidly give way to gnarled cottonwoods that meander along seasonally dry arroyos. Scruffy saltbush and desert scrub begin to dot the plains and low, rolling hills, a sure sign that you have entered the most arid section of the San Joaquin Desert. El Niño winter rains have coaxed a profusion of wildflowers from the parched soil and brought the desert to life. Your eyes are dazzled by a "crazy quilt of color" that blankets the plains and hills. "The whole plain [is] covered with great patches of rose, yellow, scarlet, orange, and blue. The colors [do] not seem to mix to any great extent. Each kind of flower like[s] a certain kind of soil best and some of the patches of one color are a mile or more across" (Mayfield 1993, p. 34). These diverse bee pastures pulsate with a collective hum in the warm spring air (Badè 1924; Minnich 2008).

As you reach the southern end of the San Joaquin Valley, the accumulated salts lighten the soil where only salt-loving species thrive, such as saltgrass and alkali sacaton, a native perennial bunchgrass. The pungent smell of annual tarplants fills the air as it thickly rings salt-scalded areas crusted with unique combinations of lichen, moss, and algae. You settle in for the evening on the glassy surface of Tulare Lake, the last stop of your flight. Herds of tule elk and pronghorn forage along the wetlands of the shoreline. Native Americans camp at the edge, net fish from tule rafts, and swim in the cool, clear water of this bountiful desert oasis.

Ecosystem Fragments: Faded Blueprints for the Future
The habitats of the San Joaquin Valley from centuries ago are mostly gone. The seasonal patterns of winter flooding and summer droughts are disrupted: Rivers are leveed and dammed, lake beds are dried and farmed. Gone are the southernmost Pacific

Coast salmon runs and the vast riparian wetlands. Less than 30 percent of the San Joaquin Valley ecosystems and plant communities remain today.

With so much loss, how can we reconstruct and rewild the diverse habitats of this unique region of California? The intact ecosystem fragments that remain today provide vital clues to understanding and rebuilding the natural ecology of the San Joaquin Valley. These fragments are faded blueprints for the future restoration of retired farmlands. Fortunately, the flora of the San Joaquin Valley has been intensively documented over the last century (Hoover 1937; Twisselmann 1956, 1967; Holland & Keil 1995; O'Dell, in review), and remaining natural patterns of vegetation have been systematically sampled, classified, and summarized (Buck-Diaz and Evens 2011; Buck-Diaz et al. 2012). This accumulation of botanical knowledge is invaluable; it guides us toward what plants are present, where they are found, and why they grow there.

Vegetation summaries lead to the development of restoration palettes that reflect the current distributions of plants, palettes rich in color and including diverse annual and perennial herbs, shrubs, and trees. These lists of species and planting density recommendations are derived from data summarized across many reference sites and indicate what to plant and where. Palettes reflect the major habitats within the San Joaquin Valley, using factors such as geography, water availability, and the degree of vegetation development (e.g., bare soil versus remnant habitat with existing vegetation).

This book describes a vision for rewilding the San Joaquin Valley as a whole but also seeks to emphasize restoration of the upland habitats and species that have been most affected by agricultural development over the past 150 years. The most common native upland vegetation types in the San Joaquin include annual forblands (wildflower fields) and diverse scrublands (e.g., alkali sink scrub, saltbush scrub, and desert scrub). The patterns of native plant species and vegetation types that remain in the San Joaquin are strongly influenced by their environmental setting, especially soil type, topography, and hydrology (Twisselmann 1956, 1967; O'Dell, in review). Other factors such as rodent (e.g., kangaroo rats; see chapter 4) burrowing, livestock grazing, and competition from nonnative annual grasses, which have come to dominate many California landscapes, also significantly influence the presence and distribution of native plant species.

Many native plant species, especially annual forbs, have strict soil texture affinities; some species grow only on sandy soils, and others grow on clay. Plants are sensitive to the amount of salt in the soil and either thrive on or avoid saline soils; these saline soils have always been here but are now more common because of the wetting and drying cycles of irrigated agriculture. North facing (cooler) and south facing (warmer) slopes of seasonal drainages create microclimates that strongly influence species composition. Local hydrology drives water availability where well-drained soils of the uplands and plains rely on variable seasonal rainfall. Hummocks (mounding) and microtopography influence rainfall ponding, particularly in vernal pools.

Annual Forblands

Annual forblands (wildflower fields) support most of the plant diversity in the San Joaquin Valley. Some years are breathtakingly showy; others are dry and dusty, with bare soil churned by rodent burrowing. These diverse annual herbs, which grow, set seed, and die in a single growing season, have adapted to frequent drought by creating seeds that can remain dormant in the soil for years during especially dry periods. They emerge from the seedbank, grow, and restock the seedbank during years of adequate rainfall.

The name *San Joaquin Desert,* coined by Germano et al. in 2011, distinguishes a portion of the San Joaquin Valley based on climate in order to guide future restoration and management. This region includes the western and southern two thirds of the San Joaquin

Table 2-1. Dominant Annual Forbland Types in the San Joaquin Desert and Species Recommended for Restoration

Type	Soil Conditions	Dominant Species Appropriate for Restoration
Sandy plains wildflowers	Sandy, nonsaline	Common fiddleneck, California mustard, tansy-leafed phacelia, common phacelia, purple owl's clover, Kellogg's tarweed, Kern tarweed, white tidy tips, and bluegrass, California goldfields, bird's-eye gilia, California poppy, valley sky lupine, short style owl's clover, field sun cup, thistle sage, vinegarweed, and small fescue
Clay plains wildflowers	Clay, saline	Leafy stemmed coreopsis, Crum's monolopia, Munz's tidy tips, Lemmon's mustard, great valley phacelia, Lost Hills crownscale, Jared's peppergrass, and bluegrass
Alkali vernal pool wildflowers	Clay, saline	Vernal pool goldfields, alkali goldfields, net peppergrass, dwarf sack clover, common tarweed, alkali barley, saltgrass, and alkali heath

Valley, the Carrizo Plain, and the Cuyama Valley to the southwest (see figure 0-1). The San Joaquin Desert supports thirty-six native annual plant species found nowhere else in the world (endemics) and thirty-three near-endemics. Most of these endemic species have a high affinity for either nonsaline, sandy soils or saline, clay soils (table 2-1).

Low-alkali playas support rare goldfields and other annual forbs, and mounded areas light your eyes with brilliant sun-tracking heads of leafy stemmed coreopsis and fields of tidy tips. The hills of the San Joaquin Desert explode with gaudy flower-covered slopes that come alive in the early spring. In certain years, you can investigate alternating, almost pure stands of purple phacelia and gold monolopia, each thriving on a specific combination of slope, aspect, and soil profile. Keep your eyes open for blazing patches of desert candle and flat terraces of the fragrant thistle sage above ephemeral streams. Each year brings different timing and amounts of precipitation to this region, and repeat surveys have shown both stability and variability across the different wildflower and grassland communities (Buck-Diaz et al. 2013).

Alkali Sink Scrub

As you meander along the San Joaquin Valley floor, you will encounter bands of alkali sink scrub where near-surface water is available year-round and the soil is moist, such as riparian zones (along rivers and streams), wetlands, and alkali sinks. The soil type is typically saline clay, and important species for restoration include bracted alkali goldenbush, iodine bush, bush seepweed, alkali heath, Mojave red sage, and saltgrass.

Alkali sink scrub can tolerate seasonal flooding during the winter but not flooding year-round or prolonged, excessively dry conditions during the summer. Successful restoration of alkali sink scrub relies on an appropriate balance of perennial soil moisture.

Saltbush Scrub

Saltbush scrub occurs along dry seasonal drainage courses and on well-drained plains. The soil type may be saline or not and of any texture. Important species for restoration of this vegetation type include allscale saltbush, spinescale saltbush, four-wing saltbush, and big saltbush.

Saltbush scrub and other woody shrubs provide vertical habitat structure on the otherwise featureless plains of the San Joaquin Desert. The shrub canopies shelter native wildlife including coyote, California ground squirrel, black-tailed jackrabbit, desert cottontail, greater roadrunner, and California quail. The importance of shrubs for native wildlife species, including those listed as threatened and endangered such as the giant kangaroo rat, Tipton kangaroo rat, and blunt-nosed leopard lizard, is examined further in chapters 5 and 6. Saltbush also offers green forage during the hot, dry summer when most other plant species are brown and dry.

Because of its tolerance of arid climates and saline soils, fast growth, a dense canopy that protects soils from erosion, and high forage and habitat value, saltbush scrub is a desirable restoration target for the San Joaquin Desert. Saltbush establishes most readily from broadcast seeding on loose, bare soils. Individuals grow fast but live only a few decades, although they are prolific, and a single individual may produce several hundred thousand seeds a year.

San Joaquin Desert Scrub

San Joaquin Desert scrub occurs on well-drained, nonsaline, sandy soils of plains and low rolling hills. Important species for restoration of these habitats include Mojave Desert California buckwheat, yellow mock aster, California ephedra, and winterfat.

California ephedra provides habitat structure for many wildlife species and serves as a nurse plant for annual forbs (Filazzola et al. 2019; Liczner et al. 2019). California ephedra shrubs grow slowly but may live for several hundred years and have been shown to readily recover from damage (Lortie et al. 2018). Consequently, they can function as stable anchors within scrub systems as a refuge from the intense midday heat.

A single California ephedra may produce several thousand brown, pine nut–like seeds a year, which are heartily consumed by birds and rodents. California ephedra produces fewer seeds than saltbush, and a high percentage of the seeds are subject to predation. These factors, and the vulnerability of ephedra seedlings to competition by dense growth of nonnative annual grasses, have suppressed natural recruitment of this species.

Challenges of Effective Restoration: Rebuilding This Old House from the Ground Up

The ecosystems of the San Joaquin Valley have been shaped by their arid climate. They are ancient, starkly beautiful, and perpetually weathered by the dry winds of time, like an old Victorian farmhouse. Land that was farmed for several decades and then retired is analogous to an old house that has been demolished, cleared to its bare foundation, and then abandoned. The solid foundation of topsoil remains, but none of the water and nutrient supply plumbing, vegetation structural frame, species diversity building blocks, or symbiotic protective roof of interacting species remain. Rebuilding an ecosystem from the ground up presents distinct challenges and requires careful planning. This work is discussed in greater detail in chapter 3 through real-life restoration project examples from the San Joaquin Desert.

We know that plant species distribution in the San Joaquin Valley is strongly influenced by topography, soil properties, and hydrology. Thus, we must attempt to match plant species with their specific tolerances to site conditions. Important soil factors include texture (sand vs. clay) and salinity (nonsaline vs. saline). Hydrology is also important because it determines whether water availability is entirely dependent on scarce rainfall (uplands and plains), whether it ponds for a brief period (vernal pools), or whether there is perennial surface or near-surface water (riparian zones, wetlands, alkali sinks). All these features could be viewed as part of the foundation, which will determine what floor plan the new house will have. It is important to quantify what those soil and hydrologic constraints are and then work with the existing conditions to select the right plant palette: the materials to build a robust and diverse vegetation frame that will support the rest of the ecosystem (figure 2-1).

In the planning stages, representative soil samples should be collected from the site for soil texture and salinity analysis. Soil probing and auguring may reveal tillage compaction layers in the subsoil that might inhibit rooting depth. Hydrologic conditions should be

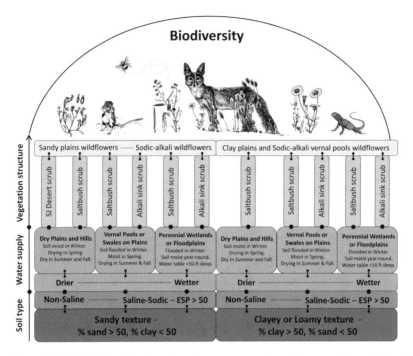

Figure 2-1. Rebuilding the San Joaquin ecosystems from the ground up. (Animal line drawings reprinted with permission from Brian Cypher and ESRP. Plant line drawings reprinted with permission from Stanford University Press.)

monitored through at least one good rainfall year to determine how wet, or not, the soils remain throughout the season. The combination of soil texture, soil salinity, and local hydrology would then be used to determine what vegetation types the site could support.

It is imperative to use an appropriate plant palette for each restoration site based on site conditions and known species combinations appropriate for the area. Once you have selected a target plant palette for your site conditions, you are ready to begin rebuilding the ecosystem. Seeds may be broadcast sown or planted with a rangeland drill. Some shrub species may be established as plug and container starts.

Invasive annual grasses, especially red brome, will be like termites, constantly challenging your building effort and chewing away at the native vegetation frame. Successful restoration necessitates control of nonnative grasses and other weeds, which may be accomplished with tools such as mowing, livestock grazing, and herbicides. The new ecosystem may be similar to but not exactly the same as the original ecosystem in function. Successful ecosystem restoration should target at least some of the endemic species of the region that dwell in related natural ecosystems. As with any house, occasional monitoring and maintenance in the form of vegetation management (weed control) will be needed.

San Joaquin Native Plant Material Sources: Getting Your Ecosystem Building Permit

Unlike crop seeds, which are abundantly available, there are few places where seeds of native plant species can be purchased for restoration purposes. The few seed producers that do exist sell seed for only a limited number of San Joaquin Desert native plant species.

Another option for obtaining high-diversity seed of native plant species is to obtain a permit and collect from federal public lands managed by the Bureau of Land Management (BLM) or U.S. Forest Service (USFS). Seeds collected from federal lands are classified by the BLM and USFS as a Special Forest Product. A Forest Products Removal Permit can be obtained from the appropriate federal land management office for commercial seed collections.

At present, only small volumes of seed are available for restoration, whether from commercial sources or federal lands. If large-scale restoration is conducted on retired farmlands in the San Joaquin Desert, it would be most cost-effective to establish local production fields at a location in the San Joaquin Valley (Borders 2009). Any new seed production fields should be established across a range of soil textures from sand to clay to accommodate a wide diversity of plant species.

Although we have extensive knowledge of the ecology of plants in the San Joaquin Valley, there is still much to be learned about the restoration of these sensitive habitats. The exploration of remnant habitats has given us a glimpse into the past, and it is up to us to rebuild the natural bounty of the San Joaquin Valley.

References

Badè, William Frederic. 1924. *The Life and Letters of John Muir*. Vol. 9. Boston, Mass.: Houghton Mifflin.

Borders, B. 2009. *A Synthesis of Native Plant Seed Production Efforts in the San Joaquin Valley, California*. Turlock: Endangered Species Recovery Program, California State University, Stanislaus.

Buck-Diaz, Jennifer, Scott Batiuk, and Julie M. Evens. 2012. *Vegetation Alliances and Associations of the Great Valley Ecoregion, California*. Final report to the Geographical Information Center, Chico State University.

Buck-Diaz, Jennifer, and Julie M. Evens. 2011. *Carrizo Plain National Monument Vegetation Classification and Mapping Project*. Unpublished report. Sacramento: California Native Plant Society.

Buck-Diaz, Jennifer, J. Ratchford, and Julie M. Evens. 2013. *California Rangeland Monitoring and Mapping: Focusing upon Great Valley and Carrizo Plain Grassland Habitats*. Report to the Natural Resources Conservation Service. Sacramento: California Native Plant Society.

Filazzola, Alessandro, Amanda Rae Liczner, Michael Westphal, and Christopher J. Lortie. 2019. "Shrubs indirectly increase desert seedbanks through facilitation of the plant community." *PLOS One* 14, no. 4.

Germano, David J., Galen B. Rathbun, Lawrence R. Saslaw, Brian L. Cypher, Ellen A. Cypher, and Larry M. Vredenburgh. 2011. "The San Joaquin Desert of California: ecologically misunderstood and overlooked." *Natural Areas Journal* 31, no. 2: 138–47.

Holland, V. L., and David J. Keil. 1995. *California Vegetation*. Dubuque, Iowa: Kendall/Hunt Publishing.

Hoover, Robert F. 1937. *Endemism in the Flora of the Great Valley of California*. Berkeley: University of California.

Liczner, Amanda R., Alessandro Filazzola, Michael Westphal, and Christopher J. Lortie. 2019. "Shrubs facilitate native forb re-establishment in an invaded arid shrubland." *Journal of Arid Environments* 170: 103998.

Lortie, Christopher J., Eva Gruber, Alex Filazzola, Taylor Noble, and Michael Westphal. 2018. "The Groot effect: plant facilitation and desert shrub regrowth following extensive damage." *Ecology and Evolution* 8, no. 1: 706–15.

Mayfield, Thomas Jefferson. 1993. *Indian Summer: Traditional Life among the Choinumne Indians of California's San Joaquin Valley*. Berkeley: Heyday Books.

Minnich, Richard A. 2008. *California's Fading Wildflowers: Lost Legacy and Biological Invasions*. Berkeley: University of California Press.

O'Dell, Ryan E. In review. "Flora of the San Joaquin Desert: present, past, and future." *Madroño*.

Twisselmann, Ernest C. 1956. *Flora of the Temblor Range*. University of San Francisco.

Twisselmann, Ernest C. 1967. "A flora of Kern County, California." *Wasmann Journal of Biology* 25, no. 1/2.

Chapter 3

Lessons Learned from Over Twenty Years of Habitat Restoration on Retired Farmlands in the San Joaquin Valley

Ellen A. Cypher, Lawrence R. Saslaw, Kenneth D. Lair, and Stephen Laymon

T HE BRIGHT MORNING SUN SKIPS ACROSS the field as Jack climbs into his weathered John Deere tractor. The first fall rains are heading in, and there is a push to finish planting before the field gets too wet. The San Joaquin Valley is a dry place; in fact, the western and southern two thirds of the valley are considered a desert (Germano et al. 2011) (figure 3-1). Rain is in the forecast, and Jack wants to make sure his tractor does not get stuck and his crops soak up every last bit of rain.

Jack has farmed cotton, oats, barley, safflower, and alfalfa on this ground for more than fifty years. He has seen a lot of things change in the valley, but one thing that has not changed on this piece of ground is the challenge of growing crops from year to year. The parched conditions have always made growing crops a challenge for Jack—nothing a little irrigation water cannot solve—but the bigger issue has always been the soil's salinity, alkalinity, and heavy clay content. Jack's land sits near the edge of what once was the mighty Tulare Lake. Jack's land and the adjacent "Sand Ridge"

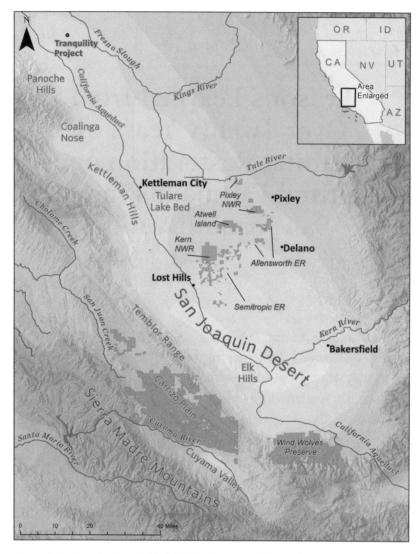

Figure 3-1. The southern half of the San Joaquin Valley and San Joaquin Desert of California. Protected areas and historical restoration projects noted. ER, Ecological Reserve; NWR, National Wildlife Refuge. (Map by Connor Shank)

form Atwell Island, home to the Yokut tribe for several thousand years (see figure 3-1). Before agricultural development and the surface water diversions and groundwater pumping that drove its expansion, rain and snowmelt from the Sierra Nevada poured down the Kaweah, Kings, and Tule Rivers each year to fill Tulare Lake. Sediment was laid down each year as the lake's waters rose in wet periods and fell in dry ones. To no one's surprise, growing crops in and around an old lakebed is not easy.

The big Deere hardly feels the drag of the small broadcast drill filled with a variety of native seeds to sow a very different crop. This is the last time Jack will plant this field. His land has recently been retired from irrigated farming and is being replaced with native plants that flourished when the Yokuts lived there. Jack's last crop, composed of shrub, wildflower, and grass seeds, is part of the first project of the Central Valley Project Improvement Act, Land Retirement Demonstration Project (LRDP). Jack's farm, along with his desire to phase out of farming, is a good match with the U.S. Bureau of Reclamation's (BOR) efforts to retire farmland that has drainage problems (and declining productivity) and to test restoration of these lands to native habitats.

The Importance of Soils, Landform, and Land Use History

Jack's farm and those of his neighbors became part of the Atwell Island LRDP site in Tulare County (see figure 3-1). A sister project, Tranquillity, was located 70 miles to the northwest in Fresno County (see figure 3-1). Both sites were located on the edges of historic lakebeds. Whereas Tranquillity historically consisted only of seasonal wetlands, the Atwell Island site was a combination of seasonal wetlands and upland desert habitats. The poorly drained, saline clay soils of the seasonal wetlands were occasionally flooded in high water years and were among hundreds of thousands of acres in the San Joaquin Valley that were "reclaimed" (drained) for agricultural use over the past 150 years.

By the end of the twentieth century, more than five decades after they were drained and tilled for agriculture, it became clear that these former wetlands created severe and persistent drainage problems for growing crops. In combination with decades of irrigation and pumping, these problems had caused toxic minerals, particularly selenium, to leach up from the underlying soil layers.

In partnership with the U.S. Bureau of Land Management (BLM) and the U.S. Fish and Wildlife Service (USFWS), the BOR purchased drainage-impaired agricultural lands from willing sellers, retired them from cultivation, and attempted to restore some for habitat, largely to control soil erosion and weed expansion. They even thought that the restored lands could offer additional economic opportunities for landowners, including livestock grazing. BLM, BOR, and USFWS believed that if they could demonstrate success at small scales, they could begin to apply these techniques more broadly across the San Joaquin Valley. Thus, the LRDP, the first effort to rewild the San Joaquin Valley, was born. As with all first-of-their-kind efforts, there were many lessons learned for what works and what should be left on the restoration shelf.

Keep in mind the difficulty Jack had growing crops on those former lake beds. Those of us who worked on the initial LRDP projects (BLM and the California State University–Stanislaus Endangered Species Recovery Program) faced similar challenges. We were tasked with creating upland habitat for San Joaquin Desert species, including kangaroo rats and kit foxes, on former seasonal wetlands. Those same clay, saline, alkaline soils that Jack struggled to grow alfalfa on were equally difficult to grow saltbush on. The heavy clay soils retain water, often making movement of people or machinery difficult during the rainy season, but they do not release that water easily to plant roots. Based on the recommendations from chapter 2—and common sense—we should have been creating wetlands on those former wetland areas. However, that was not an option because our water supply was limited, as may be the case in the current rewilding efforts driven by the Sustainable Groundwater Management Act (see chapter 1; Kelsey et al. 2018), and selenium levels were high enough to cause concern for wetland wildlife (Ohlendorf et al. 1986). Faced with this dilemma, we tested a variety of approaches for upland habitat creation at Atwell Island and Tranquillity, hoping to develop a method that would lead to large-scale habitat restoration efforts.

As was recommended in chapter 2, at both Atwell and Tranquillity we used nearby natural upland communities as templates to develop our plant palettes for restoration. Atwell and Tranquillity ultimately turned out to be quite different in soil types and vegetation communities that could be restored, but they were similar in that they had both been leveled for flood irrigation. When we looked at nearby reference sites, we saw a landscape that had natural undulations of windblown mounds, water-formed rivulets, playas, depressions, and mounds created by burrowing animals. Ground dwellers such as kangaroo rats and burrowing owls inhabited the mounds that served as refugia from floodwaters and saturated soils. Variations in topography, soil texture, salinity, and hydrology at these reference sites thus created a mosaic of plant communities. Therefore, before planting at both Atwell and Tranquillity, we constructed mounds, depressions, berms, and flood levees to mimic the natural microtopography of the reference sites.

Once the microtopography was created, the next big site preparation task was reducing the cover of weedy nonnative plant species. Irrigation on these saline and alkaline soils combined with tillage over many decades modified the soil characteristics at both Atwell and Tranquillity and eliminated beneficial soil organisms. This made both sites much more susceptible to invasion by aggressive weeds such as red brome, the dominant invader in much of the southern and western portions of the San Joaquin Valley. We also suspect air pollution may have exacerbated these invasions because weedy species are often better at using excess nitrogen to grow and outcompete native species (Weiss 1999; Brooks 2003).

Weed management as part of site preparation took on many forms. At Atwell Island, we tested disking, harrowing, burning, duration of fallowing before restoration, and flaming. Disking, plowing 6–8 inches into the ground, was successful for eliminating deep-rooted species, such as alfalfa. This was an especially important finding because our most successful restoration efforts occurred in fields where alfalfa was the last crop grown. Alfalfa needs high amounts of water to grow: 60 inches or more per year. Once that water was removed, those water-loving weed species were easily eliminated. Conversely, our restoration mixes included native plant species adapted to arid conditions of less than 10 inches of rainfall per year. Harrowing, plowing 4 inches into the ground, was more successful at sites with only sparse weed cover. Burning in late fall (November) before the start of the rainy season worked well to remove weed species before restoration planning. The duration of fallowing before restoration planting had interesting results. We found that we had to either restore the site immediately after removing the crop or wait more than five years to start restoration. Waiting allows the soil to settle and helps establish native plant species but can also lead to high weed species cover. At Atwell, we used a hot burn in late fall to remove these weed species before restoration planting. A burn like this also has the advantage of reducing the soil seedbank for weedy nonnative species. A successful alternative to disking was to pull a propane alfalfa flamer behind a tractor to kill the young alfalfa seedlings. By flaming before planting the restoration mix, we allowed the native seed to germinate without competition and the soil was not disturbed, which would have encouraged the nonnative weeds. Because flaming is more expensive, we used this method only on smaller plots of 10 acres or less to create forb-dominated "islands." We reasoned that more flaming could be done later to create additional forb islands where nonnative grasses were widespread.

Cover Crops, Herbicides, and Nurse Plants to the Rescue

Instead of fallowing at Tranquillity, we grew barley as a cover crop to control erosion and suppress weeds until we were ready to plant native seeds. As a bonus, we were able to harvest and sell the barley, and even after harvest the stubble helped retain soil moisture. The cover crop helped, but we needed a way to keep the weed seeds already in the soil from outcompeting the natives once they were planted. Our first few attempts involved similar weed control methods to those used at Atwell Island, including disking and burning, but they were not as effective at Tranquillity. The failure of burning at Tranquillity, even in combination with mowing, may have been a timing issue: We tried to take advantage of a summer wildfire because air quality restrictions precluded controlled burning. Or perhaps the issue was temperature because our handheld flamer may not have been as hot as the tractor-drawn model used at Atwell Island.

Thus, herbicides were the key to weed control at Tranquillity. But the trick was to kill weeds without killing the desirable natives. We found that the best solution was to apply broad-spectrum, preemergent herbicides (those that prevent seeds from germinating) immediately after drill seeding the native mix. We protected the native seeds by applying a form of activated charcoal in a narrow band over them before applying the herbicide (Lair et al. 2006). Although some seeds of weedy grasses fell into the drill rows and were similarly protected by the charcoal, creating the appearance of a Mohawk hairstyle along the rows, we did achieve weed control on a larger scale.

A key challenge beyond weed control is making sure there was enough moisture early on to support germination, growth, and establishment of the native seeds we had planted. The low and variable precipitation characteristic of the San Joaquin Desert climate meant that we could not be sure that rain would come when needed. But the existence of drainage problems—the very reason these lands had been retired from agriculture—meant that very little irrigation would be allowed for restoration purposes. Some arid land restoration projects have had success with compounds applied directly to the seeds or moisture-retaining gel packs buried next to the roots of transplanted shrubs, but these were not effective at Tranquillity. We found that the dryland barley we had used as a cover crop at Tranquillity also worked well as a nurse crop when planted in alternate rows with the native seeds. The nurse plants protected delicate native seedlings from drying winds and intense sunlight while also helping retain soil moisture. The nurse barley worked particularly well in conjunction with deep-furrow seeding, in which cultivator shovels on the front of the seed drill made 8-inch-deep furrows. The additional microtopography further reduced battering of seedlings by surface wind, increased moisture capture and retention, and wicked salts upward.

What Is Practical to Recreate?

Although the historic native lands of the San Joaquin and Tulare Basins displayed a wash of brilliant springtime wildflower colors in favorable years (see chapter 2), our restoration capabilities could not match the ecological processes that created that palette over thousands of years, and the native seeds were long gone from the soil after decades of farming. We have learned to accept more moderate success by focusing on just a few native species of San Joaquin Desert shrubs, annual wildflowers, and annual grasses that can jump-start the long-term recovery of functional upland habitat.

We knew that an important factor in dealing with the hot climate and variable precipitation was to use local plant ecotypes, plants that are adapted to local conditions. But the major commercial suppliers of California native seed propagate few seed stocks originating in the San Joaquin Desert (see chapter 2), and those that they do offer often come from a single collection, which can result in poor genetic diversity for that particular seed lot (see chapter 8). Another problem with many commercial seeds is that they have been propagated in a different climatic regime than our restoration site, thereby losing much of their adaptive advantage. Even when we did find seeds of desirable, local ecotypes, many were prohibitively expensive.

Because there were few commercial sources of local native seeds in the San Joaquin Valley to match the soils and climate of the Atwell Island and Tranquillity sites, we collected native seed from remnant habitats in the two regions. Our most successful plantings used native seeds that were collected within 50 miles of the restoration sites. Whereas most of the Atwell Island seed was collected from remnant habitats, then cleaned and planted directly, the Tranquillity project established an on-site nursery to increase seeds for planting. This nursery was abandoned when federal funding ended, highlighting the need for commercial seed growers to establish production plots in the San Joaquin Valley (see chapter 2).

At Atwell Island, trial and error pointed us toward a simple native mix of thirteen San Joaquin Desert species comprising eight shrubs and five herbs. The shrubs we settled on were goldenbush, iodine bush, bush seepweed, alkali heath, quailbush, allscale saltbush, spiny saltbush, and bladderpod. The herbs included wildflowers (goldfields, Sierra white layia, Great Valley phacelia, and spikeweed), and the native annual grass desert fescue (Laymon and Olsen 2011). Despite the complexity and uncertainty, some simple principles have been gleaned from our design. Ten years on, Atwell's most successful plantings were those at least 10 acres in size, seeded with at least 25 pounds per acre of locally collected seed matched to the soil type, and planted in October and November just before the late fall rains. We found that if the seedlings survived the first year and set enough seed, native vegetation on the site seemed to persist indefinitely. Our 2017 walkover surveys showed many of Atwell's plantings to be holding their own against the tough nonnative competition and to be providing habitat for native small mammals and reptiles (figure 3-2).

Figure 3-2. A fallow field at Atwell Island (Tulare County, California) in 2006 before restoration, dominated by weedy mustard (background) and fivehook bassia (foreground), and in 2017, after successful restoration, showing native herbs, native shrubs, and a wildlife trail. (Left photo by Steve Laymon; right photo by Larry Saslaw)

In contrast, more than twice as many species performed well at the Tranquillity project as at Atwell Island, but their success varied across the site. We used four subsets of native plant assemblages that each performed best in different combinations of soil chemistry (with high vs. lower levels of salt and sodium) and moisture conditions (moist vs. arid). The overall list of thirty species included twelve of the thirteen that had also performed well at Atwell Island (or their very close relatives), plus perennial grasses and more diverse forbs (Valley Flora Propagation Center 2006; Ritter and Lair 2007).

The Importance of Long-Term Management

Long after the field preparation and plantings, management of the vegetation has been critical to meeting the upland habitat objectives. We were able to establish fields of wildflowers at Atwell Island but have not recreated the natural open groundcover favored by many of the desert-adapted plants and animals. If our objective is to create upland habitats similar to those occupied by threatened and endangered species of the San Joaquin Desert and more common species, we need ongoing, annual management of the vegetation structure. And after the investment of creating alkali sink scrub and saltbush scrub vegetation communities to mimic the historic vegetation described in chapter 2, it is also important to manage fire fuel loads to minimize the risk of wildfire that will kill and eliminate the shrub layer and spread to neighboring lands.

In years when high rainfall promotes higher amounts of both native planted and nonnative weedy vegetation, livestock grazing may be used as a management tool to reduce the fuel loads and open the ground cover for the target animal and plant species. Grazing in the winter and early spring can create low vegetation and bare ground that favors San Joaquin kit fox, blunt-nosed leopard lizard, Tipton kangaroo rat, San Joaquin antelope squirrel, burrowing owl, mountain plover, Kern mallow, and San Joaquin woolly-threads. Grazing is not needed every year but only in years with above-average rainfall.

Although we initially had success with diverse wildflowers, native grasses, and shrubs at the Tranquillity project, the native herbs did not persist when we lost funding for ongoing management. The site is now dominated by nonnative grasses, but numerous stands of native shrubs remain, and native seeds may well remain in the soil seedbank. The objectives for the project area can still be achieved if we introduce grazing or other forms of weed control and supplement the native plants that remain.

Conclusions

Our work at Atwell and Tranquillity has revealed the importance of working with what you have; recognizing individual site potentials based on ancient soil formation, the native and weedy plants inhabiting those soils, and recent farming and irrigation practices; and choosing the right restoration tools. The successes and failures experienced at Atwell Island and Tranquillity offer lessons to inform future rewilding objectives and practices.

Although rewilding native plant and animal communities on previously farmed lands in the San Joaquin Valley is a daunting task, Atwell Island and Tranquillity have taught us that large-scale restoration is possible. When we match restoration practices with site-specific soil and climatic conditions, we can create sustainable plant and animal communities that approximate historic San Joaquin Desert landscapes. To do so, it is important to understand the historic landform of the site (lake bottom, adjacent alkali sink, or upslope alluvial fan), soil textures, soil chemistry, and recent tillage practices. It is also essential to consider the historic plant assemblages and plant–soil associations that evolved for that place and the animal habitat requirements in order to develop site-specific restoration objectives and practices. Simple acts of planning can make all the difference, such as taking soil samples at a site to fully evaluate the diversity of soil characteristics and better understand what is possible for revegetation and invasive species management. Newton and Claassen (2003) provide one of the best references for revegetation planners, a concise yet comprehensive guide to evaluating soils for restoration. And we should never overlook local knowledge; we have benefited greatly from the ideas and experience of local farmers and the U.S. Department of Agriculture Natural Resources Conservation Service, who know this land better than most.

Also critical has been recreating the microtopographic features typical for the historic landform (or adding new features to improve current dryland conditions); it is the foundation for seeding efforts. Weed control before planting and throughout the restoration process has also been key to success, along with moisture conservation, given how strongly annual variation in rainfall amount and timing influences seedling survival. Once the stage is set, higher seeding rates of a few locally adapted species have done best. To ensure the best results, appropriate seeds should be collected locally and propagated regionally. Finally, vegetation management before, during, and after restoration seedings and plantings will ultimately determine whether restoration objectives are met.

The recreation of historically complete plant communities may be beyond the scope of most large-scale restoration projects, or even impossible after decades of farming and in a changing climate. Nevertheless, we believe that restoration can and should be directed toward introducing more than just a few generalist native species. This is why defining objectives for a site is critical to provide direction for each restoration project. In some cases, leaving lands fallow and just managing vegetation structure, even if the composition is primarily nonnative species, may be all that is needed to provide acceptable wildlife habitat, if that is the primary objective. In short, there is not one direct route to rewilding. It is important to have a destination in mind and a route planned out, but it is also necessary to be prepared for emergencies and to be ready to detour if roadblocks are encountered.

References

Brooks, Matthew L. 2003. "Effects of increased soil nitrogen on the dominance of alien annual plants in the Mojave Desert." *Journal of Applied Ecology* 40, no. 2: 344–53.

Germano, David J., Galen B. Rathbun, Lawrence R. Saslaw, Brian L. Cypher, Ellen A. Cypher, and Larry M. Vredenburgh. 2011. "The San Joaquin Desert of California: ecologically misunderstood and overlooked." *Natural Areas Journal* 31, no. 2: 138–47.

Kelsey, Rodd, Abigail K. Hart, H. Scott Butterfield, and Dan Vink. 2018. "Groundwater sustainability in the San Joaquin Valley: multiple benefits if agricultural lands are retired and restored strategically." *California Agriculture* 72, no. 3: 151–54.

Lair, Ken, Nur Ritter, and Adrian Howard. 2006. "Use of activated charcoal to protect native seeds from herbicides (California)." *Ecological Restoration* 24: 122–24.

Laymon, S., and B. Olsen. 2011. *Upland Habitat Restoration Recommendations and Techniques for the Tulare Basin.* Alpaugh, Calif.: Bureau of Land Management; and Clovis, Calif.: U.S. Fish and Wildlife Service.

Newton, G. A., and V. P. Claassen. 2003. *Rehabilitation of Disturbed Lands in California: A Manual for Decision Making.* Sacramento: California Department of Conservation and California Geological Survey. https://www.conservation.ca.gov/dmr/SMARA%20Mines/Documents/sp123.pdf

Ohlendorf, Harry M., David J. Hoffman, Michael K. Saiki, and Thomas W. Aldrich. 1986. "Embryonic mortality and abnormalities of aquatic birds: apparent impacts of selenium from irrigation drainwater." *Science of the Total Environment* 52, nos. 1–2: 49–63.

Ritter, N. P., and K. D. Lair. 2007. *Central Valley Project Improvement Act Land Retirement Demonstration Project: A Synthesis of Restoration Research Conducted Near Tranquillity, California.* Fresno, Calif.: USDI Interagency Land Retirement Team. http://esrp.csustan.edu/publications/reports/lrdp/esrp_2007_lrdpsynthesis.pdf

Valley Flora Propagation Center. 2006. Land Retirement Demonstration Project, Department of the Interior. Last updated July 29, 2009. https://esrp.csustan.edu/projects/lrdp/vfpc/

Weiss, Stuart B. 1999. "Cars, cows, and checkerspot butterflies: nitrogen deposition and management of nutrient-poor grasslands for a threatened species." *Conservation Biology* 13, no. 6: 1476–86.

Chapter 4

Animals:
The Final Puzzle Piece
in a Functioning
Natural Community

William Tim Bean, Erin N. Tennant, Brian L. Cypher,
Lawrence R. Saslaw, and Laura Prugh

IMAGINE, FOR A MOMENT, THAT THE FARMERS of the San Joaquin Valley all stopped working today. The crops in the field would continue to grow. Irrigation, to whatever degree it was automated, would function until, bit by bit, the equipment degraded and the channels eroded. Fruits on the trees and vegetables on the vine would ripen until swollen, then slowly rot and fall to the ground. Existing pesticides would do their job for a while, and then insects and rats, birds, and other animals would eat what food was left. Some seeds would escape their notice and sprout into new plants. Tree branches would grow and tangle with each other, until the water balance reversed the trend. In ten years, or twenty, eventually the earth would be littered with decay: dead branches and rotting fruits, overgrown weeds, and soil that began to blow away. Humans on farms do not just make food. They maintain order on the land.

Amazingly, wild animals play many similar roles in shaping and structuring habitats. On farms, birds have long been valued for reducing insect outbreaks and owls for controlling rodents. In rewilding, humans will have a central role in reconstructing natural habitat through restoration (see chapter 3). But once these new natural "farms" are in place, animals will also play their role in maintaining these habitats, from controlling weeds to stabilizing rodent populations. Not only are animals important for the functional role they play in restoring natural habitats in the San Joaquin Desert, they also serve an important aesthetic purpose. As beautiful as the San Joaquin Desert can be in the middle of spring, it is the kit foxes and badgers hunting kangaroo rats, the basking leopard lizards, and the swarms of horned larks that animate this landscape and bring it to life. And finally, animals have an important policy role in rewilding. Because of the U.S. Endangered Species Act, some species are more valuable than others, and the choices we make to restore some but not others to the landscape will be dictated, at least in part, by policy.

In this chapter, we review what we know about the functions animals play in shaping natural habitats in the San Joaquin Desert. Because of its central role in the ecosystem and the abundance of research available, we will focus on the "farmer" of native animals, the giant kangaroo rat (*Dipodomys ingens*) (figure 4-1). But this is not the only actor, and ecological function is not the only axis on which to base restoration decisions. We will therefore also consider other vertebrates that have an ecological role to play in restoration. Finally, we will briefly touch on the policy and aesthetic effects of animals (native and nonnative) on the landscape.

Consider again the ways farmers control the plants on a farm: by manipulating the soil, sowing and maintaining desired seeds and plants, and weeding out undesirable ones. Many animals in the San Joaquin Desert do the same thing. Burrowing animals, the bane of many a rancher, actually do a huge service to the plant community (see figure 4-1). They aerate the soil, making it more friable and therefore more likely to hold water. They churn the seedbank, bringing long-buried seeds to the surface. They deposit nitrogen and other nutrients that they have collected away from their burrows. And they do so on a vast scale. An early estimate from Yosemite National Park suggested that pocket gophers excavated a little less than a kilogram of soil (about a shovelful) per square meter every year (Grinnell and Storer 1924). It does not sound like much, but extrapolated to the San Joaquin Desert, that equates to about 28 million tons of soil per year—enough to fill Pasadena's famous Rose Bowl thirty times over. Herbivorous animals can also change the plant community by expressing their preferences for some plants over others. Of course, the larger the species, the less selective they tend to be. But elk (and cows, in the appropriate grazing regime) can shift the system to more native plants and open habitat. Smaller animals, relying on seeds, can have an even more direct influence on plant propagation by consuming the seeds of preferred species and ignoring others. To

Figure 4-1. Both humans and animals can structure communities. On the left, humans are shown farming the land, including tilling the soil, spreading pesticides, and harvesting crops. On the right, giant kangaroo rats are at the center of an endangered ecosystem. Their burrowing creates habitat for sensitive plants and animals, their seed caching and consumption can control exotic species, and they're important prey for San Joaquin kit fox and badgers, among others. (Illustration by Piper Bean)

complicate things, many granivorous rodents store some of their preferred seed and unintentionally leave it to sprout, thereby promoting its growth. So, by burrowing and turning the soil, eating plants, and consuming or burying their seeds, animals in the San Joaquin Desert perform three of the major roles a farmer does in their more constructed landscape.

Giant kangaroo rats farm natural habitat in the San Joaquin Desert like no other species (see figure 4-1). They construct extensive underground burrows, collecting soil from well below ground and depositing it at the surface. Above ground, these burrow systems slowly grow into burrow mounds, sometimes called precincts, approximately 6 to 16 feet in diameter and up to 3 feet in height. Because giant kangaroo rats are territorial, these mounds are evenly spaced across the landscape (figure 4-2). Many other animals use the burrows, including state threatened San Joaquin antelope squirrels and federally endangered blunt-nosed leopard lizards. Recent research suggests that leopard lizards might even need the burrows for midday shade in places where shrubs are absent (Ivey et al. 2020). In doing so, they also change the soil. Soil properties are fundamentally different on burrow mounds: Calcium, magnesium, phosphorus, and nitrogen are all higher on the burrow mounds than in their surroundings. The soil is also a bit more acidic off the burrow mound. These properties persist for years after giant kangaroo rats are removed. But giant kangaroo rats do not just till the soil; they plant seeds, and weeds, too.

Giant kangaroo rats are granivores, and they like some plants better than others. Given the choice, they prefer some native seeds, such as shining pepperweed, fringed redmaids, and California goldfields, and some nonnatives, such as red brome and redstem filaree. By contrast, they avoid seeds from bristly fiddleneck and Pacific bluegrass. Giant kangaroo rats wait for the plants to go to seed, then they clip all vegetation on their burrow mounds. They harvest seeds both on and off burrow and leave them to cure in the sun in large (up to one half meter tall) stacks. Once the seeds

Figure 4-2. Giant kangaroo rats can play an important role in structuring natural communities by creating burrow mounds (sometimes called precincts). Here, in the Carrizo Plain, giant kangaroo rats have created evenly spaced burrow mounds that have different soil, plant, and invertebrate communities than the surrounding land, contributing greater diversity and ecosystem function. (Photo by Alyssa Semerdjian)

are sufficiently dried, giant kangaroo rats will store them, either on the surface in small (approximately 1 tablespoon) pit caches or in underground compartments. Although they eat most of the stored seeds, some seeds will be stolen or forgotten, or perhaps the giant kangaroo rat might die before eating the seeds.

In the process of all this farming—altering the soil, weeding, collecting seeds and planting them—giant kangaroo rats have striking impacts on the plant community, both in the spaces between burrow mounds and across the landscape. To complicate matters, these effects are influenced by rainfall, in both the current and the previous year, and by mineral concentrations in the soil. Consecutive high-rainfall years can greatly increase native and nonnative grass cover. This leads to increased grass buildup, which can suppress grass and wildflower growth in the next year. However, giant kangaroo rats help reduce this buildup, moderating the effects of high rainfall. On the other hand, the persistence of giant kangaroo rat burrow mounds increases overall grass cover; thus, with burrow mounds and active giant kangaroo rats, the net effect is mostly neutral. At the landscape level, total plant species diversity tends to be higher when giant kangaroo rat burrows are present for long periods of time, especially as differences in nitrogen on and off burrow mounds increase. As a consequence, giant kangaroo rats increase the overall diversity in landscapes where they are present, by altering topography, soil conditions, and plant species composition and cover. When they persist, they can perform many of the roles that would otherwise fall to land managers. Furthermore, not only are giant kangaroo rats important farmers of natural systems, they are prey for owls, kit foxes, and badgers; they can control shrub communities encroaching on open grasslands; and they are a large, charismatic rodent that is found nowhere on Earth besides the San Joaquin Desert. But before they can do their job, we have to get them—or animals that can provide a similar ecological role—back on site and help them thrive (see chapter 7).

Giant kangaroo rats are fairly long-lived for a small rodent. Life spans average two to three years, with a maximum of five or six. They also have evolved to withstand drought by storing excess seed in their burrow systems. In other words, once they have established themselves at a site, they tend to persist. They also seem to disperse long distances when necessary, so there are opportunities for natural recolonization. In one recent study, a pair of siblings was found nearly 5 kilometers apart (Alexander et al. 2019). This capacity for reintroducing themselves is good because any active reintroduction effort will require approval by both state and federal agencies. In many sites, therefore, reintroduction of giant kangaroo rats will be time and resource intensive. A passive approach—in other words, deliberately retiring farmlands closer to existing source populations to allow natural recolonization—may be more feasible. Even then, however, it may take years or decades before the giant kangaroo rats will return on their own. For example, after establishment of the Carrizo Plain National Monument (see figure 0-1), it took nearly fifteen years (and a failed reintroduction effort) before giant kangaroo rats functionally dominated the landscape. It took another five years to expand to fallowed farmland areas north of the monument. But giant kangaroo rats also have narrow needs for soil type and drainage, and it is unclear how they will respond to a vegetation community recently recovered on retired farmlands, particularly those with saline, alkaline, and heavy clay soils that have been irrigated and tilled for a number of years (see chapter 3). Although restoration of this iconic, endangered species should be a long-term goal, a number of other species may perform similar roles without quite the expense or effort.

From granivorous ants that collect preferred grass seeds to tule elk that reduce nonnative plant cover, the San Joaquin Desert hosts a diverse group of animals that might perform similar functional roles to giant kangaroo rats, particularly in areas where giant kangaroo rats have never existed (e.g., valley floor former lakebed locations with heavy clay soils). Although the ultimate goal of rewilding might be to have places with fully functioning, highly diverse native communities of plants and animals, achieving that level of complexity may take a very long time or be very expensive. In the meantime, piecing together individual functions by using species that are already present on the landscape could provide a bridge to rewilding.

Burrowing animals are abundant in the San Joaquin Desert. Pocket gophers perform similar roles to giant kangaroo rats, including building burrow mounds over time. California ground squirrels, too, may easily recolonize retired farmland areas or may be present already. Not only are they burrowing, granivorous rodents, but some evidence suggests that they increase local biodiversity as giant kangaroo rats do (Lenihan 2007). But the political implications of supporting California ground squirrels may be very different from those for kangaroo rats. Reintroduction of an endangered species requires a lengthy bureaucratic review, especially for a species listed at both state and federal levels. Ground squirrels, on the other hand, may be easy to move or support bureaucratically but may require very different buy-in from neighboring landowners. Depending on the landscape-level context of the property, reintroduction may be an option if nearby landowners have ground squirrels but do not want them on their land (Swaisgood et al. 2019). On the other hand, ground squirrels are often considered pests on grazed lands, and the spillover effects of ground squirrels moving onto neighboring farms may cause headaches for managers trying to maintain good relationships with owners of working lands. Other nonlisted kangaroo rat species, such as Heermann's, San Joaquin, and narrow-faced, will also serve many of the critical burrowing functions that giant kangaroo rats provide. As with plant species (see chapters 2 and 3), there are genetic considerations of source populations to take into account for animal reintroductions (see chapters 7 and 8).

Seed dispersal is another function that giant kangaroo rats perform, but many other species do, too. Farmers plant seeds in their fields to produce a crop. Many animals also spread seeds that eventually germinate and grow into plants. Granted, animals do not do this with the intended purpose of growing more plants. It is more of an accidental process, but it results in seeds being dispersed to new areas and sometimes even being deposited in more favorable growing sites. This process can facilitate the colonization of an area, such as retired farmland, by plants, and once they are established it also helps perpetuate plant populations. Thus, the dispersal of seeds by animals is an important ecological process.

Some animals passively disperse seeds that hitch a ride in their fur or feathers. This includes humans. Walk through a field of dry vegetation in the San Joaquin Desert and then count the grass and other seeds in your pants, shoelaces, and socks. Many seeds have specialized hook structures or are sticky for this very purpose.

Seeds also are passively dispersed when they are consumed (but not damaged by chewing) and then pass through the gut of an animal and are excreted intact. Some ingested seeds actually have higher germination rates because of the scarification of their seed coat by digestive juices. Elk, pronghorn, and livestock disperse vast quantities of seed in this manner. Some of these seeds have the further advantage of being deposited in a heap of fertilizer. In the spring, it is not uncommon to see elk dung or a cow patty that looks like a Chia Pet because of all the seedlings emerging from it. Finally, predators can be significant secondary seed dispersers when they consume rodents that have ingested or are carrying seeds and then excrete or regurgitate the remains including viable seeds. Kit foxes, coyotes, badgers, hawks, and owls all consume large numbers of kangaroo rats and pocket mice and therefore are potential seed dispersers. Even rattlesnakes have recently been found to excrete viable seeds.

As all of these components are added back into the system, managers can begin to restore the pyramid of life from the bottom up. Restoring native plants and topographic structure (see chapters 2 and 3) should bring ants and rodents back to the scene. By burrowing, dispersing, and consuming seeds, these animals will inevitably help create and maintain a landscape that is more representative of the wild San Joaquin. Only then will small mammals begin to support populations of badgers, coyotes, burrowing owls, and kit foxes.

Indeed, far from just skimming off the top of the food chain, predators are key ingredients to a healthy restored ecosystem. Just as herbivores and granivores can shift plant communities through selective foraging, so too can predator preferences alter the community dynamics of their prey. When predators target dominant competitors, they can help keep those dominant species in check. For example, coyotes in Texas were shown to maintain rodent diversity by suppressing the dominant Ord's kangaroo rat (Henke and Bryant 1999); in areas where coyote numbers were reduced, Ord's quickly took over. On the other hand, sometimes the presence of a dominant prey species can support high numbers of predators that are not sustainable when populations of that prey species succumb to changes in the environment. For example, a dizzying array of avian, reptilian, and mammalian predators rely on the giant kangaroo rat in the Carrizo Plain. So reliant are these predators on giant kangaroo rats that when populations occasionally go bust, as they tend to do after extended droughts, predator numbers quickly follow suit. In fact, predators declined more dramatically during the historic drought from 2012 to 2014 than plants and herbivores did (Prugh et al. 2018). After giant kangaroo rats and their predators dropped to alarmingly low numbers, several smaller rodent species increased markedly in numbers. The relationship between predators and their primary prey can thus be key in either dampening or amplifying the their individual effects on other species in the food web.

Conclusions

In summary, animals can and will perform the functions that a land manager would otherwise take on, and therefore they are a critical piece of any rewilding effort. Rather than being an added burden for managers, animals are often the key missing pieces to restoring natural function. For threatened and endangered species, landowners considering temporary fallowing or permanent land retirement who want to encourage principles of rewilding will need protections such as safe harbor agreements, policies by which landowners who promote the presence of threatened and endangered species are not subsequently punished if the population on the land decreases (see chapters 11 and 12). There is simply no good reason to encourage landowners to introduce species onto their land if it means added regulatory and financial burdens and more restrictive land uses in the future, especially on lands that have been temporarily fallowed. Neighboring landowners will also need some assurance that the animal population will not directly damage their crops or compromise food safety and that they will not be responsible for incidentally harming animals that wander onto their farms during farming activities (see chapter 11). Stakeholders should advocate a vision for animals in the San Joaquin Desert that will benefit both agriculture and other industry: no more endangered species. If enough land were restored to support multiple large populations of giant kangaroo rats, leopard lizards, kit foxes, and the suite of species that fall under their umbrella, these species could one day be removed from the endangered species list (Kelsey et al. 2018). This action will relieve landowners in this region from the threat of regulatory burdens while strengthening a unique, valuable, and underappreciated natural community.

Why do so few people value the community of native species that live in the San Joaquin Desert? Perhaps because the remnants, such as the Carrizo Plain, are hard to find and hard to get to. And perhaps because, apart from a few brilliant weeks in spring, the landscape is as harsh and uninviting as any desert. But when we have a chance to walk in the open grassland in late summer and hear tule elk bugle, grasshopper mice howl, and hundreds of giant kangaroo rats foot drum to warn each other of our presence, or when we have the opportunity to see a kit fox follow in our tracks, hoping to catch a mouse we might scare out of hiding, the people of the San Joaquin will recognize their land for the remarkable place that it is. The animals make it home.

References

Alexander, Nathan B., Mark J. Statham, Benjamin N. Sacks, and William T. Bean. 2019. "Generalist dispersal and gene flow of an endangered keystone specialist (*Dipodomys ingens*)." *Journal of Mammalogy* 100, no. 5: 1533–45.

Grinnell, Joseph, and Tracy Irwin Storer. 1924. *Animal Life in the Yosemite: An Account of the Mammals, Birds, Reptiles, and Amphibians in a Cross-Section of the Sierra Nevada*. Berkeley: University of California Press.

Henke, Scott E., and Fred C. Bryant. 1999. "Effects of coyote removal on the faunal community in western Texas." *The Journal of Wildlife Management* 63, no. 4: 1066–1081.

Ivey, Kathleen N., Margaret Cornwall, Hayley Crowell, Nargol Ghazian, Emmeleia Nix, Malory Owen, Mario Zuliani, Christopher J. Lortie, Michael Westphal, and Emily Taylor. 2020. "Thermal ecology of the federally endangered blunt-nosed leopard lizard (*Gambelia sila*)." *Conservation Physiology* 8, no. 1: coaa014.

Kelsey, Rodd, Abigail K. Hart, H. Scott Butterfield, and Dan Vink. 2018. "Groundwater sustainability in the San Joaquin Valley: multiple benefits if agricultural lands are retired and restored strategically." *California Agriculture* 72, no. 3: 151–54.

Lenihan, Colleen M. 2007. "The ecological role of the California ground squirrel (*Spermophilus beecheyi*)." PhD diss., University of California, Davis.

Prugh, Laura R., Nicolas Deguines, Joshua B. Grinath, Katherine N. Suding, William T. Bean, Robert Stafford, and Justin S. Brashares. 2018. "Ecological winners and losers of extreme drought in California." *Nature Climate Change* 8, no. 9: 819–24.

Swaisgood, Ronald R., J.-P. Montagne, C. M. Lenihan, Colleen L. Wisinski, Lisa A. Nordstrom, and Debra M. Shier. "Capturing pests and releasing ecosystem engineers: translocation of common but diminished species to re-establish ecological roles." *Animal Conservation* 22, no. 6 (2019): 600–610.

Chapter 5

Using Synthesis to Reveal Restoration Lessons Relevant to Rewilding the San Joaquin Desert

Christopher J. Lortie, Alessandro Filazzola,
María Florencia Miguel

Ecosystems in the San Joaquin Desert are home to unique flora and fauna that have changed dramatically, and they provide a profound opportunity to examine ecological processes critical to restoration of dryland ecosystems globally. Endemic, threatened, and endangered species are common in high-stress ecosystems such as these and are ecologically dependent on specific plants that provide crucial functions for these species. In desert and dryland ecosystems, shrubs play this role by providing a range of important functions for both animals (Lortie et al. 2016) and other plants (Filazzola and Lortie 2014). Building off chapters 2, 3, and 4, which documented lessons learned from individual studies and restoration projects in the San Joaquin Desert, here we aim to use synthesis to identify lessons learned from deserts and dryland ecosystems globally.

There are several ways to extract lessons learned from many studies. Synthesis allows us to aggregate evidence in ways you cannot do when looking only at individual studies, as we did with the cases of Atwell Island and Tranquillity in chapter 3. There are two ways to synthesize peer-reviewed literature: meta-analysis and systematic reviews (Lortie 2014). Systematic reviews typically document the process of searching and processing peer-reviewed literature. Extraction of evidence from systematic reviews focuses on the location, sample sizes, summary of methods used, and descriptions of the study. A meta-analysis similarly completes these steps but also adds the step of extracting a measure of the strength of evidence from each study; it gives you a quantitative statistic that helps you determine in our context which restoration practices may have the best chance of working in the San Joaquin Desert based on the similarity between sites, objectives, and methods. In this chapter, we distill lessons learned from a synthesis of systematic reviews and meta-analyses on desert and dryland ecosystems globally to inform our plans for rewilding the San Joaquin Desert. We organize the lessons into three sections: key themes that were present across the literature, concepts from fundamental theory, and specific restoration evidence from the San Joaquin Desert and California's other desert and dryland ecosystems. By examining these studies together, we can identify broad patterns that hold true across restoration efforts, not just in individual studies, to ensure that the big picture is always in focus.

Key Themes to Inform Restoration

We first examined the syntheses for specific themes and ideas relevant to restoration decision making for the San Joaquin Desert. Across all syntheses, a common set of themes emerged: plant diversity, the role of woody species, water availability, and livestock grazing.

First, the syntheses pointed to the importance of mechanisms that drive plant diversity, such as environmental filtering, the role of the physical environment selecting for species with specific traits (Le Bagousse-Pinguet et al. 2017), and positive plant interactions, the self-reinforcement effects different species can have on one another (Soliveres and Maestre 2014). These mechanisms can help us describe and predict how species and ecosystems respond to stressors such as climate change, disturbance, land cover change, and grazing and therefore may be helpful to practitioners in guiding selective management for biodiversity in desert and dryland ecosystems.

Second, local-scale management of woody structure and nitrogen deposition was important in desert and dryland ecosystems globally, particularly in those with a matrix of agricultural land use similar to that of the San Joaquin Desert. Woody species were shown to have the capacity to drive biodiversity patterns locally and shift systems from shrub-dominated to grass-dominated ecosystems depending on extent and cover (Maestre et al. 2016).

Third, desert and dryland ecosystems are particularly sensitive to the quantity of and variation in annual precipitation (Gherardi and Sala 2019), and therefore water limitation is a critical factor in restoration of these ecosystems. Water budgets, measurement of vegetation water use patterns, remote sensing, and stable isotope tracking were identified as key methods and tools that can inform evidence-based decision making for desert and dryland ecosystem restoration (Wang et al. 2012). In addition to climate, land use patterns and water recharge rates also helped explain local water availability (Scanlon et al. 2006).

Finally, syntheses that examined livestock grazing did not point to any strong conclusions. However, there is increasing evidence that grazing can increase regional diversity in desert and dryland ecosystems even if local reductions in diversity are sometimes associated with increasing grazing pressure (Filazzola et al. 2020).

Lessons Learned from Restoration Ecology Theory

The field of restoration ecology is changing. Its scope and connections with other disciplines are increasing with the urgency created by local and global human impacts on landscapes, especially in desert and dryland ecosystems. This is both a challenge and an opportunity. Reinventing the wheel can lead to new discoveries, but existing theory can serve as a launchpad for restoration planning, research, and management. Although applied research plays an important role, we can use ideas and concepts from basic theory to structure research and practice. Restoration in the San Joaquin Desert can leverage syntheses of ecological theory to frame the key concepts and ideas most relevant to achieving successful outcomes. In this section we report on syntheses that explicitly examined restoration and theory in parallel. This process highlighted the importance of defining goals and objectives; including landscape-level concepts, such as habitat connectivity, in restoration planning; and moving away from single-study lessons learned (but see chapter 3) to more generally applicable concepts.

The first key lesson revealed in these syntheses is that restoration challenges are site- and region-specific. We must clearly define our goals and objectives, which can include specific definitions of function, diversity, or sustainable endpoints. The other major lesson is that landscape-level processes cannot be overlooked even when the specific goals and objectives are locally based. Landscape-level concepts such as island biogeography, scale, and patch size are cornerstones of applied ecology and can similarly inform restoration at all scales. The theme of biogeography was echoed in a study specific to agroenvironmental subsidy planning, which revealed that we should soften agricultural lands, when possible, by including nonagricultural habitat within them to benefit wildlife movement (Donald and Evans 2006), a theme more specifically addressed in chapter 10. Second, we can use connectivity theory to inform decision making about how to facilitate wildlife movement through the agricultural matrix. Finally, Weiher (2007) concluded that we should move beyond demonstration or single-study science to inform decisions for a region.

Review of conclusions from these theory-based syntheses also revealed that investment in small patches of low-quality habitat is not recommended, consistent with basic conservation planning principles (see chapter 9), and that decision making about what restoration investments are best should explicitly include economic and socioeconomic considerations. As discussed in chapter 13, economic and socioeconomic evaluations can include assessments of the costs of different restoration techniques, contingent values, opportunity costs, and cost–benefit analyses (Wortley et al. 2013). A critical lesson is that if you do not explicitly evaluate and include social outcomes in your decision making, restoration practices will not become policy, which could limit their broad adoption.

Restoration planning should include evaluations of ecological complexity and community assembly, leading to the identification of the key factors limiting the ecological process for restoration, repair, and recovery. Planning should occur across multiple scales (e.g., local and regional), but there will be trade-offs. The extent to which we can achieve process-based and goal-oriented restoration objectives for a region depends on the spatial extent of the initiative and the timeframes available to practitioners (Rappaport et al. 2015). One solution that these syntheses identified is to prioritize planning through regional habitat rankings, a concept widely applied in conservation planning. This approach is evaluated in chapter 9 as part of identifying where across the San Joaquin Desert we can optimize land retirement for multiple benefits including habitat restoration. Planning approaches must also recognize that habitat quality is not always a direct predictor of restoration outcomes. Animals have preferences and cognitive biases that can lead to ecological traps (Hale and Swearer 2017), a scenario in which rapid environmental change leads organisms to settle in poor-quality habitats. This is a critical trade-off between habitat restoration targets without simultaneous work with the local species-specific wildlife conservation targets.

Finally, theory naturally leads to different classes of restoration strategy, namely passive versus active interventions (Wainwright et al. 2018). A key lesson from these syntheses is that a flexible strategy that incorporates both passive and active approaches is likely to be not only more cost effective but also ecologically effective because some processes operate over longer time scales and are thus best examined through passive strategies.

Lessons Learned from the San Joaquin and California Desert and Dryland Ecosystems

The San Joaquin Desert is home to many species, including several endemic plants and animals. Research on the habitat needs for these species is limited because declines occurred early in the century, and remaining habitat is often of low quality. We have a general understanding of what the habitat needs are for some of these species, but there remain many outstanding questions about what specific ingredients would make a perfect recipe for San Joaquin Desert restoration. Our synthesis of San Joaquin Valley–specific research revealed some general themes for restoration, including the need to improve habitat patch size (make the new habitats as big as possible), connectivity through remnant natural and agricultural landscapes (make all habitats as connected to one another as possible), and habitat quality (make the habitat able to sustain as many different native plant and animal species as possible). These were all themes identified in our broad synthesis of restoration theory as well.

The San Joaquin Desert has one of the highest concentrations of threatened and endangered species in the continental United States for a reason; most of the habitat for these species has been lost to agricultural and residential development (see figure 1-2 in chapter 1), and the remaining habitat remnants are often of low quality and are disconnected from one another. We know from theory and practice that smaller, lower-quality habitat patches negatively affect resident plant and animal species. For example, in the San Joaquin Desert, the blunt-nosed leopard lizard benefits from at least a 2-kilometer buffer from human development and needs at least 1,200 acres of contiguous habitat. A single San Joaquin kit fox family group needs at least 1,500 acres of habitat. A critical first step in the restoration process for these species is thus to increase the total amount of habitat, by identifying and protecting or restoring (rewilding) large tracts of land or connecting smaller tracts, restored or not, to already protected and occupied habitat (see chapter 9).

Connectivity is a key theme for plant and animal species survival globally, and the long-term survival of San Joaquin Desert plant and animal endemic species is no different. Landscape connectivity cannot be achieved through land protection and restoration alone. We need to create connectivity through agricultural landscapes (see chapters 9 and 10) by softening agricultural lands, when possible, with natural habitat interspersed with farmed crops, adapting management of agricultural lands to be as compatible as possible with species movement; and by developing specific movement corridors. Wildlife underpasses can further facilitate movement around linear human features such as roads.

Habitat quality can be improved through active restoration and management, on both natural and agricultural lands. For example, many San Joaquin Desert species need burrows to escape the heat and for food storage and predator avoidance. Burrows can be created by rodents, including species such as the giant kangaroo rat (see chapter 4), and artificial burrows can be built in places where rodents are not present or desirable (see chapter 7). When possible, restoration actions should focus on those that increase habitat quality for multiple species, especially those that serve keystone or foundational roles, such as the giant kangaroo rat (Prugh and Brashares 2012) and shrubs (Lortie et al. 2016), such as ephedra, in the San Joaquin Desert. However, there are times when managing for foundational species, such as shrubs, can have negative consequences, including increases in weedy, nonnative grasses (Lucero et al. 2019). By focusing on species with community-wide impacts, your restoration actions will be more efficient. This, in turn, will increase the abundance and diversity of a range of native plant and animal species. Improving habitat quality in the San Joaquin Desert (and all California desert and dryland ecosystems) must include management of the dominant weedy nonnative grasses, introduced during European settlement and naturalized over the past 150 years (see chapters 2 and 3). Most San Joaquin Desert endemic species, whether plant or animal, prefer bare or sparsely vegetated sandy soil. Weedy nonnative grasses, which tend to outcompete their shorter-stature and lower-productivity native plant counterparts, grow tall and form dense stands, reducing native plant cover and inhibiting the movement of and increasing the predation of native animal species. These grasses also can increase fire fuel loads, which tends to lead to hotter, more intense grass fires that can damage or kill shrub species, including those serving important foundational roles.

Management of weedy nonnative grasses can take many forms, including grazing, seeding of native plant competitors, herbicides, mechanical removal, carbon addition, and prescribed fire. Species interactions such as facilitation, competition, and herbivory are all important processes relevant to restoration efforts focused on reducing the competitive dominance of weedy nonnative grasses. In all instances, restoration efforts should first use some form of active human intervention (e.g., herbicides), followed by careful management of vegetation by species and controlled water availability.

As discussed in chapter 4, giant kangaroo rats and other rodent species can serve the role of grazer in these systems. If they are not present, cattle or other livestock can be used—in limited instances, such as in heavy rainfall years or where natural grazers such as kangaroo rats are not present—to reduce the cover of weedy nonnative species (see chapter 3). Seeding native species with resource needs similar to those of weedy nonnative grasses can reduce their competitive advantage. However, securing enough seeds for successful large-scale native plant restoration, as discussed in chapters 2 and 3, remains a challenge (Borders et al. 2011). One strategy to address this issue could include large and organized collections from remaining remnant populations (including on federal lands;

see chapter 2), which could then be commercially grown at high volumes, a similar approach to what was done by the U.S. Bureau of Land Management at Atwell Island and Tranquillity (see chapter 3). Large-scale rewilding, like that suggested in this book, may make an operation like this more economically feasible in the future. Resident animal species, such as giant kangaroo rats, preferentially feed on and encourage the growth of certain species (see chapter 4). Therefore, restoration efforts that use seeding of native species need to also address granivory by either excluding rodents from seeded plots or compensating with higher seed densities.

Herbicides and mechanical removal can be used to reduce weedy nonnative grass cover. These grasses may also be reduced through carbon addition. Nitrogen is often limiting in the soils of California desert and dryland ecosystems; when added, nitrogen is taken up more quickly by weedy nonnative grasses, which allows them to increase cover and density at the expense of native species. Carbon addition decreases nitrogen availability for native and nonnative species, which could remove their competitive advantage, although this may not be the case for all arid environments, including places similar to the San Joaquin Desert. Water addition is another tool that could help reduce nonnative weedy grass cover: Water addition may accelerate the timing of germination relative to natives, which could induce herbivory by rodents and increase weedy nongrass seedling mortality.

Interactions between plants are also an important consideration for restoration. In desert and dryland ecosystems, shrubs have been shown in some instances to facilitate the germination and establishment of other plant species under their canopies. However, the effects of different desert and dryland ecosystem shrub species in facilitating other (native) plants must be examined more broadly. Some shrub species in desert and dryland ecosystems can recover from physical damage, but not all. Understanding interactions and identifying foundation plant species can be key to conserving intact populations and accelerating the restoration of degraded ones. Revegetation of degraded desert and dryland ecosystems is constrained mainly by water availability (Elliott et al. 2014). The addition of water and nutrients to adult shrub species can result in an increase in the number of seeds produced and in seed weights. Nonetheless, identifying ideal microsites and safe sites for seedling establishment and growth is also a key consideration for restoration. In particular, lessons from research on suitable sites for shrub transplants suggest that protecting seedlings against herbivores is critical. Seeding can be a faster and more economical method than transplanting. Supplementing water to seeded shrub species can produce different species-specific effects on germination. Irrigation must be applied judiciously because nonfocal species, including weedy nonnative grasses, resident in the system can also respond to additional water. The source of seeds and seedlings was also identified as an important component of successful restoration efforts. Provenance studies suggest that local is best but that one must also incorporate seed from a broad range of environmental variables that includes genetic variability to increase the likelihood of plant establishment to a given site. This is a concept we explore for plant and animal species in more detail in chapter 8.

Restoration projects must be monitored to allow adaptive management. Monitoring is often expensive and time-consuming. However, technology-based solutions such as DNA scat dogs, wildlife cameras, telemetry, remote sensing, and artificial intelligence are increasing our ability to monitor species quickly, more accurately, and at lower costs. DNA from scat is now being used to monitor population dynamics of endemic San Joaquin Desert species such as the blunt-nosed leopard lizard, giant kangaroo rat, and San Joaquin kit fox. Wildlife cameras, when combined with new artificial intelligence–driven analytics, are being used to track animal populations, record behavior, and estimate abundance. Telemetry has been used to monitor individual species survival and movement (Lortie et al. 2020). Remote sensing technologies continue to improve and get cheaper, allowing remote assessments of habitat quality and proxies of animal abundance. For example, the burrows of giant kangaroo rats can be rapidly and effectively assessed via aerial surveys (Bean et al. 2012).

Conclusions

Restoration ecology is a rapidly advancing contemporary field of interdisciplinary research and practice. The syntheses evaluated in this chapter illuminate a set of best practices for restoration in desert and dryland ecosystems. Synthesis offers the big picture and provides a helpful framework for restoration planning and implementation at all scales from local to regional. Promoting native diversity is the critical end goal in almost all desert and dryland ecosystems. Scale cannot be ignored. Single studies can demonstrate an idea, but principles are needed to inform policy and develop generalizable restoration approaches. Restoration projects must be goal oriented. Principles can advance policies that support restoration, but only when the social costs are also incorporated. Management of social perception will further increase success rates for restoration projects. Trade-offs, triage, and rankings are a reality for restoration in the San Joaquin Desert, and ecological theory, even in a general way, can inform decision making. Benchmarks are needed to guide the work and can include ecological measures such as diversity and distribution patterns, but they also need to be grounded in flexible, realistic definitions of how long those outcomes can be realized over large areas to achieve our restoration outcomes. Restoration requires a whole-community approach. Passive and active restoration strategies are both viable pathways depending on the condition of the site and on resources such as time, space, and financial support. To support at-risk species, restoration efforts should focus on increasing habitat area, improving connectivity, and increasing the ratio of native plants to weedy nonnative ones with consistent monitoring to evaluate restoration efficacy.

References

Bean, William T., Robert Stafford, Laura R. Prugh, H. Scott Butterfield, and Justin S. Brashares. 2012. "An evaluation of monitoring methods for the endangered giant kangaroo rat." *Wildlife Society Bulletin* 36, no. 3: 587–93.

Borders, Brianna D., Brian L. Cypher, Nur P. Ritter, and Patrick A. Kelly. 2011. "The challenge of locating seed sources for restoration in the San Joaquin Valley, California." *Natural Areas Journal* 31, no. 2: 190–99.

Donald, Paul F., and Andy D. Evans. 2006. "Habitat connectivity and matrix restoration: the wider implications of agri-environment schemes." *Journal of Applied Ecology* 43, no. 2: 209–18.

Elliott, Joshua, Delphine Deryng, Christoph Müller, Katja Frieler, Markus Konzmann, Dieter Gerten, Michael Glotter, et al. 2014. "Constraints and potentials of future irrigation water availability on agricultural production under climate change." *Proceedings of the National Academy of Sciences* 111, no. 9: 3239–44.

Filazzola, Alessandro, Charlotte Brown, Margarete A. Dettlaff, Amgaa Batbaatar, Jessica Grenke, Tan Bao, Isaac Peetoom Heida, and James F. Cahill Jr. 2020. "The effects of livestock grazing on biodiversity are multi-trophic: a meta-analysis." *Ecology Letters* 23, no. 8: 1298–1309.

Filazzola, Alessandro, and Christopher J. Lortie. 2014. "A systematic review and conceptual framework for the mechanistic pathways of nurse plants." *Global Ecology and Biogeography* 23, no. 12: 1335–45.

Gherardi, Laureano A., and Osvaldo E. Sala. 2019. "Effect of interannual precipitation variability on dryland productivity: a global synthesis." *Global Change Biology* 25, no. 1: 269–76.

Hale, Robin, and Stephen E. Swearer. 2017. "When good animals love bad restored habitats: how maladaptive habitat selection can constrain restoration." *Journal of Applied Ecology* 54, no. 5: 1478–86.

Le Bagousse-Pinguet, Yoann, Nicolas Gross, Fernando T. Maestre, Vincent Maire, Francesco de Bello, Carlos Roberto Fonseca, Jens Kattge, Enrique Valencia, Jan Leps, and Pierre Liancourt. 2017. "Testing the environmental filtering concept in global drylands." *Journal of Ecology* 105, no. 4: 1058–69.

Lortie, Christopher J. 2014. "Formalized synthesis opportunities for ecology: systematic reviews and meta-analyses." *Oikos* 123, no. 8: 897–902.

Lortie, Christopher J., Jenna Braun, Michael Westphal, Taylor Noble, Mario Zuliani, Emmeleia Nix, Nargol Ghazian, Malory Owen, and H. Scott Butterfield. 2020. "Shrub and vegetation cover predict resource selection use by an endangered species of desert lizard." *Scientific Reports* 10, no. 1: 1–7.

Lortie, Christopher J., Alessandro Filazzola, and Diego A. Sotomayor. 2016. "Functional assessment of animal interactions with shrub-facilitation complexes: a formal synthesis and conceptual framework." *Functional Ecology* 30, no. 1: 41–51.

Lucero, Jacob E., Taylor Noble, Stephanie Haas, Michael Westphal, H. Scott Butterfield, and Christopher J. Lortie. 2019. "The dark side of facilitation: native shrubs facilitate exotic annuals more strongly than native annuals." *NeoBiota* 44: 75.

Maestre, Fernando T., David J. Eldridge, Santiago Soliveres, Sonia Kéfi, Manuel Delgado-Baquerizo, Matthew A. Bowker, Pablo García-Palacios, et al. 2016. "Structure and functioning of dryland ecosystems in a changing world." *Annual Review of Ecology, Evolution, and Systematics* 47: 215–37.

Prugh, Laura R., and Justin S. Brashares. 2012. "Partitioning the effects of an ecosystem engineer: kangaroo rats control community structure via multiple pathways." *Journal of Animal Ecology* 81, no. 3: 667–78.

Rappaport, Danielle I., Leandro R. Tambosi, and Jean P. Metzger. 2015. "A landscape triage approach: combining spatial and temporal dynamics to prioritize restoration and conservation." *Journal of Applied Ecology* 52, no. 3: 590–601.

Scanlon, Bridget R., Kelley E. Keese, Alan L. Flint, Lorraine E. Flint, Cheikh B. Gaye, W. Michael Edmunds, and Ian Simmers. 2006. "Global synthesis of groundwater recharge in semiarid and arid regions." *Hydrological Processes: An International Journal* 20, no. 15: 3335–70.

Soliveres, Santiago, and Fernando T. Maestre. 2014. "Plant–plant interactions, environmental gradients and plant diversity: a global synthesis of community-level studies." *Perspectives in Plant Ecology, Evolution and Systematics* 16, no. 4: 154–63.

Wainwright, Claire E., Timothy L. Staples, Lachlan S. Charles, Thomas C. Flanagan, Hao Ran Lai, Xingwen Loy, Victoria A. Reynolds, and Margaret M. Mayfield. 2018. "Links between community ecology theory and ecological restoration are on the rise." *Journal of Applied Ecology* 55, no. 2: 570–81.

Wang, Lixin, P. d'Odorico, J. P. Evans, D. J. Eldridge, M. F. McCabe, K. K. Caylor, and E. G. King. 2012. "Dryland ecohydrology and climate change: critical issues and technical advances." *Hydrology and Earth System Sciences* 16: 2585.

Weiher, Evan. 2007. "On the status of restoration science: obstacles and opportunities." *Restoration Ecology* 15, no. 2: 340–43.

Wortley, Liana, Jean-Marc Hero, and Michael Howes. 2013. "Evaluating ecological restoration success: a review of the literature." *Restoration Ecology* 21, no. 5: 537–43.

Part II

Principles of Farmland Rewilding from the San Joaquin Valley

Chapter 6

Assessing Species' Responses to Climate Change to Guide When, Where, and How to Rewild Retired Farmland

William Tim Bean, Joseph A. Stewart, Ryan E. O'Dell, and Scott Phillips

Every piece of land in the San Joaquin Valley is best suited for certain crops, and not every crop will do equally well everywhere. In some places, it is too cold for citrus. In others, the soil is saturated and too wet for pistachios. Each plant can thrive within a range of temperatures, soil conditions, and water availability specific to that species or breed. Some species need the presence, or absence, of other living things too: pollinators, soil microbes, or the lack of diseases or pests that will allow the crop to thrive. Of course, humans have become experts at modifying conditions so that land historically unsuitable for growing crops can become suitable, whether through the addition of a nutrient to the soil, modification of temperature (e.g., with greenhouses, shade, or frost protection), water availability (e.g., direct irrigation), or pest control. Many of these modifications are economically and practically feasible, and others are not: The San Joaquin Valley does not and will probably never produce much maple syrup. Understanding this set of conditions, knowing what is right for a specific type of land or how to modify that land to bring it into production, is the product of many generations of experience, study, and trial and error. Now, as the climate is changing and becoming warmer, farmers are having to reassess where the best places will be for different crops. For example, many crops in the San Joaquin Valley depend on having a certain number of cold winter days to cue flowering, including pistachios. As the climate warms, the areas suitable for producing high yields in these crops are shifting northward (Luedeling et al. 2011).

Wild plants and animals also have their own specific requirements. These are generally divided into abiotic requirements, such as climate and soil type, and biotic, such as predators, food sources, and disease. All these factors determine a species' niche, the conditions necessary for that species' existence and its role in the existence of others. Wild plants and animals also need to find their way to suitable land. Crops need only the human initiative to sow some seeds or plant a sapling. For wild species, there may be many suitable places on the planet that are not inhabited simply because the plant or animal cannot get there; there are no koalas in the eucalyptus windbreaks of the San Joaquin Valley. As with domesticated crops, the land can sometimes be modified to meet the needs of wild species (see chapters 3 and 7), but we often lack basic information about those needs (see chapters 4 and 5).

It is important to consider how climate warming is changing the suitability of the land for natural communities and species we want to save. For that reason, there is growing interest in developing climate projection maps for fifty, seventy, or one hundred years into the future to see where species might need to move or, perhaps more importantly, where the climate will be stable enough that they can stay in place. We want to ensure that the land selected for rewilding will continue to be suitable as the world gets hotter.

To understand where investment in rewilding can endure in a changing climate, we need a deep understanding of where species could thrive now if given a chance, as well as where they might need to move as the climate warms. Unfortunately, despite the time and money that has gone into studying the needs of threatened and endangered species, our understanding pales in comparison to the knowledge we have for crops. Ecologists therefore rely on shortcuts to understand the range of biotic and abiotic conditions that allow a species to thrive and use this information to predict where a species could persist now and in the future.

One shortcut that ecologists regularly rely on is correlative modeling to predict where species are most likely to be or persist, variously called species distribution models, habitat suitability models, environmental niche models, or bioclimatic niche models. Many different statistical techniques have been applied to assess a species' habitat needs, but the basic premise is the same for each. First, we identify the biotic and abiotic factors believed to limit or promote the species of interest. These factors vary, but they typically include climate, soil type, and vegetation type, all of which can play a strong role in creating the underlying conditions to which a species is adapted. Next, we compare the range of these conditions where the species is currently or was historically found to an entire region of interest. Finally, once we have estimated the relationship between the underlying environmental conditions and the species' occurrences, that relationship is projected onto a map of the environmental conditions in the rest of the region to create a map of suitability (figure 6-1). This map is essentially a prediction of the relative likelihood that the focal species could be found in a given place. High values typically mean a high probability of finding the species, and low values the opposite. Many studies have also found that areas with high suitability values often host the highest densities of individuals, or populations with high survival. In other words, these models seem to do a good job of finding suitable places for the species to live.

These models clearly can be great tools for planning where protection and restoration could be most successful under current conditions. However, these models make a series of assumptions that may not stand up to changing environmental

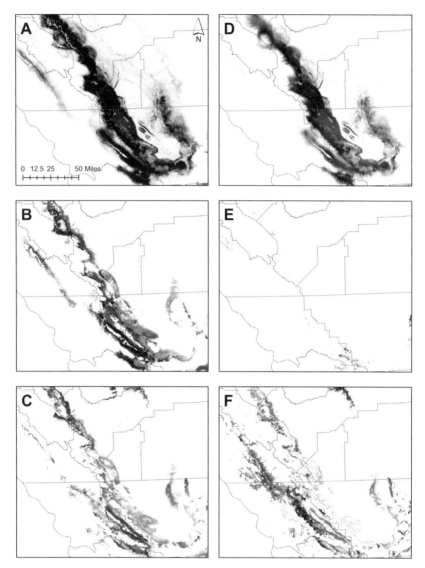

Figure 6-1. Example of alternative distribution model outcomes depending on assumptions. Black areas represent higher suitability for giant kangaroo rats. (A) Historical model built on the full range of environmental conditions in which giant kangaroo rats could persist; (B) contemporary model assuming giant kangaroo rats currently occupy the full range of suitable conditions despite loss of 95 percent of historical habitat; (C) contemporary model assuming northern and southern populations have undergone adaptation to local climate conditions; and (D), (E), and (F) projections of climate impacts in 2070 on giant kangaroo rats based on (A), (B), and (C), respectively.

conditions, including climate warming. We find strong correlations between where a species has been found in the past and the existing environmental conditions and assume there is some causation between the two, but this may not be the case. Here we summarize four complications of species distribution models. Then, we use a series of case studies from the San Joaquin Valley to illustrate how to most effectively develop and apply these models for guiding rewilding.

Caveats for Developing and Applying Species Distribution Models

Species distribution models assume that a species is able to get to every place in the region; in other words, if a suitable place is available for the species to live, it will be found there. For many animals, particularly those that fly, movement is not a major problem within areas the size of the San Joaquin Valley. However, large roads, waterways, large expanses of farmland, or major mountain ranges can all prevent species from reaching suitable habitat. In this case, a model may underrepresent the range of conditions in which a species could thrive because it will assume that all unoccupied areas are less suitable than occupied ones. This assumption may prove particularly problematic for species in the San Joaquin Desert that actually evolved in the hotter, drier conditions of the Mojave Desert to the southeast (see figure 0-1). Many plant and animal species in the San Joaquin Desert may do quite well in those conditions, but over geologic time they have become isolated in the San Joaquin Desert because they are not able to cross the Transverse Ranges. As a result, our models using current distributions would predict that they will suffer as the climate becomes warmer, when in fact they may not. As the climate of the San Joaquin Desert becomes hotter and drier (i.e., as the Mojave Desert shifts north), the species may do fine. Similarly, the impacts of humans may have reduced the available set of environmental conditions in which a species can thrive. The San Joaquin Valley has been disproportionately developed in the flattest areas with the most productive soils (see figure 1-2). These areas might support high concentrations of sensitive species if restored, as Stewart et al. (2019) showed for blunt-nosed leopard lizards, but the model will only see those areas as currently unoccupied and deem them unsuitable.

Second, these models often do not account for a species' ability to adapt to changing conditions on-site. Adaptations could take the form of shifts in behavior; for example, as it gets hotter, animals such as the blunt-nosed leopard lizard might hunt for food at cooler times of day (Ivey et al. 2020) or increasingly rely on shrubs or burrow entrances for shade (Lortie et al. 2020). Or adaptations could be evolutionary: Individuals within a population that are best adapted to hotter conditions may survive and reproduce more often, and over the course of generations, the population could evolve to cope with the changing climate. However, the ability of species to adapt to climate change on-site should not be assumed; for instance, individuals at the hot end of a species distribution may have already shifted their activity to the coolest hours of daylight available. Any additional loss of time for hunting could push them over the edge (Ivey et al. 2020).

Similarly, adaptation to rapid climate change is limited by existing genetic diversity. Take the history of selective breeding, for example. Farmers can much more easily create varieties of cotton that thrive in the sunny conditions of the San Joaquin Valley with only a little irrigation. These species evolved in open areas to begin with and do well in full sun. By contrast, many of the berries grown in California evolved beneath the shade of taller trees. It is much more difficult to breed berries that do well in full sun and much easier to build structures to give them the shade they need. By just looking at places where cotton and strawberries grow in their native conditions, we probably would not have expected them to do well in the San Joaquin Valley. But through selective breeding and behavioral modifications (for strawberries, giving them shade), these crops do fine. To the extent that species are able to adapt, then, species distribution models may underestimate suitable environmental conditions in the future. This is probably truer for species that evolved in arid environments. Indeed, a growing body of evidence suggests that where a species evolved may be the key to understanding how it will cope with a changing climate in the future. If wrong, these first two assumptions suggest a bleaker picture for species under climate change than what will come to pass.

By contrast, the other two complications may produce overly rosy predictions. First, climate is often used as a proxy for important interactions with other species. For example, coffee may be grown at a wide range of temperatures, but in hotter climates it appears to be limited by the coffee borer beetle rather than temperature. In this case, the real limiting factor is the beetle, but a climate-driven model might find only that coffee does not do well in warm areas. As the climate changes, these interactions could remain stable: As it gets hotter, the beetle does better and expands its range, reducing coffee production. In this instance, the model may be a good predictor for the future. But in other cases, the interaction (i.e., climate and the coffee borer beetle) that truly determines how well a species does may become decoupled from the climate associated with it. This may be particularly true as suitable climates move but the other environmental factors such as topography or soil type do not.

Similarly, there may be important features at individual sites that the model cannot capture. For instance, a restored farm may have higher nitrogen levels in the soil, making it more suitable for weedy nonnative grasses, such as those naturalized and dominant within most San Joaquin Desert ecosystems (see chapters 2 and 5) that outcompete a native species of concern. Or there may be spillover from pests or predators from neighboring properties. These fine-scale characteristics are much harder to capture in a large-scale model.

Habitat suitability models often produce beautiful maps that appear to show with great detail exactly where a species will and will not thrive (see figure 6-1). As appealing as these maps are, given the assumptions we have reviewed (and others we have not), they must be used with caution. Modeling is as much about the development process as it is the final map. Sitting down to identify important environmental characteristics, illuminating the most important assumptions in the model, and then assessing its usefulness in the field are just as important as the map that is produced. As we will show, using models to identify suitable habitat is an ongoing process that requires revision as new information is learned about the species and as new assumptions are discovered and tested.

Habitat Suitability Models from the San Joaquin Valley

Natural communities are often thought of as growing from the bottom up (but see chapter 4). Carnivores such as the San Joaquin kit fox consume kangaroo rats, other rodents, and insects, which in turn rely on the plant community for food. The further up the food chain, the more likely it is that interactions with other species (biotic interactions) may be more important than climate and other abiotic components. Therefore, we will start by assessing the response of the vegetation community to climate change in the San Joaquin Desert, before discussing the blunt-nosed leopard lizard and giant kangaroo rat. We chose these species for three reasons. First, they offer good insight into the important assumptions we have outlined. Second, they have received significant modeling attention, including by the authors of this chapter, and the differences in model outcomes illustrate the importance of these assumptions. Finally, the species are of both ecological and conservation importance and will therefore be central targets for rewilding.

Desert scrub plant communities provide critical habitat cover and structure for animals on otherwise featureless plains of the San Joaquin Valley and adjacent small valleys of the San Joaquin Desert. The widely scattered shrubs provide shade to stay cool in the summer and protection from predators. Saltbrush and ephedra are the two most important shrub species to animals of the

San Joaquin Desert, especially blunt-nosed leopard lizard and San Joaquin kit fox, serving a foundational role in these ecosystems. Saltbrush dominates the warmer, drier valley floor, and ephedra is found in higher areas on the edge of the western San Joaquin Desert. Both species are common throughout the southwestern United States, including the Mojave and Sonoran Deserts. The projected "business as usual" future climate in the year 2100 will be much warmer, with little change in annual precipitation, resulting in a shift from the warm San Joaquin Desert climate to a hot Mojave Desert–like climate. Although annual rainfall may stay the same on average, droughts may become longer and more severe. Because of their evolutionary history in even hotter areas, both saltbrush and ephedra should persist (Thorne et al. 2016). These shrubs will be critical for moderating the effects of hotter temperatures on other plants and animals that rely on them for shade. This is one critical example where models might miss the shrubs for the forest. A natural area with shrubs will provide much cooler temperatures than a recently plowed farm right next door. But the climate maps we have do not take these fine-scale differences into account. From a modeling perspective, these two areas will appear to have identical climates. In areas that have been plowed intensively enough to lose their native seedbed, intentional planting may be necessary to provide shade. Otherwise, these areas may appear to be climatically suitable at a large scale but, at a site level, not actually provide cool enough conditions for species to persist.

In addition, although the major vegetation types may persist, individual plant species may suffer (see chapter 2). One of those plants is the federally endangered annual forb species San Joaquin woolly-threads. It is a great example of the interaction between species—even specific plants and animals—that ultimately determine who can live where. Woolly-threads grow on loose, bare sandy patches around giant kangaroo rat burrow mounds, where competition from weedy annual grasses is reduced by clipping done by kangaroo rats and from soil disturbance caused by their burrowing (see chapter 4). Woolly-threads have several unique features that suggest they evolved in the presence of giant kangaroo rats and other rodents. Most distinctive of these is a low, branching growth form that protects it from rodent clipping and hairy, burr-like seeds that allow it to hitch a ride to other places on rodents and other small mammals. Importantly, unlike the shrub species described earlier that evolved in desert conditions, San Joaquin woolly-threads' ancestor evolved in the more moderate climate of the California coast. This species is less likely to have the genetic legacy to adapt to hotter, drier conditions, suggesting that this should not be a target species for rewilding.

San Joaquin woolly-thread has lost more than half of its historical habitat on the San Joaquin Valley floor. Most of the species is now found on San Joaquin Desert remnants in the Cuyama Valley, Carrizo Plain, and Kettleman Hills and at Jacalitos Creek and Panoche Creek (see figure 3-1). A few small, fragmented populations occur on the valley floor at Kern Water Bank (see chapter 11) and Lost Hills. Most of the remaining habitat for San Joaquin woolly-threads has been intensively invaded by weedy non-native grasses, whose fast growth smothers their slower-growing native counterparts. As a result, San Joaquin woolly-threads have become even more dependent on the clipping and soil disturbing activities of rodents and livestock grazing to keep their habitat open and bare. The ability of San Joaquin woolly-threads to find suitable habitat under the effects of climate change may be analogous to trying to get from Kettleman City to Shandon without a map and crossing the four lanes of traffic on Interstate 5 by foot—a formidable challenge indeed. San Joaquin woolly-threads will probably need to hitch a ride with us to safely get to where they need to go, in a process called assisted dispersal (see chapter 7). Assisted dispersal would involve harvesting seeds from current populations (existing range) and then sowing them on sandy soil habitat within the future San Joaquin Desert climate (projected range). Assisted dispersal and population introductions should focus on areas of sandy soils on the western leading edges of the San Joaquin Desert climate, including retired farmlands in the Cuyama Valley, northern Carrizo Plain to Shandon, and Panoche Valley (see figure 3-1).

This species illustrates the critical importance of understanding individual evolutionary history (see chapter 8). Species that have close relatives in hotter, drier climates may be less sensitive to climate change than those that are recent arrivals from cooler, wetter areas. However, deep evolutionary history is not the only consideration when projecting the impacts of climate change. The recent past can be an important factor as well, particularly for species whose distribution has recently collapsed because of human activities. What is more, San Joaquin woolly-threads may need multiple types of management if we reintroduce them into retired farmland. Reseeding will be important, but active grazing, by livestock or kangaroo rats, will also be needed (see chapter 5). On top of that, kangaroo rats and other small mammals may move seeds from one area to another. In other words, areas that appear suitable in a model may not actually have any San Joaquin woolly-threads present because there are no other species, such as livestock or kangaroo rats, to help them persist.

Giant Kangaroo Rat Case Study

Perhaps the most important species for woolly-threads, and for many other plants and animals, is the giant kangaroo rat (see chapter 4). Like most sensitive species of the San Joaquin Desert, the giant kangaroo rat has lost most of its habitat to agricultural conversion. Some estimates place the losses at more than 95 percent of their historical distribution. They feed almost exclusively on grass seeds, which they dry and store for use in the summer and fall and for years of drought. Their burrowing drastically alters the landscape, and over time the accumulation of dead plants and soil around their burrows creates easily distinguished burrow mounds.

This burrowing activity has allowed researchers to map their distribution in the San Joaquin Desert over time, using aerial surveys and inspection of recent and historical aerial photographs. Such extensive data on the distribution of a species are rarely available, so this species provides a unique opportunity to evaluate several assumptions about species distribution models.

Over the past decade, a series of studies have been conducted to characterize the relationship between giant kangaroo rat distribution and the environment. We present three of those models here to show how different assumptions produce different results. The first, and most crude, compared only the contemporary distribution with contemporary climate, vegetation type, and soil (Bean et al. 2014). This study was limited by not addressing two of the assumptions mentioned earlier: It made no attempt to control for local adaptation or the loss of suitable habitat. Despite these limitations, we present these results because many studies examining the impact of climate change on sensitive species suffer from similar problems. To control for the loss of historical habitat, a second model was created (Rutrough et al. 2019) using historical (pre-1960) aerial imagery to identify land occupied by giant kangaroo rats before the development of major irrigation projects in California. This historical model should better capture the true range of environmental conditions in which giant kangaroo rats can persist. Finally, Widick and Bean (2019) developed separate models for northern and southern populations of giant kangaroo rats. Previous research has suggested that these two populations have been reproductively isolated for more than 1,000 years (Statham et al. 2018). These two large populations persisting at two ends of the range may have undergone rapid selection. Models produced at the population scale may better reflect this local adaptation. Widick and Bean (2019) also tested whether California ground squirrels might be excluding giant kangaroo rats from wetter grasslands in the state. All these models were trained with contemporaneous climate data (i.e., the historical model used historical climate, and the modern models used modern climate) and then were projected into the future with climate models.

The results were all fairly similar for the contemporary distribution of giant kangaroo rats (see figure 6-1). All describe broad areas in the western San Joaquin Valley and the inner South Coast Ranges as suitable for the species, and under any metric they would be described as highly accurate. However, when projected into the future the differences become stark. In particular, the range-wide contemporary model becomes exceedingly pessimistic about the species' future, with only a few suitable patches remaining in the current range. Importantly, a few other areas in southern California may become suitable in the future under this model, but they are too far from contemporary populations for the species to ever get there, and by law listed species cannot be translocated outside their historical distribution (a problem not limited to giant kangaroo rats). By contrast, the historical model and a model based on an assumption of local adaptation are both far more optimistic about suitable habitat for giant kangaroo rats in the future. The first major lesson we took away from these modeling exercises was that models that appear to be fairly similar in contemporary climates may differ wildly when projected into future scenarios.

We also learned about the limits of our understanding of giant kangaroo rat ecology. The historical model was reassuring, assuming that giant kangaroo rats have maintained the ability to persist in a wider range of climates than they do currently. Surprisingly, though, the historical modeling exercise also showed that giant kangaroo rats currently occupy cooler, wetter areas than they did historically. In other words, giant kangaroo rats are now living in places that an ecologist would not have expected given their distribution in the first half of the twentieth century. That is good news; it suggests that, at least for this species, they may be able to cope with a wider range of environmental conditions than habitat models might capture. Finally, we found that California ground squirrels might be a limiting factor in wetter, more productive grasslands and that this competition might become more severe in the future. There is no way to confirm this with a correlative habitat model, but it suggests an avenue for on-the-ground research.

Taken together, these different modeling approaches provide a few important lessons for interpreting other estimates of climate change impacts. By far the most pessimistic of the models used only the current distribution for the species and assumed no ability to adapt. These two assumptions are extremely common; they are the norm. And yet there is no reason to believe that giant kangaroo rats could not persist in the kinds of climate that they did historically. If anything, we have learned that giant kangaroo rats are more flexible than we thought. A species that lives underground and comes out only at night is unlikely to suffer directly from hotter temperatures. However, hotter temperatures and longer droughts might reduce the amount of food that is available to the species. Here, again, management at a site level will be the critical factor in maintaining a natural community as the climate changes. The climate models suggest that the San Joaquin Valley should be broadly suitable for giant kangaroo rats in the future. At a site level, changes in the vegetation community, suitable soil, and possible competition with ground squirrels will probably be the central factors in their persistence.

Blunt-Nosed Leopard Lizard Case Study

Blunt-nosed leopard lizards are another endangered species endemic to the San Joaquin Desert. They offer another case study of how decisions made in species distribution model construction can lead to dramatically different results.

Blunt-nosed leopard lizards are the largest lizards in the San Joaquin Desert and are known for their bright colors and ability to run on two legs. Today, largely as a result of habitat loss, energy development, and nonnative vegetation, they have lost more than 80 percent of their historical range.

As for giant kangaroo rats, excessively wet or dry conditions are bad for blunt-nosed leopard lizards, particularly for reproduction (Westphal et al. 2016). Low-rainfall years are challenging because they result in fewer insects for them to eat. Conversely, high-rainfall years result in thick stands of weedy nonnative grasses, which limit lizard activity, including hunting. Additional mechanisms, such as burrow flooding, may also reduce fertility during wet years. Although uncertainty remains about how average rainfall may change in our region, year-to-year variability in rainfall is very likely to continue to increase. This increase in variability on its own is likely to harm blunt-nosed leopard lizards because of their sensitivity to both wet and dry years.

Weedy nonnative grasses appear to be especially problematic at the wetter end of the blunt-nosed leopard lizard's range, where the species has become locally extinct. Blunt-nosed leopard lizards have not been documented on many of the sites they once occupied in the wetter parts of their range (however, only two sites have been resurveyed exhaustively enough to confirm extinction; Stewart et al. 2019). In contrast, no local extinctions have been documented at the hot and dry end of the species' range, except for extinctions clearly caused by other factors such as conversion of habitat to farmland. This suggests that although especially dry years can cause population decline, average conditions at the hot and dry end of the species range are ostensibly still suitable.

Following common practices, Stewart et al. (2019) began by building preliminary species distribution models that assumed the Mojave Desert was available to the species but not occupied. By doing so, the model assumed that abiotic variables, such as climate and soil, explained the blunt-nosed leopard lizard's absence from the nearby Mojave Desert. Consequently, the resulting projections indicated that the hot and dry climates of the Mojave Desert are prohibitive to blunt-nosed leopard lizards and that these same hot and dry conditions will soon lead to local extinction of blunt-nosed leopard lizard in parts of the San Joaquin Desert.

However, absence of blunt-nosed leopard lizards in the Mojave does not mean that they cannot tolerate the climate there. The Mojave Desert is the home to the ancestor of blunt-nosed leopard lizards and is still occupied by closely related long-nosed leopard lizards. A more plausible explanation is that the Tehachapi Mountains (a movement barrier) (see figure 0-1) and competition from long-nosed leopard lizards (a biotic barrier) prevent blunt-nosed leopard lizards from occupying the Mojave. Accordingly, Stewart et al. (2019) chose to attribute the absence of blunt-nosed leopard lizards to movement and biotic barriers. The resulting models found that the distribution of blunt-nosed leopard lizards is limited by wet conditions but did not find dry, hot, or cold climate limits to the species range. These results agree with biogeographic data that, at present, document local extinction in association with wet conditions only. Resulting forecasts predict that the species will remain stable at the hot and dry end of its range, but suitable conditions may expand or contract at the wetter end of the range in response to drier or wetter conditions.

As with the giant kangaroo rats, these analyses provide management insights for blunt-nosed leopard lizards under climate change. In wet years, weedy nonnative grasses will need to be managed through livestock grazing, mechanical treatment (mowing), or prescribed burning. These three solutions will probably benefit other species in the area and are much more politically palatable. Again, although the model produced from this study provides a map of projected blunt-nosed leopard distribution into the future, it also illuminates specific management solutions that could mediate the worst effects of climate change on this highly endangered species.

Conclusions

Suitability models are an important tool for rewilding retired farmlands in the San Joaquin Valley. Projecting the impacts of climate change using these models is a science. But it is an inexact one, as we have shown. The choices made along the way during the modeling process can influence our projections, sometimes drastically. When contemplating the use of climate-based suitability models for rewilding efforts, we must first and foremost have a deep understanding of the species' (or community's) natural history as well as its evolutionary history. Second, the modeling process requires a clear assessment of the assumptions being made, whether they are related to the species' dispersal ability, adaptability, historical distribution, or biotic interactions. The models will produce projections in the form of maps, and these maps are best interpreted through consensus: If five different modeling approaches all project an area to be safe from the most drastic consequences of climate change, we should have more confidence in the conservation value of that land. Just as important, though, by creating models under different assumptions, we can assess which assumptions are most essential. In the case of giant kangaroo rats, we now believe that the genetic legacy of the populations is critical to projecting their response to climate change. If individual populations have adapted to local conditions, our projections are much more optimistic. Such a lesson can direct us to focused field studies to resolve the most important assumptions of any model.

Perhaps most exciting is that most of these assumptions can be assessed through rewilding. If blunt-nosed leopard lizards are truly limited by weedy nonnative grasses in the wetter parts of their range, livestock grazing, mowing, or burning will be a useful tool for the lizards as lands are restored and rewilded. If the lizards do not return or do not persist after reintroduction, this will force land managers to reassess their understanding of the species' ecology. Similarly, translocation of plants from different genetic stocks can provide strong evidence for the individual plant's ability to cope with a wide range of climates.

As we stated at the outset of this chapter, knowledge of a species' biotic, abiotic, and movement requirements is hard won. Nature is messy and complex, and even in simple agricultural systems, the ability to manage a single species rests on many lifetimes of hard study. The models used to project the impacts of climate change on the San Joaquin Desert provide an important tool for managers considering rewilding in this arid ecosystem. Just as important, the modeling process can take a very complex problem and focus it onto a few key questions for future research. These models support our own understanding of the system and can challenge some of our assumptions. And in so doing, they are a critical support tool for restoration of retired lands.

References

Bean, William T., Laura R. Prugh, Robert Stafford, H. Scott Butterfield, Michael Westphal, and Justin S. Brashares. 2014. "Species distribution models of an endangered rodent offer conflicting measures of habitat quality at multiple scales." *Journal of Applied Ecology* 51, no. 4: 1116–25.

Ivey, Kathleen N., Margaret Cornwall, Hayley Crowell, Nargol Ghazian, Emmeleia Nix, Malory Owen, Mario Zuliani, Christopher J. Lortie, Michael Westphal, and Emily Taylor. 2020. "Thermal ecology of the federally endangered blunt-nosed leopard lizard (*Gambelia sila*)." *Conservation Physiology* 8, no. 1: coaa014.

Lortie, Christopher J., Jenna Braun, Michael Westphal, Taylor Noble, Mario Zuliani, Emmeleia Nix, Nargol Ghazian, Malory Owen, and H. Scott Butterfield. 2020. "Shrub and vegetation cover predict resource selection use by an endangered species of desert lizard." *Scientific Reports* 10, no. 1: 1–7.

Luedeling, Eike, Evan H. Girvetz, Mikhail A. Semenov, and Patrick H. Brown. 2011. "Climate change affects winter chill for temperate fruit and nut trees." *PLOS One* 6, no. 5.

Rutrough, Abigail, Ivy V. Widick, and William T. Bean. 2019. "Reconstruction of the historical range alters niche estimates in an endangered rodent." *Ecography* 42, no. 10: 1742–51.

Statham, Mark J., William T. Bean, Nathan Alexander, Michael F. Westphal, and Benjamin N. Sacks. 2019. "Historical population size change and differentiation of relict populations of the endangered giant kangaroo rat." *Journal of Heredity* 110, no. 5: 548–58.

Stewart, Joseph A. E., H. Scott Butterfield, Jonathan Q. Richmond, David J. Germano, Michael F. Westphal, Erin N. Tennant, and Barry Sinervo.

2019. "Habitat restoration opportunities, climatic niche contraction, and conservation biogeography in California's San Joaquin Desert." *PLOS One* 14, no. 1.

Thorne, James H., Ryan M. Boynton, Andrew J. Holguin, Joseph A. E. Stewart, and Jacquelyn Bjorkman. 2016. *A Climate Change Vulnerability Assessment of California's Terrestrial Vegetation.* Sacramento: California Department of Fish and Wildlife.

Westphal, Michael F., Joseph A. E. Stewart, Erin N. Tennant, H. Scott Butterfield, and Barry Sinervo. 2016. "Contemporary drought and future effects of climate change on the endangered blunt-nosed leopard lizard, *Gambelia sila*." *PLOS One* 11, no. 5.

Widick, Ivy V., and William T. Bean. 2019. "Evaluating current and future range limits of an endangered, keystone rodent (*Dipodomys ingens*)." *Diversity and Distributions* 25, no. 7: 1074–87.

Chapter 7

Rewilding through Reintroduction

Brian L. Cypher, Ellen A. Cypher, David J. Germano, Erin N. Tennant, and Lawrence R. Saslaw

Tipton kangaroo rats, smaller and with one less toe on their hind foot than other kangaroo rats, including giant kangaroo rats (see chapters 4 and 6), are a charismatic and unique species of the San Joaquin Valley. Once abundant over a range of more than 1.7 million acres across the San Joaquin Valley, they are now limited to small, isolated populations in the southern San Joaquin Valley, at places such as Kern National Wildlife Refuge (see figure 3-1). Like many other threatened and endangered species in the San Joaquin Desert, their range has declined by more than 95 percent because of agricultural expansion and urbanization (see figure 1-2). The question now is, can we bring them back to some of that range even if we restore their natural habitats? Reintroduction is going to be part of that answer in many places, but it is not without its challenges.

In 2010, eighty Tipton kangaroo rats were reintroduced to a site in the Kern National Wildlife Refuge (see figure 3-1). Forty of them were fitted with radio collars so that researchers could track their movements and survival as they explored and settled into their new (but actually, their old) home. Several days after release, the researchers tracked one of the kangaroo rats to a large shrub. Expecting to see the animal or its burrow, the researcher moved branches around to peer under the bush. That is when he realized that his hand was about 12 inches above a very fat rattlesnake. Fortunately, the snake did not strike, probably because it had a bellyful of kangaroo rat (with a little radio transmitter on the side) and was quite content. And so it goes for some kangaroo rats. This fate befell at least two of the other collared kangaroo rats and probably other reintroduced animals.

As this story suggests, we can encounter unexpected challenges when reintroducing species. But in many areas of the San Joaquin Valley, where species such as the Tipton kangaroo rat have been completely lost and with the nearest remaining population miles away across inhospitable agricultural lands, reintroduction will be essential to meet any rewilding vision. Species simply will not be able to get there on their own. What makes a successful reintroduction? When and why should it be conducted? And how is it best done? In this chapter, we address those questions and offer examples to help illustrate the many factors that will influence whether a reintroduction effort will be successful.

What Is Reintroduction, and Why Is It Necessary?

Reintroduction is the act of returning a species to an area where it once occurred but is no longer present, usually because people have moved in and removed all the habitat for other land uses such as agriculture or housing. This act of returning a species to its ancestral area is called by other names too: *translocation, assisted colonization, assisted dispersal, repatriation, restocking,* and *de-extinction.* All of these are valid, but they can be more or less appropriate in specific contexts. For example, *repatriation* generally is used when captive animals are released into the wild. *Assisted colonization* or *dispersal* can refer to introducing an animal even to areas where it historically never occurred, a strategy discussed in chapter 6 for helping a species adapt to climate change. However, *reintroduction* is the most widely used and universally understood term, and here we use it to mean returning a species to ancestral areas.

Reintroduction is conducted for several reasons. The most common reason is to reestablish and recover a species' population where the potential for natural recolonization of a site by a species is low, usually because the site is far from existing populations or is not connected to occupied areas. In the early days of wildlife conservation, reintroduction was used to return game species to areas where they had been eliminated, usually because of overharvesting. For example, reintroduction efforts for white-tailed deer in the eastern United States and moose in the Rocky Mountains and New England in the early twentieth century have been immensely successful.

Less often, reintroduction has been used to return rare, nongame animals to areas from which they have been lost. Perhaps the most famous example from North America has been the reintroduction of gray wolves to the Yellowstone ecosystem. The success of this effort can be attributed largely to wolves' extreme adaptability and ability to disperse and recolonize large landscapes. As for the wolf, reintroductions of many species to ancestral areas where habitat remains or can be restored are probably essential for preventing extinction in the long term. Most of the very few reintroduction efforts of plants and animals in the San Joaquin Valley have been for this purpose, including for San Joaquin woolly-threads (see chapter 6), Bakersfield cactus (see chapter 14), giant kangaroo rats (see chapters 4 and 6), and tule elk.

Individuals also may be moved to an area where the species persists but in low numbers, in order to increase the size or genetic diversity of an existing population. For example, the Florida panther was reduced to as few as thirty individuals by the 1990s by habitat loss and hunting. Once it was realized that this population was declining, because of disease caused by reduced genetic diversity, cougars from Texas were introduced into Florida to boost genetic diversity. This introduction seems to be working, with a growing population and decreasing prevalence of disease. This has also been attempted in the San Joaquin Valley, where San Joaquin kit foxes were translocated from Bakersfield to the Elk Hills (see figure 3-1), where fox numbers were declining. Small populations of Bakersfield cactus have also been enhanced with propagated plants (see chapter 14). Given that many of the remaining subpopulations of threatened and endangered species in the San Joaquin Valley are small and isolated, this kind of direct introduction to increase gene flow and population size could be a vital part of recovering these populations and rewilding parts of the San Joaquin Valley (see chapter 8).

The value of reintroducing certain species to areas where they formerly lived is not restricted to the rare and endangered. Some more common species play a vital ecological role for the health of whole communities. These are commonly referred to as keystone or foundational species, or ecosystem engineers. For example, consider the beaver. Beavers are well known and increasingly valued for the role they play in creating and maintaining wetlands through their dam building. These wetlands in turn provide key habitats for a large community of other wildlife. Their activity can also benefit people by enhancing water storage and release in mountain watersheds. Reintroducing species that play important functional roles, such as beavers, may end up being particularly useful for rewilding efforts on retired farmlands in the San Joaquin Valley, where their activity can restore important aspects of the ecosystem. For example, reintroducing common burrowing species such as California ground squirrels, pocket gophers, or Heermann's kangaroo rats to former farmlands as part of restoration efforts could help loosen compacted soils, create shelter for many invertebrates and reptiles, and provide prey for raptors and carnivores (see chapter 4). In fact, many of the rarest species in the San Joaquin Valley will ultimately depend on the burrows these species create. An example of how successful this can be occurred in San Diego, California, where reintroduced California ground squirrels created burrows that then were used by reintroduced burrowing owls, a declining species of special concern in California.

How Should Species Be Reintroduced?

Although reintroduction of some species may be an essential task in thoughtfully and strategically rewilding parts of landscapes, as in the San Joaquin Valley, several important factors must be considered. Two of the most important are where it is appropriate to do so and what animals should be used as the source for reintroduction.

WHAT ARE APPROPRIATE SITES FOR REINTRODUCTIONS?

Species should be reintroduced only to sites that have the necessary ingredients for the species to survive and that increase the prospects for the successful establishment of a population. This is perhaps obvious, but it's easier said than done. The full ecological needs of species are often not fully understood. Also, sites that may seem suitable based on our best available knowledge may have hidden challenges or missing pieces that are revealed after the fact. Therefore, it is important to start with good foundations for selecting sites. The International Union for the Conservation of Nature and others (IUCN/SSC 2013; Houde et al. 2015) recommend considering the following factors in selecting sites for reintroductions:

- Favor areas within a species' historic range, except when evidence and predictions suggest population survival will depend on moving to new areas as climate changes.
- Ensure sufficient area in suitable habitat.
- Have high-quality habitat.

- Understand and mitigate potentially large, unnatural sources of mortality.
- Be prepared to actively manage sites where needed.

Species reintroductions should focus on areas within a species' historic range, because the habitat conditions within that range are more likely to be suitable for that species. Historically occupied areas are most likely to include and support all the abiotic and biotic characteristics that are necessary for the species in question to survive and reestablish a sustaining population. When not all factors that determine success are known (which is usually the case), where the species was before is a good proxy for suitability (see chapter 6 as it relates to habitat suitability modeling). In some cases, the reasons will be obvious. For example, in the San Joaquin Valley it would not be appropriate to introduce giant kangaroo rats or Bakersfield cactus to the center of the valley. These areas used to be covered by wetlands and have heavy clay soils. Both of these species are adapted to sandy soils and were never found in that part of the valley. Thus, reintroduction of these species would probably never succeed. In other cases, the factors that make an area unsuitable may be unknown but nevertheless would explain why the species did not occur there historically. In making this decision, it is worth considering whether it is simply natural physical barriers that might have prevented occupation in the past. If this is the case, then, perhaps known historic range is not the only factor to consider, especially as the climate changes.

Even within the historic range, it is important to ensure that the habitat quality at a proposed reintroduction site is high enough that a population of the reintroduced species can meet critical life history needs, such as finding food, cover, and water. Considering all factors that determine habitat quality is important to avoid learning too late that one aspect necessary for survival is missing. A relevant example from the San Joaquin Valley is the translocation of kit foxes to the Elk Hills in western Kern

County (see figure 3-1) in the late 1980s. Half of the reintroduced animals were released in hilly, rugged terrain, not typical for kit foxes. Most of these animals quickly dispersed from the release area or were killed by coyotes and bobcats. Researchers later realized that kit foxes have a hard time avoiding predators in more rugged terrain. Habitat quality is essential, and so is the amount. Different species need different sized areas as individuals and in order to support viable populations. Therefore, it is critical to reintroduce species only to areas where the amount of suitable habitat is sufficient for a self-sustaining population. For example, Tipton kangaroo rats may need only about 40 acres of good habitat to sustain a population. However, blunt-nosed leopard lizards and San Joaquin antelope squirrels probably need at least 1,000 acres, and San Joaquin kit foxes and tule elk probably need at least 15,000 acres. For species that need very large areas, such as elk and foxes, connectivity is a critical ingredient in agricultural landscapes where there will be very few or no continuous patches of suitable habitat of adequate size (see discussion of softening the agricultural landscape in chapter 10).

Sometimes, establishing suitable habitats in large enough patches is not enough. In many cases, it is necessary to plan for and implement active management to maintain habitat suitability for reintroduced species. This is especially true in the San Joaquin Valley—and California more generally—where weedy nonnative grasses and other plants have come to dominate the landscape and cannot be fully eliminated from restoration areas (see chapter 5). Dense, nonnative grass cover is a problem for many species in the San Joaquin Valley and may need to be controlled through some method such as livestock grazing. In 2006, approximately 144 Tipton kangaroo rats were translocated to the Allensworth Ecological Reserve (see figure 3-1), where they had once occurred. All seemed fine, as the reintroduced animals persisted for several years. But after some wet winters, much of the reserve became covered with dense populations of weedy nonnative grasses. The kangaroo rat population subsequently began to decline, and no individuals have been found on that site since.

Other key management needs can include enhancements that help a small, reintroduced population avoid predation while it gets established. For example, for the kit foxes reintroduced to the Elk Hills, where predation from coyotes and bobcats was a problem, providing escape cover and artificial dens could have given the foxes a chance and perhaps led to a successful reintroduction. Likewise, giant kangaroo rat reintroductions to the places such as the Carrizo Plain, which have failed because of predation, could have benefited from the initial protection provided by artificial burrows. Human management of the surrounding landscape can also be a factor. Channelization of water courses through agricultural lands directs floodwaters to natural lands in some areas. Flooding from such channelization has significantly affected reintroduced populations of riparian brush rabbits and reduced the suitability of sites such as the Allensworth Ecological Reserve and Pixley National Wildlife Refuge (see figure 3-1) for reintroductions of Tipton kangaroo rats and other species. All these factors and others should be considered when planning reintroductions. Given the expense and other inherent challenges of any reintroduction effort, planning to curtail these additional challenges could be well worth the time.

WHAT ARE APPROPRIATE SOURCE POPULATIONS?

Just as important as the selection of reintroduction sites is the selection of source populations. The source population should be large enough that it would not be adversely affected by the removal of individuals for reintroduction elsewhere. A large, demographically robust source population is more likely to have "surplus" individuals that would have dispersed anyway. Identifying such a population could be challenging for some rare species for which only small populations remain. In these situations, captive breeding or propagation may be necessary. California condors, riparian brush rabbits, and Bakersfield cactus are all examples of species for which captive breeding or propagation contributed significantly to reintroduction efforts. In other cases, individuals have become available for reintroduction when they were "salvaged" from areas where the habitat was about to be destroyed by development. The Tipton kangaroo rats reintroduced to the Allensworth Ecological Reserve came from such a site. Salvaged giant kangaroo rats and Bakersfield cactus also have been reintroduced to new sites.

The source population, or at least the individuals removed for a reintroduction effort, should be free of disease. This is typically accomplished by conducting a health check on individuals captured or collected for reintroduction. Disease is a particular concern if individuals are being introduced into an area with an existing population of the species. For example, kit foxes in Bakersfield have been suggested as a source population for reintroduction or population enhancement efforts, but many kit foxes in this population have sarcoptic mange, which is 100 percent fatal if an infected fox is not treated. Reintroducing foxes infected with mange would result in a failed effort and could threaten other nearby fox populations if infected foxes from the reintroduced population dispersed.

Finally, the source population should be genetically appropriate (see chapter 8). One concern here is that individuals locally adapted to conditions in the source population area may not fare well in a given reintroduction area if conditions are appreciably different. Conversely, many remaining populations in the San Joaquin Valley are small and isolated because of habitat loss and fragmentation. These populations are susceptible to deleterious genetic effects from inbreeding and genetic drift. Introducing new individuals into such populations may improve genetic fitness, with increases in survival and reproduction. A dramatic example of this improvement was recently observed among Sierra Nevada red foxes, where immigration by individuals from outside the Sierra Nevada improved reproduction in the existing population, which had been exhibiting inbreeding effects.

WHY ARE PLANT REINTRODUCTIONS SO CHALLENGING?

Reintroductions involving plants seem like they should be easy: Just disperse some seed or plant some young plants, add some water, and watch them grow, as you do with tomatoes in your home garden. However, for a variety of reasons plant reintroductions are inherently difficult, and to date very few efforts in the San Joaquin Valley have been successful (see chapters 2 and 3). Delano grape grower Jack Zaninovich really loved wildflowers. He even led a fundraising effort to purchase several of his favorite wildflower hotspots in Kern and Tulare counties, which were then donated to The Nature Conservancy. Knowing that California jewelflower—so named because of its striking maroon buds—was rare, he collected seeds from two small populations that were soon to be destroyed, grew them in this garden to produce seed, and then scattered seeds in two of the parcels he had helped to protect. After a decade about a dozen jewelflower plants were found in one of the new sites, but no plants have been seen now for more than thirty years. Years after Jack's effort, researchers tried again, this time in the foothills of Santa Barbara County. They sowed 4,000 seeds in each of two sites, resulting in populations of forty-eight and sixty-four plants two years later. By six years after the initial introduction, the jewelflower populations were down to three and five plants, respectively, and have not been observed in the twenty-five years since. California jewelflower is not an isolated case. An analysis of 249 attempts worldwide to establish new populations of rare plants concluded that translocated plants averaged 52 percent survival after one year but declined in successive years (Godefroid et al. 2011). Successful long-term establishment has very rarely been documented.

Not all plant reintroductions have been unsuccessful in the San Joaquin Valley. Reintroduction and reestablishment of Bakersfield cactus has been extremely successful. Once reduced to about thirty populations, with some consisting of as few as three plants,

Figure 7-1. Interns at Wind Wolves Preserve planting Bakersfield cactus during a high school service learning program. (Photos by The Wildlands Conservancy)

the cactus has rebounded, with twelve newly established populations and six existing populations that have been successfully enlarged (see chapter 14 as an example at the Wind Wolves Preserve; figure 7-1).

Can Reintroduction Help Rewild the San Joaquin Valley?

Reintroduction can help to more rapidly establish populations of animals and plants and restart ecosystem processes on retired farmland in the San Joaquin Valley. Reintroduction is particularly necessary for species for which source populations are too far from restoration sites for natural colonization to occur. Using reintroduction to establish additional populations of rare species could contribute immensely to reducing extinction risk for these species and facilitating their recovery.

Reintroduction efforts are notoriously expensive and success rates frustratingly low, particularly for first attempts, which often

Figure 7-2. Tule elk being released at the Wind Wolves Preserve in Kern County. (Photo by Melissa Dabulamanzi)

are more of a learning experience. Thus, extensive planning, including the careful selection of reintroduction sites and source populations, can increase the potential for successful reintroduction. Finally, early coordination with any agencies (federal, state, and local) from which permits or permissions might be necessary, and with neighboring landowners, will facilitate reintroduction efforts and help avoid or reduce problems and delays.

A number of reintroduction efforts with various species have been attempted in the San Joaquin Valley, and most have not been successful. Efforts with Bakersfield cactus and giant kangaroo rats are notable but limited exceptions. Tule elk are a fascinating example of restoration of a native species in the San Joaquin Valley. Historically, they were abundant, numbering in the thousands. Because of a combination of habitat loss and overharvesting, only two to four individuals may have remained by 1870 (McCullough 1969). These animals were captured and placed on a private reserve, where their numbers slowly began to increase again. In the 1900s, individuals were translocated to a number of other locations throughout their historic range. There are now approximately 5,700 individual Tule elk (California Department of Fish and Wildlife 2018). Some populations have been so successful that they are now harvested, in part for recreation but also because they have become an agricultural pest in some locations. One of the successful reintroduction sites is the Wind Wolves Preserve (see chapter 14), where there are currently about 300 Tule elk (figure 7-2). As former agricultural lands in the San Joaquin Valley become available and are restored, hopefully there will be many more stories of reintroduction successes.

References

California Department of Fish and Wildlife. 2018. *Elk Conservation and Management Plan*. Sacramento: California Department of Fish and Wildlife.

Godefroid, Sandrine, Carole Piazza, Graziano Rossi, Stéphane Buord, Albert-Dieter Stevens, Ruth Aguraiuja, Carly Cowell, et al. 2011. "How successful are plant species reintroductions?" *Biological Conservation* 144, no. 2: 672–82.

Houde, Aimee Lee S., Shawn R. Garner, and Bryan D. Neff. 2015. "Restoring species through reintroductions: strategies for source population selection." *Restoration Ecology* 23, no. 6: 746–53.

IUCN/SSC. 2013. *Guidelines for Reintroductions and Other Conservation Translocations*. Version 1.0. IUCN Species Survival Commission.

McCullough, Dale R. 1969. *The Tule Elk, Its History, Behavior, and Ecology*. University of California Publications in Zoology, 88. Berkeley: University California Press.

Chapter 8

Genetic Considerations for Rewilding the San Joaquin Desert

Jonathan Q. Richmond, Dustin A. Wood,
and Marjorie D. Matocq

Approximately 10,000 years ago to as recently as 3,000 years ago, humans in different parts of the world began to cultivate plants for food. Of course, these early farmers knew nothing about Gregor Mendel's peas or genetics, but they seem to have known that by breeding plants with sweeter and juicier fruits, for example, they could make those traits more common in successive generations of plants. Corn domestication is one of the most amazing examples of how prehistoric agriculturalists used their skillset to create a plant that looks nothing like the wild teosinte plant ancestor from which it is derived (Yang et al. 2019). Most of the modified traits associated with crop domestication, such as larger fruits or seeds, easier harvesting, and reduction of bitter taste, were already complete by the time of historic Egyptian and Mayan agricultural civilizations. In fact, agriculture in the San Joaquin Valley is an extension of the same types of genetic modification of wild plants that has occurred over many millennia. King Tutankhamun would surely be proud.

But long before prehistoric farmers ever removed plants from their wild habitats and placed them into human-managed environments, the natural environment selected for traits that increased the ability of individual plant species to pass their genes on to the next generation. This continuous process of natural selection can operate only if heritable variation exists for the trait and if at least some of that variation makes individuals better able to survive and reproduce. If so, the favorable variants increase in frequency, and ultimately the population becomes better adapted to its local environment. Yet variation in the underlying genetic code originates from random mutations, with most being either harmful or neutral. Only occasionally are these changes beneficial. In this way, trait evolution resembles the proverbial house of cards: One wrong mutation with little other variation to work with, and the whole house comes down, but one right mutation and the house improves. Variation in the DNA sequences (the "cards"), and therefore variation in the trait itself (the "house"), provides the material for natural selection to operate. The more material there is for natural selection to act on, the greater the evolutionary potential of a species to cope with a changing environment.

Understanding how genetic variation within a species is distributed across a landscape is an important consideration for ecosystem restoration and the maintenance of biological diversity. This is particularly true of landscapes that support high numbers of threatened and endangered species such as the San Joaquin Desert, where habitat continues to shrink and become more fragmented as humans continue transforming the natural landscape. Depending on the severity of habitat loss and fragmentation, the ability of plants and animals to exchange genes across different populations (i.e., gene flow) can be reduced or even eliminated if gaps grow too large or the habitat in between becomes too disturbed.

It turns out that well before the San Joaquin Valley was converted to agricultural fields, there were numerous natural gaps that constituted movement barriers for arid-adapted terrestrial species. Some of the biggest barriers were several large lakes and their interconnected wetland and riparian areas, surrounded primarily by arid saltbush habitat (see chapter 2). These wetted areas and other geophysical features were big influences on how individuals of different species were able to move their genes around this landscape (Matocq et al. 2012; Bainbridge et al. 2017; Richmond et al. 2017; Statham et al. 2019). Populations occurring on opposite sides of a barrier became more genetically differentiated than those on the same side of the barrier, given that gene flow was limited to populations on the same sides. The extent of these habitats also expanded and contracted during periods of wetter and drier climate over many tens of thousands of years, ensuring fluctuation in both the location and the timing of when the populations could mix. The genetic legacy of current populations is therefore a result of this ancient history coupled with more recent human-mediated change across this region. The biggest problem with these more recent changes is the severity and rate at which they have taken place; evolution cannot keep pace in maintaining genetic variability through the mutational process (Charlesworth 2020), and space is becoming more limited.

Thus, if we aspire to preserve biodiversity, rewilding efforts in highly altered landscapes such as the San Joaquin Valley must consider the underlying genetic variability of the species in jeopardy. Genetic variability in space and time reflects the adaptive capacity of a species and the degree to which habitat fragmentation is reducing population health and adaptability. This information should be combined with more traditional modes of conservation planning to guide rewilding efforts, including the selection of areas to restore habitat (see chapter 6) and methods for species reintroductions (see chapter 7). Without considering the inherent capacity of these populations to adapt over time, we risk reducing or, at worst, preventing long-term recovery of populations.

The State of Wildlife Genomics

Our ability to collect, analyze, and use genetic data for planning is light-years ahead of where it was even fifteen years ago. Different types of genetic data and analyses can be used to identify patterns of genetic variability and adaptive capacity and the processes that underlie the maintenance of each. Researchers have been able to move from collecting information about tiny fractions of the genome to very large or even full genomes of individual plants and animals (so-called next-generation or high-throughput DNA sequencing), all at lower cost, with less effort, and with greater speed than ever before. The technology is advancing so rapidly that complete genome sequencing is now more efficient for a wild lizard or grasshopper than it was for humans in the early 2000s.

These emerging methods allow researchers to precisely measure how genetic variation is generated, maintained, and distributed across the landscape. Which method to use depends on the research question being asked (Hunter et al. 2018). We can target specific genes of interest or capture and characterize variation in random subsets of the genome. We can also focus on parts of the genome that are neutral passengers reflecting processes such as gene flow or parts of the genome that are functional and reflect past or ongoing responses to natural selection (Caballero and García-Dorado 2013; Wilbert et al. 2020). But all the methods available are capable of recovering many hundreds of thousands to even millions of variable genetic markers that make it possible to understand both the genetic history of a species and its adaptive potential for future environments. One of the biggest advantages of using next-generation methods is that the precision and confidence in almost any metric of genetic diversity increases dramatically with greater representation of the genome simply because there are more data available to tell the story. The more of the book you are able to read, the more you understand the story.

Are There Genetic Alarm Bells When Habitat Shrinks in Size and Quality?

As habitat patches decrease in size and quality, the number of individuals of plants and animals that can be supported by local resources decreases rapidly. Shrinking habitat area also increases competition for the resources that are left, reduces population size, and makes it more difficult to find mates that are not a third or fourth cousin. The latter leads to inbreeding, which for very good reasons is generally avoided by all animals. Inbreeding can result in the expression of harmful genetic variation that negatively affects an individual's ability to survive and reproduce. When a population remains large, harmful alleles (different versions of a gene) can persist at low frequency without expressing themselves, remaining "hidden" from natural selection by their dominant, nonharmful counterparts (Reed and Frankham 2003). That is, the dominant allele is always expressed even if another recessive (i.e., nondominant) and potentially harmful allele is present. As a result, an individual carrying a recessive harmful allele can still be healthy but transmit the allele to its offspring without ever knowing. It is like a drawer full of hundreds of socks where twelve colors are predominant, but two or three socks have an awful thirteenth color that lurks in the background. That thirteenth color is hard for the fashionista to tease out unless two show up, side by side, in the dirty laundry.

On the other hand, with a small, closely related population, many individuals can be carriers of the same recessive, harmful alleles, and the likelihood of them reproducing increases simply because there are fewer mates to choose from. This means that their offspring have a greater chance of inheriting two copies of the same harmful allele, in which case the son or daughter would suffer the consequences of expressing that suboptimal or perhaps lethal allele. This is precisely the case with sickle cell anemia, a disease affecting the ability of red blood cells to deliver oxygen to the body: The parents of an afflicted individual each carry one recessive copy of the mutated gene but rarely show symptoms of the condition, whereas their offspring who inherit the same harmful allele from both parents will suffer the effects of sickle cell anemia.

Plants generally follow the same rules as observed in animals when it comes to the effects of inbreeding. However, many plants, such as the San Joaquin woolly-thread, have evolved an ability to self-pollinate, an extreme form of inbreeding that guarantees reproductive success during times when cross-pollination from insects or wind is not working or other conditions prevent cross-breeding. This offers a good short-term strategy, but over the long haul it can lead to extinction due to the accumulation of harmful mutations, or genetic load (Charlesworth and Willis 2009; Slotte et al. 2013). This is why many plant species that can self-pollinate typically have a built-in mechanism to avoid it but still maintain it as an emergency backup system. Unfortunately, selfing is something that may be unavoidable as patch size becomes smaller and the separation from nearby populations increases. For plants, it is better to mate with yourself in hopes that your options are better the next time around.

Isolated habitat patches can also lead to a loss of genetic diversity in local populations through random changes in allelic variation from one generation to the next, a process known as genetic drift. In a closed population (i.e., one that cannot receive migrants from other populations), genetic drift results in a loss of allelic diversity: Some alleles randomly rise in frequency to the point of fixation, in which case all individuals share the same allele of a given gene, whereas others are randomly lost. The smaller the population size, the more rapid the effects of genetic drift, particularly if immigrants are unable to resupply lost genetic variation because of habitat fragmentation. Reductions in genetic diversity can translate to reduced evolutionary potential in the face of things such as climate change or emerging diseases, such as snake fungal disease in California kingsnakes or the most recent rabbit hemorrhaging disease in black-tailed jackrabbits, that can lead to population declines or even local extinction (Chapman et al. 2009; Caballero and García-Dorado 2013; Frankham et al. 2017).

The degree of connectivity between habitat patches is often key to preventing the loss of genetic diversity, particularly when patch sizes become small. This is because plants and animals often counteract the effects of inbreeding and genetic drift by functioning as a collective network of interconnected subpopulations, or a metapopulation, where individuals are capable of dispersing and passing their genes throughout the network (figure 8-1; Hanski and Gilpin 1991). If one side of the network is affected by a random event such as a fire or flood, dramatically reducing or even causing the local extinction of subpopulations on that side of the network, individuals from the unaffected side can then repopulate and infuse those areas with new genetic variation once the habitat recovers. Even changes in food availability or increased competition in different parts of the network can cause local declines or extinctions, which can then be counterbalanced by immigrants arriving from more densely populated areas that are close by.

Now come to grips with the fact that biology is messy; in reality, factors such as habitat patch size, density of individuals per patch, movement capacity in different parts of the network, or the ability of local populations to "give back" to the overall metapopulation are highly variable. So real-life systems are never neat and tidy. Metapopulations can also have a "mainland–island" type of structure, where island populations rely on mainland propagules for persistence and are expected to go extinct unless they can be rescued by colonizers from mainland sources (see figure 8-1). The key to this choreography, whether it be mainland–island or network-like, is that core habitat nodes remain connected such that individuals can move within the system. Once the habitat linkages are broken and patch size decreases, the dynamics of the entire metapopulation begin to degrade into an island-like system, and genetic diversity begins to decline. Unfortunately, these islands are no place to honeymoon or drink piña coladas.

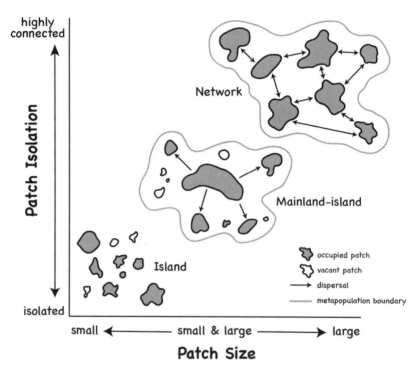

Figure 8-1. Examples of different types of metapopulation structure. In an idealized network structure, migrants disperse back and forth between different occupied habitat patches, patch sizes tend to be larger, and gene flow connects populations throughout the network. In the mainland–island structure, a large mainland source provides migrants that disperse to island sinks, with island populations experiencing cycles of extinction–recolonization or bottleneck–augmentation. Gene flow can but does not always occur in all available islands. With island structure, metapopulation dynamics cannot exist because of small patch size and the inability for dispersing individuals to transmit their genes between patches. Before land conversion in the San Joaquin Desert, the dynamics would have resembled more of the network or mainland–island types of structure for most species. However, as land conversion has led to habitat loss and fragmentation, these systems have eroded to a more island-like structure, where metapopulation dynamics no longer exist across the full landscape.

Cheetah: The Poster Child for the Effects of Small Population Size and Inbreeding

The cheetah is an iconic species of the Serengeti in Africa, accelerating from 0 to 97 kilometers per hour in a matter of seconds and reaching speeds of up to 120 kilometers per hour. It is a Ferrari with a beating heart and sharp teeth. Unfortunately, this cat is at risk of extinction due to habitat loss, poaching, and inbreeding. A recent study quantified the genetic similarity between cheetahs from Namibia and Tanzania, showing that they are at the back of the pack in nearly every measure of genetic diversity (Dobrynin et al. 2015). In fact, cheetahs are so genetically similar that any individual in need of a kidney transplant could get one from any other, even total strangers, without having to worry about tissue rejection (O'Brien et al. 1985).

Hassle-free organ transplants might seem like a good thing, but they mean that you are bad at fighting disease and probably lack variability in the genes that determine immunity. In cheetahs, extremely low genetic variability and inbreeding might also explain the elevated rates of juvenile mortality, poor success of captive breeding (until recently), increased susceptibility to disease, and high prevalence of malformed sperm in males (most definitely *not* a good thing). Because of these problems, it is highly probable that inbreeding and low genetic variation are limiting the cheetah's evolutionary potential and accelerating its path to extinction, alongside habitat loss and poachers.

So why is the cheetah in such dire genetic straits? The data clearly show that the lineage has experienced multiple bottlenecks at different points in the species' history, which happens when only a small portion of a population survives a catastrophic event or when only a few individuals disperse into a new area (i.e., a founder effect). In either situation, the last survivors of a population or founders of a new one contain only a minute fraction of the original gene pool, which means that they may be genetically ill-equipped to cope with selection pressure in their new or future environment.

Although the exact causes of the bottlenecks in the cheetah lineage may never be known, we can say for sure that they have had lasting, detrimental effects on this declining species. In fact, the cheetah is a good example of the types of genetic problems that many other species face when forced into small, isolated populations, including those in the San Joaquin Valley.

The Genetic Legacy of a Landscape in Decline

Genetic studies on plant and animal species of the San Joaquin Desert reveal some of these same phenomena affecting the cheetah, but with different causes. In the San Joaquin Desert, bottlenecks and founder events are driven by intensive flood–drought cycles, a result of the El Niño Southern Oscillation that operates on a time scale of every two to seven years. This has led to a boom-and-bust population cycle for many species in the San Joaquin Desert, a pattern now entrenched in their natural history (Williams et al. 1993; Germano and Saslaw 2017). Extended droughts often lead to severe bottlenecks (i.e., the bust) in these species, followed by severe winter rainfall events that fuel resources and lead to dramatic and rapid population rebounds (i.e., the boom). Historically, busts would have been followed by booms created by successful reproduction of remaining survivors and a functional metapopulation dynamic that supported broad dispersal of individuals into the bottlenecked populations or depopulated areas (see figure 8-1).

Unfortunately, because of land conversion, habitat fragmentation, and introduction of weedy nonnative grasses, connectivity has been disrupted and species have a much more difficult time rebounding in the wake of these flood–drought cycles (Germano et al. 2012), which are becoming more common and extreme with climate change (Westerling et al. 2006; Seager et al. 2007; Dettinger 2011). But perhaps the future is not so bleak for even the rarest of species in the San Joaquin Desert, given their potential to be saved by rewilding retired agricultural lands.

Genetic Data as a Prioritization Tool for Identifying Restoration Sites

Key questions about rewilding involve the identification of lands that are best suited for retirement and the prioritization of their alternative future uses (see chapters 1 and 9). Genetic information can play a key role in identifying the most critical parcels to reestablish natural patterns of genetic connectivity. It can also help identify the most diverse, most locally adapted, or most genetically related source populations from which to draw individuals to establish or augment existing populations. If captive breeding is necessary to establish or augment populations (as with the riparian brush rabbit), genetics can identify the most genetically diverse founders as a basis to establish a breeding program that maximizes retention of genetic variation. Finally, genetics can be an integral part of monitoring programs to ensure that target levels of variation are being maintained as an indicator of population health and adaptive potential. Therefore, genetics can play a central role in every phase of rewilding to maximize the potential for self-sustaining populations.

A main consideration would be the targeting of lands that are geographically close to existing core populations of threatened and endangered species, where core populations occupy larger, higher-quality patches and are shown through genetic analysis to possess a significant proportion of the total genetic variation of a given region. Fortunately, there are quite a few threatened and endangered species in the San Joaquin Desert that have similar habitat needs, and because little undisturbed natural habitat still exists, there is probably considerable overlap in what remains of the core ranges for many species (Stewart et al. 2019). We also know that there is considerable overlap in the genetic structure of different plants and animals across this landscape, as well as geographic areas where genetic diversity tends to be higher or lower and where ancestry is mixed between different populations (Good et al. 1997; Bainbridge et al. 2017; Richmond et al. 2017; Statham et al. 2019). As suggested in chapter 7, selecting parcels that are close to core areas of high genetic diversity and admixture increases the probability that migrants will harbor genetic variation that is locally adaptive for that area. A capacity for natural dispersal could also mean that less human intervention will be needed to maintain that diversity and prevent inbreeding.

Natural dispersal could also be facilitated by targeting parcels that can be connected through habitat corridors and that were identified through landscape genetic methods as previous thoroughfares for gene flow before land conversion. Connectivity is critical for reactivating source–sink dynamics and plays into the concept of rewilding as it applies to restoring ecosystem function (Perino et al. 2019; see chapter 1). It also does not necessarily need to be limited to the periphery of crop fields; chapter 10 discusses the potential to increase permeability through ecological intensification, where surrounding natural habitat becomes integrated into the farmscape itself via internal corridors. This strategy may fare better for larger vertebrates (e.g., kit fox and other mammals; Warrick et al. 2007) that are already using agricultural fields to some extent and are less prone to smaller-scale disturbances such as increased soil moisture near or within crop fields, presence of invasive species that adhere to the artificially watered environment, or greater susceptibility to vehicular activity. Because genetic data have the potential to identify where movement corridors existed in the historic landscape, this information can be used as a guidance tool for conducting the ecological intensification experiment (see figure 8-1).

Genetic Considerations for Translocation or Assisted Dispersal to Restored Lands

One of the most critical roles for genetics in rewilding these landscapes is the selection of individuals for translocation or reintroduction (see chapter 7). This is important because the last thing managers want to do is introduce maladaptive genetic variation to an ecosystem they are attempting to resurrect. For example, if a pathogenic soil microbe happens to occur on a restored parcel, we would not want to introduce a plant species that lacks the genetic variability necessary to combat that pathogen (assuming we know what that variability is, say for genes involving the immune response; Wilbert et al. 2020). So what other factors go into identifying suitable source populations? One guiding principle is that candidate sources should be as genetically diverse as possible, even for self-fertilizing plants such as San Joaquin woolly-threads that have low diversity to begin with. More diversity translates to more raw material for selection to act on, which leads to greater evolutionary potential. For the recipient population, there should also be some sense about the number of individuals needed to establish and maintain its viability. That number that can be estimated with genetic data from other surviving populations.

The success rate of translocation efforts might also be increased by matching genotypes to the current environment for a particular area. An initial strategy could be to recolonize restored land from sources that are as genetically similar as possible to the population that used to occur in that area, which often means that sources will be from nearby sites. This is because genetic similarity tends to decay with geographic distance in dispersal-limited species, a pattern geneticists refer to as isolation by distance (Nei 1972). Attempts at genotype matching increase the likelihood that the reintroduced genetic variation evolved under an environmental background that is consistent with the restoration site and works toward restoring the natural genetic structure that developed long before the land was ever used to grow nuts and citrus.

Chapter 6 also presents good arguments for considering what the environment of an area might look like under plausible climate scenarios. Like habitat and climate forecasting, we can also use genetic forecasting to predict the types of genetic variation that might increase individual survivorship under future climate projections (Prober et al. 2015). For example, because more arid conditions are predicted to extend farther north in the San Joaquin Desert than they do today, we can identify parts of the contemporary range of, say, the blunt-nosed leopard lizard or giant kangaroo rat, where the climate currently matches that future scenario (Stewart et al. 2019; Widick and Bean 2019). Using genome-wide association studies, we can then identify whether specific genetic variation already exists in lizards that occur in those areas by comparing them with other lizards collected in the more northern, wetter parts of the range. If unique alleles exist at genes that are involved with heat tolerance, water retention, or some other physiological function associated with heat stress, we can infer that those alleles might be adaptive in a more arid climate (Marra et al. 2014). Such information could be valuable for guiding reintroductions.

Related to genetic forecasting is the concept of genetic rescue, a technique normally used to improve the fitness of small populations by moving individuals from other areas to increase genetic diversity (Frankham 2015; Whiteley et al. 2015). This might be necessary to avoid founder effects on rewilded parcels and could also be a way to introduce adaptive genetic variation as described earlier. With genetic rescue, the idea is that only a few individuals are needed to inoculate an area with new genes, so few that the introduced variation does not swamp out the genetic diversity that is already in the population. This gives selection room to tinker with different genetic possibilities. If it turns out that the genetic rescuers have brought something to the table that selection favors, that variation is then going to increase in frequency in the population. To date, the technique has been used to good effect in Florida panthers (Johnson et al. 2010), bighorn sheep (Hogg et al. 2006), prairie chickens (Westemeier et al. 1998), and wolves (Fredrickson et al. 2007).

Fortunately, many endemic species in the San Joaquin Desert have ancestral origins and close evolutionary relatives in the hotter, drier Mojave Desert to the east–southeast (Bradford 1992; Mercure et al. 1993; Germano et al. 2011; Richmond et al. 2017). Knowing this kind of genetic information can provide important clues to understanding how these species might cope with the changing climate. We cannot build structures to shade lizards as we can for strawberries, but the genetic legacy of many species in the San Joaquin Desert may already be casting its own "shade" by increasing their tolerance to future environmental conditions. In other words, these species may already have the genetic tools they need to survive (Barrett and Schluter 2008). What is even better is that the two shrubs that the blunt-nosed leopard lizard is commonly associated with, saltbush and ephedra, also have evolutionary histories that are tied to the Mojave Desert (Filazzola et al. 2017; Westphal et al. 2018).

As a last measure, it is a good idea to test the efficacy of rewilding through genetic monitoring (Flanagan et al. 2018). We need to be able to measure the success of the effort so that we know we are not spinning our wheels. Monitoring could enable stakeholders to answer questions such as "Are populations losing genetic diversity faster than would be expected under normal conditions, and if so, is there a means for recovery?" "Are animals moving and interbreeding across the rewilded areas and at sufficient levels?" "Are certain alleles increasing in frequency as a result of a changing environmental variable, such as aridity or temperature?" Genetic monitoring techniques have advanced so rapidly that it is now straightforward to sequence the same, large set of genetic markers repeatedly and reliably over successive generations to improve the likelihood of long-term population viability.

Conclusions

Genetic data are a powerful and important tool for guiding rewilding efforts and for monitoring the recovery outcomes of those efforts. When used in conjunction with historic species' distribution records and predictive habitat suitability modeling, genetic information adds a key piece to the puzzle that will increase the probability of successful ecosystem restoration.

References

Bainbridge, Sue, Ryan O'Dell, and Bruce Baldwin. 2017. "Population genetics and genetic structure in San Joaquin wooly threads (*Monolopia congdonii*)." Bureau of Land Management, UC Berkeley Grant/ Cooperative Agreement no. L12AC20073. Unpublished.

Barrett, Rowan D. H., and Dolph Schluter. 2008. "Adaptation from standing genetic variation." *Trends in Ecology & Evolution* 23, no. 1: 38–44.

Bradford, David F. 1992. "Biogeography and endemism in the Central Valley of California." In: *Endangered and Sensitive Species of the San Joaquin Valley California: Their Biology, Management, and Conservation*, edited by D. F. Williams, S. Byrne, and T. A. Rado, 65–79. Sacramento: California Energy Commission.

Caballero, Armando, and Aurora García-Dorado. 2013. "Allelic diversity and its implications for the rate of adaptation." *Genetics* 195: 1373–84.

Chapman, J. R., S. Nakagawa, D. W. Coltman, J. Slate, and B. C. Sheldon. 2009. "A quantitative review of heterozygosity–fitness correlations in animal populations." *Molecular Ecology* 18, no. 13: 2746–65.

Charlesworth, Brian. 2020. "How long does it take to fix a favorable mutation, and why should we care?" *The American Naturalist* 195, no. 5: 753–71.

Charlesworth, Deborah, and John H. Willis. 2009. "The genetics of inbreeding depression." *Nature Reviews Genetics* 10, no. 11: 783–96.

Dettinger, Michael. 2011. "Climate change, atmospheric rivers, and floods in California: a multimodel analysis of storm frequency and magnitude changes 1." *Journal of the American Water Resources Association* 47, no. 3: 514–23.

Dobrynin, Pavel, Shiping Liu, Gaik Tamazian, Zijun Xiong, Andrey A. Yurchenko, Ksenia Krasheninnikova, Sergey Kliver, et al. 2015. "Genomic legacy of the African cheetah, *Acinonyx jubatus*." *Genome Biology* 16, no. 1: 1–20.

Filazzola, Alessandro, Michael Westphal, Michael Powers, Amanda Rae Liczner, Deborah A. Smith Woollett, Brent Johnson, and Christopher J. Lortie. 2017. "Non-trophic interactions in deserts: facilitation, interference, and an endangered lizard species." *Basic and Applied Ecology* 20: 51–61.

Flanagan, Sarah P., Brenna R. Forester, Emily K. Latch, Sally N. Aitken, and Sean Hoban. 2018. "Guidelines for planning genomic assessment and monitoring of locally adaptive variation to inform species conservation." *Evolutionary Applications* 11, no. 7: 1035–52.

Frankham, Richard. 2015. "Genetic rescue of small inbred populations: meta-analysis reveals large and consistent benefits of gene flow." *Molecular Ecology* 24, no. 11: 2610–18.

Frankham, Richard, Jonathan D. Ballou, Katherine Ralls, Mark Eldridge, Michele R. Dudash, Charles B. Fenster, Robert C. Lacy, and Paul Sunnucks. 2017. *Genetic Management of Fragmented Animal and Plant Populations*. Oxford: Oxford University Press.

Fredrickson, Richard J., Peter Siminski, Melissa Woolf, and Philip W. Hedrick. 2007. "Genetic rescue and inbreeding depression in Mexican wolves." *Proceedings of the Royal Society B: Biological Sciences* 274, no. 1623: 2365–71.

Germano, David J., Galen B. Rathbun, and Lawrence R. Saslaw. 2012. "Effects of grazing and invasive grasses on desert vertebrates in California." *Journal of Wildlife Management* 76: 670–82.

Germano, David J., Galen B. Rathbun, Lawrence R. Saslaw, Brian L. Cypher, Ellen A. Cypher, and Larry M. Vredenburgh. 2011. "The San Joaquin Desert of California: ecologically misunderstood and overlooked." *Natural Areas Journal* 31, no. 2: 138–47.

Germano, David J., and Lawrence R. Saslaw. 2017. "Rodent community dynamics as mediated by environment and competition at a site in the San Joaquin Desert." *Journal of Mammalogy* 98: 1615–26.

Good, Sara V., Daniel F. Williams, Katherine Ralls, and Robert C. Fleischer. 1997. "Population structure of *Dipodomys ingens* (Heteromyidae): the role of spatial heterogeneity in maintaining genetic diversity." *Evolution* 51, no. 4: 1296–310.

Hanski, Ilkka, and Michael Gilpin. 1991. "Metapopulation dynamics: brief history and conceptual domain." *Biological Journal of the Linnean Society* 42, no. 1–2: 3–16.

Hogg, John T., Stephen H. Forbes, Brian M. Steele, and Gordon Luikart. 2006. "Genetic rescue of an insular population of large mammals." *Proceedings of the Royal Society B: Biological Sciences* 273, no. 1593: 1491–99.

Hunter, Margaret E., Sean M. Hoban, Michael W. Bruford, Gernot Segelbacher, and Louis Bernatchez. 2018. "Next-generation conservation genetics and biodiversity monitoring." *Evolutionary Applications* 11, no. 7: 1029–34.

Johnson, Warren E., David P. Onorato, Melody E. Roelke, E. Darrell Land, Mark Cunningham, Robert C. Belden, Roy McBride, et al. 2010.

"Genetic restoration of the Florida panther." *Science* 329, no. 5999: 1641–45.

Marra, Nicholas J., Andrea Romero, and J. Andrew DeWoody. 2014. "Natural selection and the genetic basis of osmoregulation in heteromyid rodents as revealed by RNA-seq." *Molecular Ecology* 23, no. 11: 2699–2711.

Matocq, Marjorie D., Patrick A. Kelly, Scott E. Phillips, and Jesus E. Maldonado. 2012. "Reconstructing the evolutionary history of an endangered subspecies across the changing landscape of the Great Central Valley of California." *Molecular Ecology* 21, no. 24: 5918–33.

Mercure, Alan, Katherine Ralls, Klaus P. Koepfli, and Robert K. Wayne. 1993. "Genetic subdivisions among small canids: mitochondrial DNA differentiation of swift, kit, and arctic foxes." *Evolution* 47, no. 5: 1313–28.

Nei, Masatoshi. 1972. "Genetic distance between populations." *The American Naturalist* 106, no. 949: 283–92.

O'Brien, Stephen J., Melody E. Roelke, L. Marker, A. Newman, C. A. Winkler, D. Meltzer, L. Colly, J. F. Evermann, M. Bush, and David E. Wildt. 1985. "Genetic basis for species vulnerability in the cheetah." *Science* 227, no. 4693: 1428–34.

Perino, Andrea, Henrique M. Pereira, Laetitia M. Navarro, Néstor Fernández, James M. Bullock, Silvia Ceauşu, Ainara Cortés-Avizanda, et al. 2019. "Rewilding complex ecosystems." *Science* 364, no. 6438.

Prober, Suzanne Mary, Margaret Byrne, Elizabeth H. McLean, Dorothy A. Steane, Brad M. Potts, Rene E. Vaillancourt, and William D. Stock. 2015. "Climate-adjusted provenancing: a strategy for climate-resilient ecological restoration." *Frontiers in Ecology and Evolution* 3: 65.

Reed, David H., and Richard Frankham. 2003. "Correlation between fitness and genetic diversity." *Conservation Biology* 17, no. 1: 230–37.

Richmond, Jonathan Q., Dustin A. Wood, Michael F. Westphal, Amy G. Vandergast, Adam D. Leaché, Lawrence R. Saslaw, H. Scott Butterfield, and Robert N. Fisher. 2017. "Persistence of historical population structure in an endangered species despite near-complete biome conversion in California's San Joaquin Desert." *Molecular Ecology* 26, no. 14: 3618–35.

Seager, Richard, Mingfang Ting, Isaac Held, Yochanan Kushnir, Jian Lu, Gabriel Vecchi, Huei-Ping Huang, et al. 2007. "Model projections of an imminent transition to a more arid climate in southwestern North America." *Science* 316, no. 5828: 1181–84.

Slotte, Tanja, Khaled M. Hazzouri, J. Arvid Ågren, Daniel Koenig, Florian Maumus, Ya-Long Guo, Kim Steige, et al. 2013. "The *Capsella rubella* genome and the genomic consequences of rapid mating system evolution." *Nature Genetics* 45, no. 7: 831–35.

Statham, Mark J., William T. Bean, Nathan Alexander, Michael F. Westphal, and Benjamin N. Sacks. 2019. "Historical population size change and differentiation of relict populations of the endangered giant kangaroo rat." *Journal of Heredity* 110, no. 5: 548–58.

Stewart, Joseph A. E., H. Scott Butterfield, Jonathan Q. Richmond, David J. Germano, Michael F. Westphal, Erin N. Tennant, and Barry Sinervo. 2019. "Habitat restoration opportunities, climatic niche contraction, and conservation biogeography in California's San Joaquin Desert." *PLOS One* 14, no. 1: e0210766.

Warrick, Gregory D., Howard O. Clark, Patrick A. Kelly, Daniel F. Williams, and Brian L. Cypher. 2007. "Use of agricultural lands by San Joaquin kit foxes." *Western North American Naturalist* 67, no. 2: 270–77.

Westemeier, Ronald L., Jeffrey D. Brawn, Scott A. Simpson, Terry L. Esker, Roger W. Jansen, Jeffery W. Walk, Eric L. Kershner, Juan L. Bouzat, and Ken N. Paige. 1998. "Tracking the long-term decline and recovery of an isolated population." *Science* 282, no. 5394: 1695–98.

Westerling, Anthony L., Hugo G. Hidalgo, Daniel R. Cayan, and Thomas W. Swetnam. 2006. "Warming and earlier spring increase western US forest wildfire activity." *Science* 313, no. 5789: 940–43.

Westphal, Michael F., Taylor Noble, Harry Scott Butterfield, and Christopher J. Lortie. 2018. "A test of desert shrub facilitation via radiotelemetric monitoring of a diurnal lizard." *Ecology and Evolution* 8, no. 23: 12153–62.

Whiteley, Andrew R., Sarah W. Fitzpatrick, W. Chris Funk, and David A. Tallmon. 2015. "Genetic rescue to the rescue." *Trends in Ecology & Evolution* 30, no. 1: 42–49.

Widick, Ivy V., and William T. Bean. 2019. "Evaluating current and future range limits of an endangered, keystone rodent (*Dipodomys ingens*)." *Diversity and Distributions* 25, no. 7: 1074–87.

Wilbert, Tammy R., Jesús E. Maldonado, Mirian T. N. Tsuchiya, Masoumeh Sikaroodi, Brian L. Cypher, Christine Van Horn Job, Katherine Ralls, and Patrick M. Gillevet. 2020. "Patterns of MHC polymorphism in endangered San Joaquin Kit foxes living in urban and non-urban environments." In *Conservation Genetics in Mammals*, 269–98. Cham, Switzerland: Springer.

Williams, Daniel F., David J. Germano, and Walter Tordoff III. 1993. "Population studies of endangered kangaroo rats and blunt-nosed leopard lizards in the Carrizo Plain Natural Area, California." Report 93-01, State of California, Department of Fish and Game, Wildlife Management Division, Nongame Bird and Mammal Section.

Yang, Chin Jian, Luis Fernando Samayoa, Peter J. Bradbury, Bode A. Olukolu, Wei Xue, Alessandra M. York, Michael R. Tuholski, et al. 2019. "The genetic architecture of teosinte catalyzed and constrained maize domestication." *Proceedings of the National Academy of Sciences* 116, no. 12: 5643–52.

Chapter 9

Strategic Selection of Lands for Rewilding to Optimize Outcomes and Minimize Costs

T. Rodd Kelsey, Benjamin P. Bryant, Adrian L. Vogl,
Abigail K. Hart, and H. Scott Butterfield

In the early 2000s, what has been described as California's modern gold rush was beginning to speed up in California's deserts. The rush was to take advantage of abundant and intense sunlight and wind to generate renewable energy and help California meet its goal of 60 percent renewable energy by 2030 and 100 percent by 2050. By 2011, several projects had been developed, and more than eighty solar and wind projects were in the permitting process. This was also about the time voices of dissent over what this development would mean for nature were becoming louder. California's deserts cover 22 million acres, within which is the largest expanse of remaining intact ecosystems in the lower forty-eight states. Rather than being, as many assume, nearly lifeless, these deserts are one of the most biologically diverse regions in the state. They are home to the ancient desert tortoise, iconic golden eagle, and desert bighorn sheep. Many of the species within them are already on the brink of extinction because of agricultural development and other human endeavors that have cut up this landscape. The solar and wind projects threatened to make this fragmentation and habitat loss much worse. The projects being planned and implemented were very large, with many existing and planned developments covering thousands of acres.

This is an ironic conflict, given that the environmental community stands in favor of renewable energy as essential for slowing down climate change and easing the impact it will have on entire communities and landscapes. In this case, however, the concern for many was not that the energy development would take place but that it would be done in a poorly planned way and result in unnecessary impacts to nature. Specifically, if the projects were not planned in a coordinated way to take greatest advantage of already-degraded former agricultural lands and located to minimize their impact on wildlife movement, then they would have unnecessary, severe impacts on the desert natural community. On the other hand, with smart planning in advance to identify the areas of least conflict for energy development, impacts to these natural ecosystems could be minimized, and the permitting process for project development could be made easier, cheaper, and faster, benefiting all involved.

Fortunately, state and federal agencies took a step back, and by working with the environmental community they began developing a comprehensive plan for renewable energy development in the desert that would accommodate the scale of expansion needed while protecting the natural resources of the desert. In 2016, this plan was released: the Desert Renewable Energy Conservation Plan. This plan lays out a roadmap for the development of renewable energy on more than 350,000 acres in consolidated areas of the desert while minimizing the impacts on desert ecosystems. It also lays the foundation for more streamlined and cheaper permitting processes for the energy companies and agencies.

This kind of regional planning to balance outcomes between multiple benefits and to avoid unnecessary costs is urgently needed to ensure that the large land use transition beginning in the San Joaquin Valley achieves the best outcomes and minimizes the costs.

Some of the lessons learned from the desert example are already being applied in the San Joaquin Valley, with careful planning for least-conflict solar development footprints (Pearce et al. 2016). There are also some efforts under way to plan for land use change in ways that achieve multiple benefits. But these efforts have not been integrated, and none have been developed for making the most out of planned agricultural land retirement.

A key reason that advanced, landscape-scale planning is needed is that the large land use changes that will be necessary to achieve groundwater sustainability in the San Joaquin Valley will come with costs, particularly to the agricultural economy and workers dependent on agriculture. If they are done well, these costs can be minimized. There are also important societal benefits that could be achieved. Like the Mojave, the San Joaquin Valley has high potential for renewable energy development on former agricultural land. There is also a great need to increase recreational opportunities for underserved communities and to reduce air and water pollution in a region with some of the most severe agriculture-related human health problems in the country. Some of these benefits can be created together. For example, human health and recreational opportunities can be created simultaneously with rewilding efforts. But identifying and achieving the most appropriate balance can happen only if the opportunities are assessed and planned for in advance. There will also be important trade-offs between costs and benefits that should be considered as these communities contemplate where and how to change land use. These trade-offs can be managed and shaped by analytically supported planning in advance of the inevitable land use change.

Planning for Rewilding to Maximize Benefits and Minimize Costs
The focus of rewilding the San Joaquin Valley is on restoring natural landscapes in order to recover natural systems that have been lost and, in particular, to save many unique and imperiled species from extinction. This challenge is the opposite of the challenge cre-

ated by energy development in the deserts, where the objective was to optimally protect key parts of the natural landscape. For rewilding, the key challenge is identifying where we could restore natural habitats to create the most benefit for these natural systems and how much to restore given inevitable trade-offs and resource limitations. Ideally, the costs and trade-offs will be minimized or mitigated while the potential benefits are maximized. However, that depends on where things happen on the landscape, rather than simply the total amount of cultivation, land retirement, or restoration. For any single land use, some places will be better than others. For example, how suitable an area is for San Joaquin Desert species depends on soil types, slope of the land, microclimates, and other biophysical attributes, and these must be used in guiding where and how to restore parts of the landscape (see chapters 2 and 6). At the same time, some areas will be more suitable for sustaining economically viable agricultural production because of soil and water availability. The trade-offs between these land uses and their benefits vary across the landscape. All else being equal, the best rewilding outcomes can be achieved by retiring agriculture and restoring natural habitats in areas that have the potential for the highest habitat value and that are less suitable for agriculture.

The size and configuration of restored areas are also important factors for the success of rewilding and its effects on the surrounding landscape. The long-term habitat value of a restored area is strongly influenced by its patch size, or how connected it is to other areas of natural habitat and the habitat value of interstitial agricultural lands. Overall, the larger a natural area is, the larger the number of species and individuals it can support and sustain, and this is especially true for several of the San Joaquin Desert species. Also, habitat islands closer to each other and to large intact areas of natural habitat or, better yet, connected via corridors through the agricultural landscape, sustain biodiversity better than those that are more isolated (Hilty et al. 2019). This is in large part because of dispersal between patches and the dynamics of immigration and emigration that maintain populations and "rescue" small populations in isolated areas (see chapter 8, figure 8-1). By extension, it is also true that fragmentation of natural landscapes into many small, isolated patches contributes to the loss of biodiversity and ecological function (Haddad et al. 2015). Furthermore, mosaics of natural habitat and agricultural land can support high biodiversity as long as those agricultural lands are hospitable or at least not directly or indirectly affecting the health and survival of wildlife in adjacent natural areas (Mendenhall et al. 2014; see chapter 10).

For all these reasons, an important goal of rewilding is targeting land restoration to areas where larger, more connected patches of habitat can be created at the least additional cost to other values, including the economic costs of retiring agricultural land. This means selecting areas with the greatest current and future potential habitat suitability, consolidating land retirement into large blocks, and ideally building on existing natural and protected lands to maximize the average size and connectedness of natural areas to increase the likelihood of population persistence (see chapter 6), dispersal (see chapter 7), and genetic exchange (see chapter 8). This also means taking maximal advantage of restoring lands whose long-term economic viability as croplands is hampered by poor land quality or lack of reliable water. Ideally, the value of areas as habitat and the trade-offs with agricultural economic value would be considered alongside other values, such as human health concerns, and potential for other benefits or land uses. This is the kind of planning that has put renewable energy development in California's deserts on a more sustainable, balanced path.

There is not yet such an established landscape-scale planning effort in place for the San Joaquin Valley. Decisions made at the local level in isolation and without coordination at a regional scale are more likely to result in a highly fragmented and haphazard pattern of land use change that at best does not take advantage of opportunities to reap potential benefits and minimize long-term costs and, at worst, exacerbates problems the valley already faces. Achieving optimal outcomes that result in balancing multiple land uses and their benefits while minimizing trade-offs will require proactive, region-wide planning. To do this, stakeholders need a systematic way to integrate different objectives into spatial planning. In the following case study, we illustrate such a strategic planning approach for the valley that shows how habitat value on retired lands can be optimized while the net additional economic impacts of agricultural land retirement are minimized. We also estimated greater soil carbon sequestration and potential for air and water quality benefits in the form of reductions in nitrogen application that will come with a transition from cultivation to restored habitat. These co-benefits can be tied to incentive programs that ease the transition through strategic land retirement and restoration to rewild the San Joaquin Valley (Bryant et al. 2020). The results of this case study represent one plausible scenario but not the only one. They also do not fully explore the potential for optimizing other benefits beyond habitat value and economic losses. But the approach taken can easily accommodate additional goals, and it is a good illustration of how more comprehensive planning could be done.

Strategic Land Restoration for Habitat Value in the San Joaquin Valley
This case study is explicitly designed to help collaboration between agencies, conservation organizations, and agricultural land managers and inform planning that helps achieve rewilding in ways that benefit communities in the valley. To do this, we needed to estimate how much land is likely to come out of production due to limited water supplies, where that retirement is likely to occur, and where the best places to restore habitat are relative to these patterns of land retirement. We used established methods in an innovative way that can be easily replicated for guiding on-the-ground action. Our recommendations should not be considered "the" answer in terms of where and how much retired agricultural land should be used to

restore as natural habitat. Rather, they provide a plausible starting point for how and where to get the most benefits from rewilding at the least additional economic cost to the agricultural community. They also provide the basis for local and state agencies to begin targeting investments for incentivizing farmers in making this transition, thus mitigating the economic costs of lost agriculture and covering the costs of restoration for public benefit. In some places, projected agricultural land retirement may align well with opportunities for habitat restoration. However, in other cases the best lands for habitat may not overlap with areas of likely retirement. In these cases, conservation or government actors could collaborate to provide compensation to achieve consolidated retirement of specific agricultural land to meet habitat goals, thereby directing land retirement to places where it can provide multiple benefits while avoiding retirement in areas less suitable for habitat. This analysis simultaneously incorporates water-constrained land use change modeling with optimized site selection that provides realistic scenarios at a fine scale, making it particularly useful for local planning. Not only does combining these approaches improve our ability to plan for better outcomes in the San Joaquin Valley, it presents an approach that can be generalized to other water-stressed agricultural landscapes. The full analysis and results of this study can be found in Bryant et al. (2020).

How Much and Where Is Land Likely to Be Retired?

Optimizing the benefits of rewilding through multibenefit planning requires first understanding what the landscape would look like in the absence of strategic planning. Although the trajectory of land use change in the San Joaquin Valley is uncertain, we need to know where lands are likely to come out of production simply as a function of water availability and land suitability.

In order to estimate how much land will need to come out of production in the long-run because of the Sustainable Groundwater Management Act (SGMA), we applied the Statewide Agricultural Production (SWAP) model (Howitt et al. 2012). Using SWAP, we estimated the change in acreage of irrigated agriculture needed to meet groundwater sustainability targets in ten groundwater regions of the San Joaquin Valley. The SWAP model simulates annual agricultural production based on predicted annual water supplies under SGMA and agricultural market trends for different crops. From these estimates we derived the average annual acreage of cultivation predicted under future SGMA conditions, as well as acres likely to be fallowed (including annually fallowed or permanently taken out of production, i.e., retired). To predict where those irrigated agricultural lands are most likely to be retired in each of the regions, we considered multiple spatially varying indicators of agricultural suitability, including aspects of land quality (e.g., salinization), surface water rights, and degrees of groundwater dependence and historical extraction. Lands with worse soil and water characteristics were assumed to be the most likely to be permanently retired to achieve sustainable groundwater use. These attributes that broadly determine overall agricultural suitability were mapped across the whole valley with publicly available data (Bryant et al. 2020).

In a comprehensive analysis (summarized in chapter 11), Hanak et al. (2019) predict that between 535,000 and 780,000 acres of agricultural land would need to be fallowed either temporarily or permanently in the San Joaquin Valley to end groundwater overdraft. The exact amount will depend on approaches taken to balance water supplies and demands; cost-effective projects to increase water supplies combined with liberal water trading policies will help minimize the amount of fallowing needed to meet groundwater sustainability targets (Hanak et al. 2019). We calculated similar impacts with SWAP, which predicted that approximately 210,000 acres of agricultural land would need to be permanently retired, and 395,000 acres would be fallowed annually by 2040 to achieve sustainable groundwater use across the valley (Bryant et al. 2020).

However, our analysis suggests that the amount of permanently retired land may be less than valley residents have feared, representing only 28 to 40 percent of necessary land fallowing. Notably, the temporary fallowing we predicted due only to SGMA would be in addition to what will also result from natural and policy-driven variability in water availability.

Importantly, the acreage of permanently retired land is only 4 percent of the currently cultivated landscape overall. When looking at the permanently retired area and temporarily fallowed areas together, we expect approximately 14 percent of the total land area to be out of production in any given year. This impact will not be felt equally across groundwater regions in the San Joaquin Valley, as the proportion of predicted land retirement ranges from 0 to 8 percent of the total area across the ten regions because of existing surface water supplies, dependence on groundwater, and cropping patterns. Also, the total area to be restored for rewilding will occur only on a subset of otherwise retired lands. These distinctions are relevant for a few reasons. First, the total area of retirement is likely to be small relative to agricultural production overall. Second, having more retired land available than would be used for restoration offers the flexibility to exchange some areas for others. Land that would otherwise be retired but would not provide high-quality habitat can be maintained in production, in exchange for retiring and restoring another property. Finally, the larger acreages of land to be temporarily fallowed in many years because of land quality and water supplies create significantly more flexibility for consolidating retirement in certain areas in exchange for maintaining greater agricultural productivity in others. In other words, in exchange for cultivating land more frequently in some areas, other land could be retired and restored, thus freeing up those water supplies for the other cultivated lands. This will work only if water trading policies and other mechanisms are enabling, rather than disabling, factors (see chapter 11; Hanak et al. 2019).

*Where Are the Optimal Areas to Strategically Restore Retired
Agricultural Lands for Rewilding?*

Our objective was to identify consolidated areas of agricultural land
that, if restored to natural vegetation, could provide high-quality
habitat while minimizing the economic impact of retiring those
lands. To do this we used open-source spatial conservation planning software, Prioritizr (Hanson et al. 2019), to optimize the selection of lands for restoration based on habitat quality, proximity to
existing natural areas, and potential economic value. The economic
value of land was determined based on the average gross revenue
of current crop types and whether the land is predicted to be vulnerable to retirement. Lands identified as vulnerable to retirement
based on land quality and water availability were considered the
least costly by discounting the potential gross revenue by 90 percent (Bryant et al. 2020).

It is difficult, if not impossible, to plan individually for all the
wildlife species that could benefit from restoring landscapes.
Thus, it is useful to identify a single or small suite of species to
plan around, in effect serving as umbrella species for a broader
natural community; this approach is common in conservation
planning. We focused on the habitat needs of five endangered
arid upland species that we chose to represent the habitat needs
of more than thirty-five listed plant and animal species that
occupy the once-abundant upland desert scrub and grassland
habitats of the region: San Joaquin kit fox, giant kangaroo rat,
Tipton kangaroo rat, blunt-nosed leopard lizard, and San Joaquin
woolly-threads. We used habitat suitability maps (see chapter 6)
for these five species and selected the areas identified as in the top
10 percent of potential suitability (Stewart et al. 2019). For these
species, the goal should be to create enough habitat that is connected to other high-quality natural areas to support a population
of each species that can persist and thrive over time. The U.S.
Fish and Wildlife Service set explicit habitat protection goals for
each of these species that were deemed necessary for biological

and legal recovery, which would enable removing these species from the endangered species list (Williams et al. 1998). Based on those goals, we propose an objective of restoring 25,000 acres of high-quality habitat for each of the five focal species. If there were no overlap in high-quality habitat between the species, this would mean identifying 125,000 acres total. However, if there is overlap in high-quality habitat, the acreage identified could be smaller. Given that larger areas of habitat and those closer to or connected with existing natural areas will result in better conservation outcomes, we also sought to select land for restoration that was adjacent to existing wildlife preserves and natural areas, including national wildlife refuges, state wildlife areas, conservation easement lands, and unprotected natural areas.

By optimally selecting lands for strategic restoration at the least economic cost, we identified 48,000 acres of land that together achieve the goal of 25,000 acres per target species. About half of this area was selected from lands predicted to be retired in any case. However, the emphasis on avoiding fragmentation and capitalizing on sites that serve multiple species resulted in selecting approximately 24,000 acres for strategic restoration that are not otherwise expected to be retired. This is despite there being significant areas of unselected retired land, which would be expected to be less costly and thus have a lower overall economic impact on the region. However, the existence of unused retired lands and large areas prone to temporary annual fallowing points to opportunities for proactive engagement with water districts and the farming community to consolidate retirement in some areas for their habitat value while maintaining cultivation in less valuable habitat areas (see chapter 11). This would be instead of securing additional retirement above and beyond that imposed by SGMA. However, this more collaborative outcome is unlikely to be achieved unless explicitly planned for and incentivized in advance. This study provides guidance for this type of planning by highlighting specific areas of focus.

All the existing agricultural lands identified as optimal for restoring habitat at the lowest cost are in the southern part of the San Joaquin Valley, in Kern, Tulare, Kings, and western Fresno counties. In this southern landscape, three geographic hubs emerged as priorities for strategic restoration (figure 9-1). One potential hub of strategic land restoration is in southwestern Tulare County, where this study identified approximately 7,000 acres that are both likely to be retired and excellent for habitat restoration. Restoring habitat in this area would build on existing protected lands, such as Pixley National Wildlife Refuge and Tule Elk State Natural Reserve (see figure 3-1). North central and western Kern County is also a hub with significant opportunities for strategic restoration around existing habitat areas including the Kern National Wildlife Refuge, Semitropic Ecological Reserve, and Kern Water Bank (see figure 3-1). These areas include opportunities to create new habitat areas that would add to natural lands along portions of the historic Buena Vista lakebed and the Lost Hills. If implemented in these areas, new habitat in Kern County would significantly increase habitat connectivity across the southern San Joaquin Valley and to the north in Pleasant Valley. The northern part of Pleasant Valley is the other high-value area for strategic restoration (figure 9-1). However, like western Kern County, this is an area where the study did not predict much permanent retirement. So restoration here would require planning and incentives to either swap with other areas where retirement is more likely or increase cropping frequency on some areas of Pleasant Valley while retiring key sites in order to minimize overall reductions in agricultural production. Pleasant Valley has limited water supplies, and significant temporary annual fallowing is expected under SGMA; thus, it is an important place to consider the second alternative. Importantly, restoration in Pleasant Valley would be highly ecologically significant because establishing new protected natural areas here would increase connectivity between existing natural lands to the north and south.

Although this analysis identified three core areas where retiring

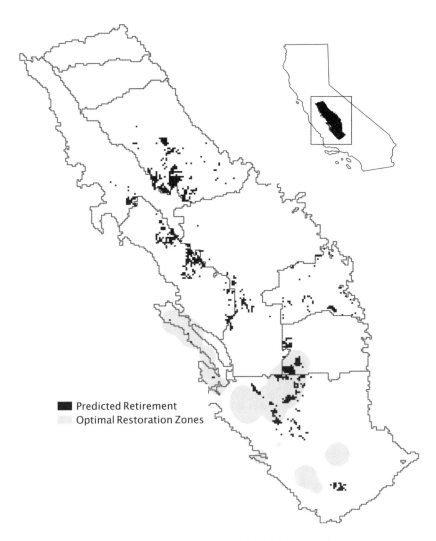

Figure 9-1. Over the next twenty years we predicted that more than 200,000 acres of farmland will be permanently retired to meet the requirements of the Sustainable Groundwater Management Act. The areas most likely to be retired based on land quality and water availability are shown in black here. There's an opportunity to restore some of this area to upland habitat. The best outcome will be to select areas where the restored lands can be consolidated into large reserves and where the habitat value will be highest while minimizing the overall economic impact of taking that land out of production. These optimal areas for land restoration are shown in gray.

agricultural lands to reduce water demand and restoring it to natural habitat would be optimal, it does not mean there are no other important opportunities across the valley. The choice of hubs was driven in part by how good the habitat could be if restored and also by the greater amount of already protected nature preserves. Fewer protected, natural areas exist to the north except the Grasslands Ecological Area and San Luis National Wildlife Refuge. Nevertheless, the Westside groundwater basin to the north is expected to need temporary annual fallowing of up to 48,000 acres of agricultural land to meet groundwater sustainability goals. This could create valuable opportunities to restore upland habitats along the western margins of the valley, creating an important wildlife area and corridor.

What Community and Environmental Benefits Could Come with Restoration?

In addition to providing an alternative land use that can be incentivized through public and private funding programs focused on habitat restoration and endangered species recovery, restoration can bring additional societal benefits. In this case study, we examined two related benefits: reduced nitrogen application, which would ultimately improve water and air quality, and the potential for increased carbon sequestration, with associated reduction in greenhouse gas emissions, in restored lands.

The ecosystem benefits of land restoration can extend to positive impacts on human health at the local and regional scales. Pollutants associated with agricultural activities contribute significantly to several major health issues in the region, with large health disparities relative to the rest of California. Therefore, the health benefits that may emerge from reductions in agriculture-related exposure to air or water pollution would be highly valuable. In particular, reducing the byproducts of nitrogen application in agriculture may yield important benefits. Nitrogen is commonly applied as a fertilizer in agricultural production, but when applied in excess it can lead to water and air quality degradation. Leaching and runoff of nitrogen fertilizer and manure applied to farm fields is responsible for the majority of groundwater nitrate concentrations in the San Joaquin Valley (Harter et al. 2017). The San Joaquin Valley contains two of the most nitrate-contaminated aquifers in the United States, and almost 95 percent of residents rely on groundwater for drinking (Balazs et al. 2011). Unfortunately, nitrate in drinking water is the most common environmental exposure associated with blue baby syndrome, the death rates from which have been reported to be as much as 140 percent above the state average in the San Joaquin Valley. Land retirement at any scale will contribute to reducing this problem and others. In this study, we estimated that excess nitrogen application would decrease by 19,000 tons annually with the predicted 210,000 acres of agricultural land retirement by 2040. This is 9 percent of the excess nitrogen applied each year in the San Joaquin Valley. However, if land retirement were strategically targeted to reduce impacts of excess nitrogen for the most vulnerable populations, in ways similar to the approach used to target habitat restoration, the human health benefits could be even more significant.

Agricultural land retirement could also contribute meaningfully to meeting California's climate change mitigation goals. Agricultural activities account for about 10 percent of greenhouse gas emissions in California, including more than 50 percent of nitrous oxide (largely from applied nitrogen fertilizer), a greenhouse gas that is 300 times more potent than carbon dioxide in its effect on climate warming. A considerable amount of this impact comes from the release of carbon from the soil and an overall lack of soil carbon storage. To assess greenhouse gas impacts of land retirement and restoration, this study used the Land Use and Carbon Scenario Simulator to track changes in soil carbon storage over time until 2100, comparing a future with the scale of restoration described earlier (48,000 acres) to one without. We assumed a steady rate of land retirement and restoration (along with other predicted shifts in agricultural land use) between 2020 and 2040.

Restoration increases carbon stored in soils and natural vegetation and improves sequestration of soil carbon through reduced tilling. Restoring 48,000 acres of retired farmland to grassland or shrubland has the potential to increase soil carbon storage by more than 1.6 million metric tons of carbon over the next eighty years. On a per-acre basis, restored grasslands and shrublands would contribute an additional 70–330 tons of carbon per acre on average. This is the equivalent of taking more than 300,000 cars off the road in 2020. Therefore, restoring even a small portion of the land expected to be retired will contribute significantly to California's goal to become carbon neutral by 2045 (Bryant et al. 2020).

Conclusions

This study illustrates how strategic planning can consider multiple outcomes to proactively shape landscapes to provide a suite of benefits rather than allowing one concern alone (i.e., economics) to drive outcomes in a haphazard manner. The success achieved for energy development with the proactive Desert Renewable Energy Conservation Plan can be replicated now to plan for groundwater sustainability in the San Joaquin Valley, enabling a future that balances economic prosperity, habitat restoration goals, and human health.

Even though we examined impacts of strategic retirement on carbon and nitrogen, we ultimately considered only two outcomes as part of the optimization process: habitat provisioning and cost to the agricultural economy. The same analytic tools used in this case study can be extended to consider other environmental, health, and economic objectives that are shaped by land use—not just in separate studies but simultaneously. Fundamentally, all that is needed is an ability to represent how benefits associated with different land uses vary in space. These could range from the nitrogen and carbon benefits already discussed to different types of habitat (e.g., wetland or riparian), energy development, groundwater recharge, and reducing human health impacts.

Indeed, many of these are being considered by various groups already, and although more holistic integration is lacking, the potential is high. The kind of approach presented here could be combined with other efforts. The Environmental Defense Fund has developed a tool (Bourque et al. 2019) to help large landowners identify priority parcels that can benefit recharge and provide habitat, and Sustainable Conservation has developed tools to help irrigation districts identify the best places to conduct groundwater recharge operations on agricultural lands. Point Blue Conservation Science, in partnership with The Nature Conservancy and NASA, is working to improve the targeting of flooded fields for groundwater recharge and wildlife habitat. Most of these efforts consider only a small number of objectives, but they could readily be brought together to improve holistic planning to remove key barriers and achieve a multibenefit landscape (see chapter 11).

Conversely, many challenges will always be present. Land and livelihoods are not commodities and hold special value. So, although analytical support will be essential for examining and then implementing the possibilities to get the best outcomes for the San Joaquin Valley, costs and benefits will vary from what are assumed by any planning process. Local knowledge and engagement will always be crucial, both ethically and from an effectiveness standpoint. Nevertheless, analytically supported planning has a key role to play in guiding those engagements to develop a new land use mosaic in the San Joaquin Valley that has the potential to protect nature and improve outcomes for people of the region in cost-effective and ethical ways.

Forty years from now and possibly even sooner, the San Joaquin Valley is going to be a very different landscape than it is right now. This will lead to profound impacts on food production and the communities that depend on agriculture for their livelihood. The challenge of feeding a growing global population is daunting, and it remains essential to maintain, if not increase, productivity in many agricultural landscapes. However, this can be balanced with recovering and maintaining natural systems and the ecosystem functions they provide, such as pollination and pest control services, climate regulation, and clean water. Fortunately, it may be possible to achieve these goals simultaneously. Given the stakes, we underscore the urgency to consider the fate of the San Joaquin Valley and other intensively cultivated landscapes where production exceeds sustainable limits or will in the future and to take advantage of the opportunity to redesign these landscapes to rebalance agricultural, environmental, and social benefits. We can do this by deliberately redesigning these areas with natural systems as inherent and vital components in ways that account for the specific needs and constraints of these places and by treating them as demonstrations of collaborative reconfiguration of unsustainable landscapes in ways that help protect biodiversity and human well-being.

References

Balazs, C., R. Morello-Frosch, A. Hubbard, and I. Ray. 2011. "Social disparities in nitrate-contaminated drinking water in California's San Joaquin Valley." *Environmental Health Perspectives* 119, no. 9: 1272.

Bourque, Kelly, Anna Schiller, Cristóbal Loyola Angosto, Lindsay McPhail, Wendy Bagnasco, Andrew Ayres, and Ashley Larsen. 2019. "Balancing agricultural production, groundwater management, and biodiversity goals: a multi-benefit optimization model of agriculture in Kern County, California." *Science of the Total Environment* 670: 865–75.

Bryant, Ben P., Rodd T. Kelsey, Adrian L. Vogl, Stacie A. Wolny, Paul Selmants, Tanushree Biswas, and H. Scott Butterfield. 2020. "Shaping land use change and ecosystem restoration in a water stressed agricultural landscape to achieve multiple benefits." *Frontiers in Sustainable Food Systems* 4: 138.

Haddad, Nick M., Lars A. Brudvig, Jean Clobert, Kendi F. Davies, Andrew Gonzalez, Robert D. Holt, Thomas E. Lovejoy, et al. 2015. "Habitat fragmentation and its lasting impact on Earth's ecosystems." *Science Advances* 1, no. 2: e1500052.

Hanak, Ellen, Alvar Escriva-Bou, Brian Gray, Sarge Green, Thomas Harter, Jelena Jezdimirovic, Jay Lund, Josué Medellín-Azuara, Peter Moyle, and Nathaniel Seavy. 2019. *Water and the Future of the San Joaquin Valley*. San Francisco: Public Policy Institute of California.

Hanson, J. O., R. Schuster, N. Morrell, M. Strimas-Mackey, M. E. Watts, P. Arcese, J. Bennett, and H. P. Possingham. 2019. *Prioritizr: Systematic Conservation Prioritization in R*. R package version 4.1.4.3. Available at https://github.com/prioritizr/prioritizr

Harter, Thomas, Kristin Dzurella, Giorgos Kourakos, Allan Hollander, Andy Bell, Nick Santos, Quinn Hart, et al. 2017. "Nitrogen fertilizer loading to groundwater in the Central Valley." Final report to the fertilizer research education program, Projects: 11-0301.

Hilty, Jodi A., Annika T. H. Keeley, Adina M. Merenlender, and William Z. Lidicker Jr. 2019. *Corridor Ecology: Linking Landscapes for Biodiversity Conservation and Climate Adaptation*. Washington, D.C.: Island Press.

Howitt, Richard E., Josué Medellín-Azuara, Duncan MacEwan, and Jay R. Lund. 2012. "Calibrating disaggregate economic models of agricultural production and water management." *Environmental Modelling & Software* 38: 244–58.

Mendenhall, Chase D., Daniel S. Karp, Christoph F. J. Meyer, Elizabeth A. Hadly, and Gretchen C. Daily. 2014. "Predicting biodiversity change and averting collapse in agricultural landscapes." *Nature* 509, no. 7499: 213–17.

Pearce, Dustin, James Strittholt, Terry Watt, and Ethan Elkind. 2016. *A Path Forward: Identifying Least-Conflict Solar PV Development in California's San Joaquin Valley*. Berkeley, Calif.: Center for Law, Energy & the Environment. https://scholarship.law.berkeley.edu/cleepubs/1

Stewart, Joseph A. E., H. Scott Butterfield, Jonathan Q. Richmond, David J. Germano, Michael F. Westphal, Erin N. Tennant, and Barry Sinervo. 2019. "Habitat restoration opportunities, climatic niche contraction, and conservation biogeography in California's San Joaquin Desert." *PLOS One* 14, no. 1: e0210766.

Williams, Daniel F., Ellen A. Cypher, Patrick A. Kelly, Karen J. Miller, Nancy Norvell, Scott E. Phillips, and Gary W. Colliver. 1998. *Recovery Plan for Upland Species of the San Joaquin Valley*. Washington, D.C.: U.S. Fish and Wildlife Service.

Chapter 10

The Role of Diversifying Farmland Management in Rewilding the San Joaquin Valley

Claire Kremen, T. Rodd Kelsey, and Sasha Gennet

Even if rewilding in the San Joaquin Valley is implemented successfully at large scales, most of the landscape will remain in intensive agriculture. In the San Joaquin Valley, more than 3 million acres will remain in production, and the ultimate success of rewilding efforts will depend on how the surrounding agriculture is managed. Protected regions surrounded by agriculture may be vulnerable to the management practices used. For example, in Germany, protected areas within an agricultural matrix suffered the loss of more than 75 percent of insect biomass over thirty years. Habitat cover in the protected areas and the surrounding region did not change greatly over this time period, but pesticide use may have intensified (Hallmann et al. 2017).

Thus, to maximize the chances that large investments in rewilding natural landscapes are successful and to capitalize on opportunities to create multiple benefits for nature and people, remaining farmlands must be managed with strategies that are complementary to and compatible with restoration on retired farmlands. We need to identify how farmlands can be managed to reduce negative effects of agriculture on restored areas, to provide additional habitat or resources for target species, and to improve landscape-level permeability and connectivity between restored and conserved regions. These changes in management should be implemented in ways that retain or increase farmland productivity and profitability (Kremen and Merenlender 2018). Maintaining production and profitability will be especially important if the agricultural footprint in the San Joaquin Valley shrinks while expectations remain to produce the same amount of food.

Fortunately, history shows us that we can increase production without expanding agricultural land use. Since the emergence of the Green Revolution in the 1960s, intensive agriculture has dramatically increased food production while still reducing expansion of agriculture into natural areas by producing large amounts of food on the most productive lands (land sparing; Stevenson et al. 2013). However, this has been accomplished through agricultural management increasingly dominated by monocultures of the same crops over large areas and industrial-scale inputs. This form of agriculture relies on chemically and mechanically intensive methods to deal with pest outbreaks and declining soil fertility, both of which are exacerbated by these intensive methods. Such intensive methods are precisely the kinds of management that can have the most devastating impacts on nature. For example, we are now seeing global declines in invertebrate populations (Hallmann et al. 2017; Wagner 2020), with agrochemical pollutants considered among the primary causes. Many of the insects being lost are vital to the function of ecosystems, and many of them are important sources of pollination and pest control for crops (Kremen et al. 2002; Rusch et al. 2016; Dainese et al. 2019). Likewise, this trend toward more intensive agriculture appears to be a significant contributor to ongoing declines in other wildlife, stream pollution, and the occurrence of coastal and marine dead zones.

The good news is that recent evidence suggests we can also intensify crop production by harnessing ecological processes such as natural pest control. Such ecological intensification (i.e., relying on management techniques that use natural processes to increase agricultural production) can boost yields, reduce environmental harms from farming, and increase biodiversity in the broader landscape (Kremen and Merenlender 2018). For example, flower strips at farm edges, which support natural predators of crop pests, allowed farmers in Asia to reduce pesticide usage by 70 percent while increasing yields by 5 percent and profits by 7.5 percent (Gurr et al. 2016). Integration of permanent prairie strips into corn and soy monoculture in the Midwestern United States reduced leaching of nitrates by 84 percent and phosphorus by 89 percent, cleaning up waterways with conversion of only 10 percent of the land area to deep-rooted prairie plants that soak up these pollutants. Conservation tillage to reduce soil disturbance reduces erosion and runoff, increases soil water holding capacity, and builds soil organic carbon (Busari et al. 2015).

Other ecological intensification methods such as cover cropping, intercropping, and hedgerow addition also increase crop and noncrop diversity over space and time. Increasing plant diversity on and around farmlands may provide more habitat and resources for some species, and indeed, farms using these diversification practices exhibit higher levels of biodiversity (Kremen and Miles 2012). Restoration or maintenance of natural habitat patches within farms and farming landscapes can also be an important part of ecological intensification; for example, these habitat patches export pollinators and natural predators of crop pests that increase crop yields in nearby crops. In fact, having the right ratio of natural habitat to farmland (around 1:4, or 20 percent natural habitat) can lead to net gains in production and profitability. Thus, rewilding agricultural landscapes is compatible with an ecological intensification strategy and with the concept of diversified farming systems that rely on suites of techniques to promote ecosystem services and sustainable agriculture by diversifying crop and noncrop vegetation from within-field to landscape scales (Kremen et al. 2012; Rosa-Schleich et al. 2019).

Increasing the vegetative diversity of farmlands through ecological intensification could also make farmlands more permeable
to wildlife and thus increase the connectivity of wildlife populations living in otherwise separated natural or restored regions. Linear habitat strips along field edges, riparian corridors, and even
"islands" of natural habitat as steppingstone habitat patches can
simultaneously provide benefits to farmers, such as pollination
services, while improving the ability of target wildlife to navigate
across otherwise impenetrable landscapes. Critically, increasing
landscape permeability can maintain gene flow, increase population persistence, and permit range movements in response to climate change for target wildlife species, which will be essential for
long-term population persistence and adaptation (see chapter 6).

At first glance, management of remaining agricultural lands
might appear unrelated to rewilding of retired agricultural lands.
But different forms of agricultural management will have vastly different impacts on the success of rewilding projects. On one hand,
highly simplified, chemically intensive agriculture can have significant impacts on surrounding natural lands, either by directly
affecting species through agricultural pollutants or by creating biological deserts with low permeability for many species. An alternative future can come from ecological intensification, leading to
much more diversified farms and landscapes that will reduce off-
farm impacts to improve environmental quality, create resources
and habitat for some species, and potentially increase permeability
of farming landscapes for wildlife.

Farms as Habitat

The habitat value of farms can come from the crops themselves,
cover crops used seasonally to improve soil health, and farm edge
or strip plantings that provide resources different wildlife need.
However, the degree to which the farms can deliver these benefits, and in turn benefit from the increased diversity, varies with

the crop types, farmland elements, and scale of implementation of diversified management.

Farmlands themselves can provide valuable, surrogate habitat for many different species of wildlife, supplementing the habitat provided by surrounding natural lands. In some cases, farmlands are providing important resources for one component of a species' needs (e.g., food) while adjacent natural lands provide for other needs (e.g., cover, breeding sites). However, the value of farmlands is highly dependent on the crop itself and its management. One important example from the San Joaquin Valley is the importance of irrigated farmlands for certain bird species. Swainson's hawks (an imperiled species in California) are now highly dependent on farmlands. Adult survival and reproduction in Swainson's hawks are strongly associated with having agricultural foraging sites, especially alfalfa, near their nesting sites (Briggs et al. 2011). This pattern is probably an important reason why we see high densities of Swainson's hawks persisting in the southern Sacramento Valley, where there are abundant trees in windbreaks and along riverine corridors, but not in much of the San Joaquin Valley, where farmland trees or windbreaks and riparian corridors are now rare. Similarly, other migratory birds rely heavily on agricultural lands as habitat during migration (Golet et al. 2018).

The potential value of farmland is not limited to birds. Kit foxes use orchards and other farmlands to supplement their prey base. Thus, restoration or practices such as providing artificial den sites in farmlands (especially in orchards) might increase their use and facilitate kit fox movement between isolated patches of natural lands. However, farmers would also need to avoid using rodenticides, which directly and indirectly harm carnivores such as the kit fox. Alternatively, farmers could use ecologically based rodent management practices, such as use of owl boxes and trapping.

There is also good evidence that a greater diversity of crops may support a wider array of species within farmlands. For pollinators, a recent study in the San Joaquin Valley found higher diversity of native bee species on farms growing multiple crops than on mono-culture squash farms. Farms were otherwise similar in surrounding landscape and pesticide use. Even native squash bees that special-ize on and pollinate squash were found in greater abundance on polyculture farms, presumably because although they obtain pol-len exclusively from squash, they need other flowering plants to provide nectar later in the day when squash flowers have closed (Guzman et al. 2019). Globally, growing multiple crops on the farm and in the farming landscape increases pollinator diversity and abundance, and this effect is in addition to positive effects on pol-linator biodiversity of organic management and natural habitat in the surrounding landscape (Kennedy et al. 2013). Also, patterns of field size, another reflection of variability in the landscape, can have profound impacts on wildlife diversity. For example, Fahrig et al. (2015) found that farming landscapes composed of smaller fields on average may increase overall diversity across different kinds of wildlife, including birds, butterflies, other insects, and spiders.

Crop diversity can occur over time as well as space. Crop rota-tions, including the use of cover crops, add to crop diversity over time and can increase species diversity. Fallowing has also been asso-ciated elsewhere with increased bird species richness (Van Buskirk and Willi 2004). However, we do not know of studies in the San Joa-quin Valley that have investigated the relationship between rotations, cover crops or fallowing, and biodiversity or wildlife. Intermittently fallowed fields can also be managed with seasonal (fall, winter, and spring) flooding to provide excellent and vitally needed habitat for migratory waterbirds (Golet et al. 2018). This kind of flooding will also provide groundwater recharge benefits that are critically needed in the San Joaquin Valley, where groundwater overdraft is severe and current laws require achieving more sustainable use.

Historically, not only was there more natural land remaining within and on the boundaries of agricultural areas, but there were also greater amounts of small, uncultivated areas along field mar-gins and in corners of fields where soils were less productive. In the drive to plant all parts of the farm (fencerow-to-fencerow farming), much of that patchy habitat along field edges has been lost. Although these small patches and linear margins of seminatural vegetation, such as hedgerows and windbreaks (figure 10-1), do not support the full community of native wildlife that need larger, intact areas of native habitat, they do contribute meaningfully to the abundance and diversity of native wildlife in the landscape. They also can serve as steppingstones and connecting corridors between larger natural areas.

In the northern Central Valley of California, hedgerows of native flowering shrubs have been shown to increase the abundance, diversity, and persistence of native bees (Morandin and Kremen 2013), including approximately fifty species that are valuable pollinators to nearby crops. The communities of pollinators that persist in hedgerows even resemble the natural pollinator communities found in nearby natural lands (Kremen and M'Gonigle 2015). And the more, the better; networks of restored hedgerows create higher pollinator persistence in the landscape (Ponisio et al. 2019).

Beyond insect communities, hedgerows and windbreaks also increase the diversity of birds and other species. As noted earlier, the value of farm fields for hunting by Swainson's hawks depends on having nesting trees nearby. Also, the overall variety and abundance of birds are known to increase in agricultural landscapes when woody vegetation is maintained along field margins.

Farms as Matrix

What is on the farm clearly matters. So do the spatial configuration and management of those farmlands. If inhospitable or even dangerous for wildlife, farms create barriers between and damage to protected and restored areas. Alternatively, with more diversified, ecological management they can create a supportive matrix that connects and buffers natural or restored areas, thereby supporting rewilding efforts. Specifically, it is important to manage farmlands

Figure 10-1. Farm edge plantings, such as hedgerows, create highly valuable habitat for many species and when installed over larger areas can play a vital role in landscape connectivity for wildlife. Hedgerows are also well documented to support diverse wildlife species that provide important pollination and pest control services for the adjacent farm fields. In this image, a farm field in Yolo County was transformed in 2006 (before) with the installation of a hedgerow, seen here in 2013 (after).

so that they are permeable to wildlife movements, containing elements such as unfenced riparian corridors that serve as connectors between wild areas. These natural movement pathways provide the critical linkages between habitat nodes, enabling genetic exchange between population subunits (see chapter 8) and facilitating population shifts in response to climate change (see chapter 6). Furthermore, farmlands should be managed to buffer natural areas from the effects of pollutants, pesticides, invasive species, fire, and other disturbances rather than pose threats to natural areas. That can be done by creating physical buffers of seminatural vegetation or topographic features (e.g., berms) between high-intensity farm fields and high-value habitat. It can also come from adjusting or reducing biocide use and active management of natural and seminatural vegetation.

Most historic movement pathways in the San Joaquin Valley, primarily riparian corridors, have been heavily degraded or eliminated to maximize planted acres on fertile bottomland soils. Although these riparian corridors historically occurred on about 90,000 acres in the southern San Joaquin Valley (Warner and Hendrix 1984), the valley currently supports few or perhaps no remaining pathways for animals to move freely (Spencer et al. 2010). Furthermore, many farms in California, especially those that produce fresh-market specialty crops where food safety concerns run high, use fencing to deter movement of animals through fields or along natural corridors. In a study in the nearby Salinas Valley, 75 percent of all natural corridors were found to be impermeable to wildlife movement because of fencing (Gennet et al. 2013).

Although current conditions for connectivity are poor in the San Joaquin Valley, restoration of these corridors is technically feasible. Elsewhere in California it has been shown to be valuable both for migratory or dispersing wildlife such as bobcats, deer, and mountain lions and as breeding or resident habitat for birds, reptiles, amphibians, and other species. As climate changes, the value of these areas as move-through and live-in habitat will increase still further as cool, mesic, and ecologically resilient safe harbors.

Biocides are great at what they do, targeting agricultural pests of all sorts. However, they can also have widespread impacts on nontarget, native species via direct lethal or sublethal effects and sometimes through bioaccumulation. Each of these could have significant and counterproductive effects on the very species rewilding aims to recover if not avoided on lands adjacent to restoration sites, including wildlife corridors.

Of concern is the use of anticoagulant rodenticides, which are used widely in residential and agricultural landscapes. Rodents that consume these chemicals can become prey for native carnivores such as San Joaquin kit fox, as well as raptor species such as Swainson's hawk. The result is bioaccumulation of the ingested poison, leading to health effects such as mange, disorientation leading to vehicle strikes, and direct mortality from poisoning (Nogeire et al. 2015).

For aquatic species, biocides and fertilizers can pose acute risks. One notable example is the herbicide atrazine, commonly used to control nonnative weed species. This chemical is now well understood to cause reproductive deformities and other impacts in amphibians, fish, and reptiles, even changing individual animals from female to male (Hayes et al. 2010). Restoration efforts that include waterways could be affected by nearby use of this chemical.

Pollinating insects, both native and managed (e.g., honeybees), are severely affected by other classes of biocides that are contributing to the global decline in invertebrates, including pollinators. Among these are neonicitinoids (e.g., imidacloprid), which are systemic pesticides that attack insects' central nervous systems. Although California has curtailed new uses of this class of chemicals, they are still in use for some of the high-value specialty crops grown in the San Joaquin Valley. Organophosphates (e.g., chlorpyrifos) are another class of pesticides with significant nontarget effects on mammals and other vertebrates. Chlorpyrifos was recently banned in California because of neurotoxicity in humans, but other organophosphates remain widely used. Widespread and concentrated use of these chemicals undoubtedly has consequences for a range of wildlife species in and around the San Joaquin Valley.

To counteract the effects of pesticides on wildlife in natural areas near farms, it is important to use farm methods that reduce or eliminate biocide use. As discussed earlier, integrating native plant hedgerows and maintaining or restoring natural habitat patches in the landscape can promote vertebrate and invertebrate predator communities that help control pests and reduce the need for pesticides. In addition, other ecological intensification techniques that include diversifying the landscape—for example, mixed crops, crop rotations, varietal mixtures, and flower strips—have been shown to promote natural enemy communities and reduce pest abundance and pest damage. Such techniques can be used to reduce pesticide use and thus create farming systems with fewer negative impacts on adjacent natural lands.

Ecosystem Service Benefits from Natural Lands and On-Farm Habitats

In a recent global synthesis, studies from around the world showed that decreases in diversity and abundance of pollinators and wildlife (which are natural enemies of agricultural pests) are reducing the pollination and pest control services that farmers get from nature and reducing crop yields (Dainese et al. 2019). Retained or restored natural habitats within and around agricultural landscapes can increase crop yields, probably by serving as a source of pollinators and natural enemies to crop fields.

Studies in California are consistent with these results. In the Central Valley, increased levels of natural habitat in farmlands have been shown to increase native bee diversity and abundance and increase the pollination services provided to many crops, including watermelon, tomato, and almond (Kremen et al. 2004). When native pollinators are supported in agricultural landscapes, growers are able to import fewer and reduce their reliance on European honeybees—which are increasingly in short supply because of diseases—thereby reducing their costs (Kremen et al. 2002; Morandin et al. 2016) and the potential for honeybees to harm native bees by competing for floral resources (Cane and Tepedino 2017).

Diversified Farming's Role in Rewilding

Creating a diversified farming landscape to complement rewilding efforts can occur by integrating ecological intensification techniques into farms and farming landscapes, from within field to the whole farm to the entire landscape (Kremen et al. 2012). At the smallest scale (within field), ecological intensification techniques dictate crop choice over space and time and can increase crop diversity through intercropping (two or more crops grown together to improve production of one or both crops), polyculture (multiple crops grown in a field), and crop rotation (growing a sequence of crops over time, including cover crops, or having fallow rotations). Within fields, noncrop plants such as sweet alyssum can also be planted to improve pest control. At intermediate scales (around fields, whole farm), ecological intensification techniques increase diversity through noncrop plantings, such as hedgerows, flower strips, and windbreaks planted at field edges, along roads, or around outbuildings, and riparian plantings next to streams, ditches, and tail-water ponds. Here there is the option to use a native plant palette (see chapter 2) to maximize the benefits for native wildlife (Long et al. 2017). Finally, at the largest scale (entire landscape), protection and restoration of native habitat elements can be included in agricultural landscapes to provide services such as pollination (Garibaldi et al. 2014). Landscape-scale diversification can also be an emergent property of multiple farms adopting ecological intensification practices, growing different crops, and using asynchronous crop rotations and fallowing. At this scale, the benefits to each individual farm and farmer are likely to begin increasing well beyond what any farmer acting alone could achieve.

Although diversified farms can increase long-term sustainability, improve resilience to climate change, and decrease reliance on expensive and sometimes harmful inputs (Rosa-Schleich et al. 2019), many barriers prevent more widespread adoption. In California, where several recent foodborne pathogen outbreaks were traced to specific farms, one of the most significant barriers is the perception that hedgerows, riparian buffers, and other natural habitats may harbor wildlife that cause food safety risks. Even though research does not support this conclusion (Karp et al. 2015), fear of failing a food safety audit and consequent lost revenue motivates growers to eradicate such areas on their farms rather than to plant them. Because specialty crop growers do not have access to crop insurance as row crop growers do, the inability to sell a crop may be a total financial loss for the season and may jeopardize future sales through reputational damage.

Implementing diversification practices also requires more labor, either initially (such as hedgerow installation) or long-term (such as harvesting from diverse cropping systems). Labor is not only a major cost for growers but is increasingly difficult to obtain in California. Finally, it takes time for farmers to learn how to farm in this manner, and the underlying ecological processes that ensure the success of ecological intensification, such as forming healthy soils and colonization of below- and above-ground habitats by beneficial organisms, take time. During this transition, productivity and profits may fall first, only to rebound later. Without a ready source of credit or an incentive payment to tide growers through the initial difficult period, many growers will be unwilling or unable to make the leap.

Acknowledging that serious impediments exist to adoption of diversified farming systems requires that conservation managers and agencies work to find creative solutions to counter these barriers. First, it is critical to identify and document diversification practices that maximize production and minimize input use, thus increasing profitability (Rosa-Schleich et al. 2019). One promising avenue is to site noncrop plantings either in areas that are never planted (around outbuildings or along field edges and roads) or in regions of the farm that are less productive because of unfavorable drainage, soil type, or topography. Using less productive lands for noncrop plantings can increase profits, both because these areas may then supply critical ecosystem services such as pollination that improve crop yields and because the costs of using inputs and labor on these less productive areas are eliminated. In the San Joaquin Valley, the need to permanently fallow some lands to achieve groundwater sustainability presents a valuable opportunity to convert even small retired areas to islands of natural habitat on the farm. Second, documenting how these practices affect long-term sustainability of soils and water use, as well as climate change adaptation, could be important to some farmers, particularly those who own their land. Enhancement of soil organic matter through cover cropping, for example, can increase the capacity of fields to store water and resist drought. Third, additional studies should be conducted on potential wildlife vectors of foodborne pathogens, and food safety auditors and farmers should be educated about best management practices to avoid food safety risks (Karp et al. 2015). Fourth, there could be beneficial job-securing repercussions with the need to reorganize the labor force on diversified farms to employ a smaller number of permanent, well-trained, full-time workers rather than a larger number of seasonal workers. Fifth, it will be necessary to work with government agencies to provide accessible incentive programs, particularly to manage the transition period from conventional intensive agriculture to more diversified systems.

The desired biodiversity outcomes of rewilding in the San Joaquin Valley will be improved through simultaneous transition of the remaining agricultural lands to ecological intensification, creating a diversified farming system across the agricultural landscape. This diversified farming landscape would then help buffer the restored lands from exposure to high temperature, wind, dust, and pollutants from agricultural lands. The diversified agriculture may provide additional habitat and resources for some target species and increase permeability, thus increasing the likelihood of gene flow and population rescue effects for targeted endangered species. For this reason, encouraging ecological intensification techniques, in order to create a landscape of diversified agriculture, should be considered as an integrated part of the long-term solution for biodiversity conservation and rewilding of the San Joaquin Valley. To this end, conservationists need to consider not only incentives for taking land out of production for rewilding but also a package of support for adopting ecological intensification practices, which could involve research, incentives and market development, and outreach. Such incentives could create goodwill and support in the community, particularly if they support practices that increase farmland profitability (i.e., by maintaining or increasing productivity while decreasing costs) and the long-term agricultural sustainability of the soil and water.

References

Briggs, Christopher W., Brian Woodbridge, and Michael W. Collopy. 2011. "Correlates of survival in Swainson's hawks breeding in northern California." *The Journal of Wildlife Management* 75, no. 6: 1307–14.

Busari, Mutiu Abolanle, Surinder Singh Kukal, Amanpreet Kaur, Rajan Bhatt, and Ashura Ally Dulazi. 2015. "Conservation tillage impacts on soil, crop and the environment." *International Soil and Water Conservation Research* 3, no. 2: 119–29.

Cane, James H., and Vincent J. Tepedino. 2017. "Gauging the effect of honey bee pollen collection on native bee communities." *Conservation Letters* 10, no. 2: 205–10.

Dainese, Matteo, Emily A. Martin, Marcelo A. Aizen, Matthias Albrecht, Ignasi Bartomeus, Riccardo Bommarco, Luisa G. Carvalheiro, et al. 2019. "A global synthesis reveals biodiversity-mediated benefits for crop production." *Science Advances* 5, no. 10: eaax0121.

Fahrig, Lenore, Judith Girard, Dennis Duro, Jon Pasher, Adam Smith, Steve Javorek, Douglas King, Kathryn Freemark Lindsay, Scott Mitchell, and Lutz Tischendorf. 2015. "Farmlands with smaller crop fields have higher within-field biodiversity." *Agriculture, Ecosystems & Environment* 200: 219–34.

Garibaldi, Lucas A., Luísa G. Carvalheiro, Sara D. Leonhardt, Marcelo A. Aizen, Brett R. Blaauw, Rufus Isaacs, Michael Kuhlmann, et al. 2014. "From research to action: enhancing crop yield through wild pollinators." *Frontiers in Ecology and the Environment* 12, no. 8: 439–47.

Gennet, Sasha, Jeanette Howard, Jeff Langholz, Kathryn Andrews, Mark D. Reynolds, and Scott A. Morrison. 2013. "Farm practices for food safety: an emerging threat to floodplain and riparian ecosystems." *Frontiers in Ecology and the Environment* 11, no. 5: 236–42.

Golet, Gregory H., Candace Low, Simon Avery, Katie Andrews, Christopher J. McColl, Rheyna Laney, and Mark D. Reynolds. 2018. "Using ricelands to provide temporary shorebird habitat during migration." *Ecological Applications* 28, no. 2: 409–26.

Gurr, Geoff M., Zhongxian Lu, Xusong Zheng, Hongxing Xu, Pingyang Zhu, Guihua Chen, Xiaoming Yao, et al. 2016. "Multi-country evidence that crop diversification promotes ecological intensification of agriculture." *Nature Plants* 2, no. 3: 1–4.

Guzman, Aidee, Marissa Chase, and Claire Kremen. 2019. "On-farm diversification in an agriculturally-dominated landscape positively influences specialist pollinators." *Frontiers in Sustainable Food Systems* 3: 87.

Hallmann, Caspar A., Martin Sorg, Eelke Jongejans, Henk Siepel, Nick Hofland, Heinz Schwan, Werner Stenmans, et al. 2017. "More than 75 percent decline over 27 years in total flying insect biomass in protected areas." *PLOS One* 12, no. 10: e0185809.

Hayes, Tyrone B., Vicky Khoury, Anne Narayan, Mariam Nazir, Andrew Park, Travis Brown, Lillian Adame, et al. 2010. "Atrazine induces complete feminization and chemical castration in male African clawed frogs (*Xenopus laevis*)." *Proceedings of the National Academy of Sciences* 107, no. 10: 4612–17.

Karp, Daniel S., Sasha Gennet, Christopher Kilonzo, Melissa Partyka, Nicolas Chaumont, Edward R. Atwill, and Claire Kremen. 2015. "Comanaging fresh produce for nature conservation and food safety." *Proceedings of the National Academy of Sciences* 112, no. 35: 11126–31.

Kennedy, Christina M., Eric Lonsdorf, Maile C. Neel, Neal M. Williams, Taylor H. Ricketts, Rachael Winfree, Riccardo Bommarco, et al. 2013. "A global quantitative synthesis of local and landscape effects on wild bee pollinators in agroecosystems." *Ecology Letters* 16, no. 5: 584–99.

Kremen, Claire, Alastair Iles, and Christopher Bacon. 2012. "Diversified farming systems: an agroecological, systems-based alternative to modern industrial agriculture." *Ecology and Society* 17, no. 4.

Kremen, Claire, and Adina M. Merenlender. 2018. "Landscapes that work for biodiversity and people." *Science* 362, no. 6412.

Kremen, Claire, and Leithen K. M'Gonigle. 2015. "Small-scale restoration in intensive agricultural landscapes supports more specialized and less mobile pollinator species." *Journal of Applied Ecology* 52, no. 3: 602–10.

Kremen, Claire, and Albie Miles. 2012. "Ecosystem services in biologically diversified versus conventional farming systems: benefits, externalities, and trade-offs." *Ecology and Society* 17, no. 4.

Kremen, Claire, Neal M. Williams, Robert L. Bugg, John P. Fay, and Robin W. Thorp. 2004. "The area requirements of an ecosystem service: crop pollination by native bee communities in California." *Ecology Letters* 7, no. 11: 1109–19.

Kremen, Claire, Neal M. Williams, and Robbin W. Thorp. 2002. "Crop pollination from native bees at risk from agricultural intensification." *Proceedings of the National Academy of Sciences* 99, no. 26: 16812–16.

Long, Rachel F., Kelly Garbach, and Lora A. Morandin. 2017. "Hedgerow benefits align with food production and sustainability goals." *California Agriculture* 71, no. 3: 117–19.

Morandin, Lora A., and Claire Kremen. 2013. "Hedgerow restoration promotes pollinator populations and exports native bees to adjacent fields." *Ecological Applications* 23, no. 4: 829–39.

Morandin, Lora A., Rachel F. Long, and Claire Kremen. 2016. "Pest control and pollination cost–benefit analysis of hedgerow restoration in a simplified agricultural landscape." *Journal of Economic Entomology* 109: 1020–27.

Nogeire, Theresa M., Joshua J. Lawler, Nathan H. Schumaker, Brian L. Cypher, and Scott E. Phillips. 2015. "Land use as a driver of patterns of rodenticide exposure in modeled kit fox populations." *PLOS One* 10, no. 8: e0133351.

Ponisio, Lauren C., Perry de Valpine, Leithen K. M'Gonigle, and Claire Kremen. 2019. "Proximity of restored hedgerows interacts with local floral diversity and species' traits to shape long-term pollinator meta-community dynamics." *Ecology Letters* 22, no. 7: 1048–60.

Rosa-Schleich, Julia, Jacqueline Loos, Oliver Mußhoff, and Teja Tscharntke. 2019. "Ecological-economic trade-offs of diversified farming systems: a review." *Ecological Economics* 160: 251–63.

Rusch, Adrien, Rebecca Chaplin-Kramer, Mary M. Gardiner, Violetta Hawro, John Holland, Douglas Landis, Carsten Thies, et al. 2016. "Agricultural landscape simplification reduces natural pest control: a quantitative synthesis." *Agriculture, Ecosystems & Environment* 221: 198–204.

Spencer, W. D., P. Beier, K. Penrod, K. Winters, C. Paulman, H. Rustigian-Romsos, J. Strittholt, M. Parisi, and A. Pettler. 2010. *California Essential Habitat Connectivity Project: A Strategy for Conserving a Connected California.* Sacramento: California Department of Fish and Wildlife.

Stevenson, James R., Nelson Villoria, Derek Byerlee, Timothy Kelley, and Mywish Maredia. 2013. "Green Revolution research saved an estimated 18 to 27 million hectares from being brought into agricultural production." *Proceedings of the National Academy of Sciences* 110, no. 21: 8363–68.

Van Buskirk, Josh, and Yvonne Willi. 2004. "Enhancement of farmland biodiversity within set-aside land." *Conservation Biology* 18, no. 4: 987–94.

Wagner, David L. 2020. "Insect declines in the Anthropocene." *Annual Review of Entomology* 65: 457–80.

Warner, Richard E., and Kathleen M. Hendrix, eds. 1984. *California Riparian Systems: Ecology, Conservation, and Productive Management.* Berkeley: University of California Press.

Part III

Socioeconomic and Political Dimensions of Rewilding the San Joaquin Valley

Chapter 11

Managing Changes in Water and Land Use to Benefit People and Nature

Ellen Hanak, Brian Gray, Jelena Jezdimirovic,
and Peter Moyle

In our work with valley stakeholders over the past several years, we frequently heard concerns about the potential negative consequences of large reductions in irrigated farmland, the main way to reduce groundwater demand. To limit these reductions, many stakeholders are focusing first on Sustainable Groundwater Management Act (SGMA) strategies that augment water supplies, including groundwater recharge (Hanak et al. 2020). But we also consistently heard hopes that the fallowing that must occur not be piecemeal and unplanned, but instead done in ways that maximize an array of economic, social, and environmental benefits. Stakeholders recognized that this would be a heavy lift, requiring new approaches to planning and much greater coordination than ever before among the many individuals and agencies that own, manage, and regulate water and land.

Drawing on an in-depth study of solutions to water scarcity (Hanak et al. 2019), this chapter explores opportunities for shifting toward multibenefit stewardship of fallowed farmlands as part of a comprehensive effort to tackle the San Joaquin Valley's resource management challenges. We first describe an approach known as reconciliation ecology to achieve multiple benefits for people and nature, and we summarize the range of uses and potential benefits of lands likely to come out of crop production. We then identify planning, regulatory, funding, and technical tools that can help move the management of natural resources toward reconciliation and the steps needed to launch an ambitious regional multibenefit planning effort.

Multibenefit Resource Stewardship and Reconciliation Ecology
Without careful planning, growing water scarcity in the San Joaquin Valley could increase conflict between human and environmental uses of water. Land fallowed to achieve groundwater balance could contribute to dust and weed problems that compromise air quality and neighboring farmland. And the region could miss out on many possibilities for improvements that require more coordinated decisions about water and land use, from harnessing floodwaters for recharge, to keeping the most valuable farmlands in production, to reaping the most benefits from lands to be fallowed.

Improving ecosystem health as part of the coming change presents both special challenges and distinct promise. The transformation of the region's historic network of rivers, wetlands, and desert ecosystems over the last two centuries has resulted in a growing list of imperiled native plant and animal species. Efforts to protect these species have had mixed success. And these efforts have at times generated conflict, pitting farmers and others against federal and state agencies and environmental organizations focused on species protection.

Reconciliation ecology—the science of inventing, establishing, and maintaining new habitats to conserve species diversity in places where people live, work, and play (Rosenzweig 2003)—offers the prospect of shifting this trajectory in a positive direction. Reconciliation ecology emphasizes strategies that increase the habitat value for native plants and animals both within and outside traditional protected areas. And by seeking approaches that benefit people and nature, it holds promise for expanding partnerships and reducing controversy over the use of water and land for ecosystems and species.

Beyond improving conditions for native plant and animal species, reconciliation ecology can provide additional benefits, including enhanced groundwater recharge, improved air and water quality, increased soil health and carbon storage, new recreational opportunities, and additional flood protection. Projects that bring multiple benefits offer opportunities to share costs and leverage more sources of funding. As the Kern Water Bank (see below) experience shows, groundwater recharge and banking facilities can also create intermittent habitat for sensitive species. Pooling funds for flood protection infrastructure with riparian and floodplain habitat improvements can result in larger projects that are more effective at meeting both objectives (Opperman et al. 2017). Broader, long-term plans for ecosystem management can also bring more regulatory flexibility for landowners, producers, and water managers. These benefits offer significant motivation for diverse stakeholders to come together and develop creative solutions to reinvigorate the San Joaquin Valley's natural environment.

Recharging Groundwater and Providing Habitat: The Kern Water Bank
Groundwater recharge projects may be especially well suited to a multibenefit approach. One particularly effective example is the Kern Water Bank, one of the state's largest water banks, with storage capacity of 1.5 million acre-feet, approximately 7,000 acres of recharge ponds, eighty-five recovery wells, and a canal that connects these facilities with the California Aqueduct. Bank members purchase surface water for recharge when available and make withdrawals when needed.

In 1997, the Kern Water Bank Authority established a Habitat Conservation Plan (HCP) under the federal Endangered Species

Act and a Natural Community Conservation Plan (NCCP) under California law to provide co-benefits for native plants and animals from the management of its recharge facility. Under these agreements, the bank has restored 17,000 acres of farmland to native San Joaquin Desert and intermittent wetland habitat. The agreements also designate more than 3,000 acres as a conservation bank. By allowing landowners to purchase credits as mitigation for their own projects, these banks help consolidate habitat, which is especially valuable for many San Joaquin Desert species (see chapter 9).

The conservation agreements focused on the site's potential for managing vegetation to improve habitat for San Joaquin Desert species. This work has been successful, with an abundance of desert species now found on-site. The recharge ponds also serve as intermittent wetlands, in wet years hosting dozens of species of waterbirds that desperately need the habitat along their migration. Bank managers hypothesize that the recharge lands' topography makes them particularly suitable as wetland habitat. Whereas recharge basins are typically highly engineered structures with evenly contoured sides and depths, the Kern Water Bank's basins have more natural, sloping contours and varying water depths, which provide more diverse habitat.

The Kern Water Bank also provides a good example of how managing vegetation on retired farmland can provide multiple benefits. In this case, conservation activities focused on keeping the weedy nonnative grasses under control, primarily with cattle grazing. This has helped prevent air quality and pest problems while creating habitat for San Joaquin Desert species.

At least a quarter of the valley's 202 agricultural and urban water suppliers had one or more recharge basins on their lands in 2017, and managers we surveyed reported considerable interest in expanding this tool on suitable lands (Hanak et al. 2018). Although few projects will be on the scale of the Kern Water Bank, many will present opportunities to achieve the multiple benefits of water supply, water storage, and intermittent wetland habitat enhancement for birds and San Joaquin Desert species (figure 11-1).

Figure 11-1. Long-billed dowitchers forage in the shallow waters of the wetlands at the Kern Water Bank. The bank provides critical wetland habitat for migratory shorebirds, such as these dowitchers. (Photo by John Parker)

Managing Fallowed Farmlands for Multiple Benefits

There are many potential uses for irrigated farmland that will be temporarily or permanently fallowed to help end groundwater overdraft, and reconciliation ecology approaches can point stakeholders in promising directions.

By design, these lands will have little or no dedicated, ongoing water use. Potential uses currently envisaged include solar energy (Wu et al. 2019) and multibenefit restoration of historic riparian, wetland, and desert ecosystems (Kelsey et al. 2018). But even if these ambitious targets are met, this would at best account for two thirds of all land likely to be fallowed by 2040 (figure 11-2). Managing the transition successfully will require identifying strategies that can yield the greatest benefits from all formerly irrigated farmlands.

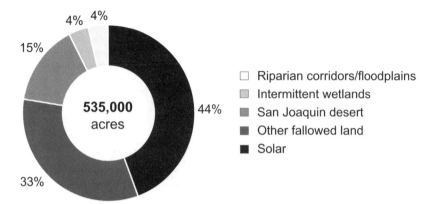

Figure 11-2. Potential uses of formerly irrigated lands. Planning will need to identify strategies that can yield the greatest benefits from all formerly irrigated farmlands. This figure assumes that 535,000 acres of irrigated farmland will be fallowed by 2040 under the Sustainable Groundwater Management Act. This is the estimated reduction if roughly one quarter of the valley's historical groundwater deficit is filled by augmenting supplies. If land fallowing needs to be larger—because of either a higher future water deficit or limited success in augmenting supplies—the area in "other fallowed land" would probably expand more than the other categories. (Data from Hanak et al. 2019 with updated solar energy estimates from Wu et al. 2019)

Here are our rough estimates of potential uses of these lands:

- **Expanding solar energy.** California's climate mitigation goals could be a boon for managing retired farmland, which has suitable acreage for cost-effective, utility-scale solar energy development. The state has committed to provide all electricity from carbon-free sources by 2045. Meeting the more ambitious goal of full electrification (including the vehicle fleet) could convert roughly 235,000 acres of retired farmland to solar development (Wu et al. 2019). This would require significant supporting investments in the electrical grid. Solar energy is one of the few options for generating significant revenues on retired farmland and can incorporate techniques such as wildlife-friendly fencing and greater space below and between panels to provide functional habitat (Phillips and Cypher 2015).

- **Reducing flood risk and expanding riparian corridors and floodplains.** Some retired farmland, perhaps 20,000 acres, may be suitable for multibenefit projects that reduce flood risk, increase groundwater recharge, and expand riparian corridors and floodplains.
- **Creating intermittent wetlands.** Dedicated recharge areas that can also serve as intermittent wetlands may expand, perhaps by 20,000 acres.
- **Recovering the San Joaquin Desert.** As described in other chapters (see chapters 1, 9, and 15), land retirement presents an opportunity to recover this unique ecosystem.
- **Managing other fallowed land.** The remaining land to be fallowed (175,000 acres or more) exceeds the scope of these energy and habitat plans. Some acreage could accommodate new housing or industrial developments if they rely on urban water savings to meet their water needs. But without proactive planning, much could be fallowed haphazardly.

The shape of the landscape—and the benefits from fallowed land—will depend on how and where fallowing occurs (see chapter 9). There will be choices between permanently retiring farmlands or temporarily fallowing them in rotation for shorter periods. Either way, achieving multiple benefits from these lands will depend on the level of coordinated stewardship.

The Stewardship Toolkit

Stewarding the San Joaquin Valley's water and land resources to benefit people and nature will require new approaches to planning and a focus on practical, cost-effective solutions. Here we discuss pathways and tools that can facilitate this transition: broad-based planning, regulatory flexibility, financial incentives, and technical support.

BROAD-BASED PLANNING

Broad-based planning will be essential to manage scarce water resources effectively for freshwater ecosystems (Mount et al. 2019) and to steward the region's lands. Realizing groundwater recharge's potential requires protecting highly suitable lands from development and selecting lands that protect groundwater quality. Planning is also essential to keep the most valuable farmlands in production.

Today, land use planning tends to be locally driven, with only limited consideration of water resources. City planners focus on decisions within their boundaries and in the adjacent unincorporated areas where they are likely to expand. County planners focus on unincorporated areas, primarily farmland, open space, and small rural communities. City and county general plans devote little attention to water, and water agencies' only role has been to certify that water is available to support new development (Hanak 2010).

With the SGMA, more coordination must occur at the basin scale, involving groundwater sustainability agencies (GSAs) and their many stakeholders—farmers, business and community groups, environmental nonprofits—along with city and county land use planners and others.

For many key land use decisions, a broader regional planning effort is also needed. Many ecological patterns are regional (Huber et al. 2010), and this is probably the appropriate scale for mapping the most suitable lands for solar energy development, recharge investments, and the retirement of salt-impacted lands.

Regional planning can also help assess the land use implications of valley-wide surface water trading, a tool that can lower the economic costs of reducing groundwater use. Without such trading, there would be little fallowed land in the valley's wetter, northern half. By shifting some fallowing from south to north, trading expands possibilities to repurpose farmland for floodplain restoration and habitat corridors.

Ownership, Management, and Local Incentives

Planning must consider not only how to incentivize landowners to make multibenefit land fallowing decisions but also who would own and manage lands. Many farmers are unlikely to want to continue owning and managing them, because the required skill set and legal risks are quite different from those of farming. One option is to convert permanently retired farmlands into public lands, owned and managed by federal or state agencies with existing land assets and expertise. Another possibility is for water districts or GSAs to purchase the land, making the water available for use elsewhere within districts. Alternatively, the retired farmland might remain with the current landowner but with a conservation easement that restricts the land use of the property and helps support native plant and animal habitat goals. Local land trusts or government agencies such as resource conservation districts could support management of these properties. Temporarily fallowed lands would not change hands, but farmers could receive support to manage them for wildlife and other benefits, such as soil health.

Another key consideration is the fiscal implication for local governments. In a land use workshop we held in 2019, county officials expressed concerns about the potential loss of property tax revenues from some land use changes that could otherwise be beneficial for the regional economy. Surface water trading that shifts the location of land fallowing to another county is one example. Another is the conversion of cropland to solar energy, which has been exempt from property tax under California law. Finding ways to make local governments whole may be necessary for these strategies to succeed.

A regional effort will require scaling up the coordination between various parties and looking beyond wildlife habitat to include other societal values, such as water supply and flood management, water and air quality, and outdoor recreation. Importantly, landowners must be treated as true partners and given both voice and choice in the process, and local governments will need incentives to support change.

REGULATORY FLEXIBILITY

Another challenge is overcoming regulatory hurdles. Environmental regulations are designed to protect public health and the natural environment. But they can also increase the time and cost of permitting without improving decision making. Different regulations can also be in conflict. Chapter 12 features several cases in which regulatory assurances made large-scale restoration possible. Here we review three key areas where flexibility is essential: implementing large, multibenefit projects, simplifying the environmental permitting process, and protecting landowners seeking to steward fallowed lands from regulatory risk.

FACILITATING LARGE, MULTIBENEFIT PROJECTS

Implementing reconciliation ecology principles on a large scale requires a framework for managing land and water for the benefit of multiple species while allowing for other economic uses. Although administration of state and federal endangered species acts (ESAs) has traditionally focused on conservation of single species, both state and federal laws allow for a broader perspective on species protection and habitat management.

The most noteworthy examples are HCPs, created under the authority of the federal ESA, and NCCPs, which contribute to the implementation of the California ESA and related state laws. Both allow economic uses of land and water resources while also managing for the benefit of multiple species and are typically approved for at least several decades. A key provision is the authorization of localized negative impacts ("take") to listed species, as long as the overall project meets requirements to protect these species.

The Kern Water Bank illustrates the HCP/NCCP approach. This agreement authorizes the impacts of the recharge project's operations (e.g., flooding, groundwater withdrawals, vegetation management, infrastructure construction) on listed species in recharge basins, given the protections put in place on other lands designated as sensitive habitat and conservation banks. This proactive approach makes it easier to manage flexibly to increase wildlife benefits rather than managing in order to avoid attracting listed species into the area.

The HCP/NCCP process is expensive and protracted, however, making it less suitable for small projects. Countywide or even regional HCP/NCCPs, in which individual landowners can participate, could broaden ecosystem planning and realize economies of scale in permitting costs.

Another tool to facilitate integrated regional management is the state's Regional Conservation Investment Strategy. This planning process facilitates conservation investments by linking them to the creation of mitigation credits. It is intended to be a speedier alternative to the NCCP process, though without the regulatory assurances for specific activities. It is under exploration in the Kaweah Basin in the southern Sierra Nevada to help manage future land conversions under SGMA (see chapter 12).

Simplifying Permitting of Restoration Projects

Restoration project proponents must currently go to multiple agencies to get permits, resulting in a lengthy and costly process. Establishing expedited permitting processes for some actions can help. So can programmatic permits, issued on a regional basis for activities that are substantially similar in nature. To get past the challenges of each agency having its own set of requirements, work is under way to develop expedited review processes that meet multiple state and federal agency requirements at once (Sustainable Conservation 2018).

Protecting Landowners from Regulatory Risk

Landowners will also need better protections from regulatory risk when stewarding fallowed farmland.

Conversion of fallowed farmland into temporary habitat can bring regulatory risks for landowners if these lands attract listed species. Safe harbor agreements with the California Department of

Fish and Wildlife (CDFW) and the U.S. Fish and Wildlife Service or similar Voluntary Local Programs established with the CDFW could address this risk (see the tricolored blackbird case in chapter 12). These agreements seek to promote the conservation of listed species while assuring landowners that no additional regulatory burdens will be imposed for habitat improvements that attract these species. Neighbors may also protect themselves from liability for affecting species that stray onto their property.

Without these programs, incentives remain strong for farmers to till or apply herbicides to fallowed lands to make them less attractive to listed species, an approach that not only limits habitat and soil health benefits but also increases the risk of air quality problems. One promising initiative, now in early stages, is the development of a programmatic safe harbor agreement to cover multiple species in the southern San Joaquin Valley.

State and local laws that protect prime farmland could conflict with the need to convert large amounts of land to other uses. Most notably, the California Environmental Quality Act guidelines, as well as some local ordinances, require protecting farmland meeting certain soil quality standards if it has been used for irrigated agriculture in the recent past. Those wanting to convert such lands to other uses must fund the acquisition or protection of other prime farmland.

Mitigation fees for land development can help fund multibenefit stewardship of fallowed lands. But mitigation requirements on prime farmland that is being transitioned to other land uses could increase the costs of stewarding these lands.

SGMA's implications for rural communities may also make it necessary to reconsider other policies designed to protect farmland. This includes relaxing the requirements of the Solar Use Easement Act, which prohibits cities and counties from acquiring easements for solar installations on prime farmland.

The presence of animals can pose a real risk to farms' ability to comply with food safety regulations or related practices required by buyers (see chapter 10). Gennet et al. (2013) showed that the conversion of riparian habitat in the Salinas Valley may be accelerating because of on-farm practices that are meant to promote food safety but are not well-founded in science. The authors recommended an evidence-based, adaptive approach to manage farms for both food safety and ecological health.

Financial Incentives

Stewarding water and land for multiple benefits will require funding. Multiple sources already contribute to restoration: surcharges on water use, mitigation fees paid by land developers, grazing fees from livestock owners, and state and federal grants. An even wider range of programs can be tapped to support this work.

Water, Land, and Energy Use Fees

The Central Valley Project Improvement Act restoration fee on water use—now about $10 per acre-foot for agricultural customers and $20 for urban and energy sector customers—supports various regional stewardship efforts, from managed wetlands, to San Joaquin River restoration, to restoration of San Joaquin Desert ecosystems such as Atwell Island (see chapter 3). Surcharges on other surface water projects could make similar contributions elsewhere (Hanak et al. 2014). Under the SGMA, GSAs can introduce fees on groundwater use to cover the costs of management. One innovative idea in Kern County is to use these fees to acquire land from willing sellers and retire the associated groundwater allocation (Pottinger 2018). Farmers get flexibility to pay a surcharge to pump more than their allocation, and the GSA can find the most suitable lands to retire, ideally where it can get multiple benefits such as recharge or habitat.

Livestock grazing on fallowed lands is important for vegetation management; grazing fees can also bring in modest revenues to support land management. Mitigation requirements for various types of land development are already used to acquire habitat and may be particularly useful for managing lands to support listed species.

The market for carbon credits, in which where energy users pay others who can reduce greenhouse gas emissions or store carbon more cheaply, has potential to fund numerous land stewardship practices. Riparian forest and upland restoration, rangeland management, and planting cover crops on fallowed lands can all store carbon. Today, credits for these activities are limited mainly to private, voluntary markets; significant expansion is possible if California authorizes these activities under its cap-and-trade program for large emitters, as is now the case with forestry projects.

STATE AND FEDERAL GRANTS AND TAX CREDITS

In recent years, voter-approved state general obligation bonds have made hundreds of millions of dollars available for ecological stewardship grants to local agencies, nonprofit organizations, and farmers. Several state programs also provide landowners with property tax credits for dedicating land to habitat, and federal income tax deductions are available for donations of money, land, and, in some limited cases, water rights.

State and federal programs also support farmers—and sometimes local agencies and nonprofits—to steward their lands. The state programs are recent and fairly small, funded by the cap-and-trade program and bonds. Much larger federal programs have been in place for decades under the Farm Bill. Although both emphasize investments on active farmland, they can support the management of fallowed lands to provide wildlife habitat and minimize consequences such as the loss of soil health and the proliferation of weeds.

Nationwide, U.S. Department of Agriculture (USDA) conservation programs already support stewardship of lands that are temporarily fallowed or protected under longer-term easements.

Some western states, including Colorado, Idaho, Kansas, and Nebraska, have used the Conservation Reserve Enhancement Program, which involves joint federal and state funding, as a mechanism to fallow land to reduce irrigation water use (Jezdimirovic and Hanak 2019).

Changes introduced with the 2018 Farm Bill increase the USDA's capacity to provide this help. Funding for the Environmental Quality Incentives Program, the largest conservation program used by farmers in the valley, has increased, and the program is now open to local water management agencies and associations. Funding has tripled for the innovative Regional Conservation Partnership Program, which leverages public and private dollars to tackle regional conservation challenges. And throughout the Farm Bill, conservation program descriptions have been updated to include soil health and carbon sequestration as targeted outcomes.

Although further changes in program rules could be helpful, state and local stakeholders have begun partnering with the USDA to use its programs to help the region's farmers make beneficial land transitions as it addresses scarcity (see chapter 12).

State grants to help implement the SGMA could also support the stewardship of lands coming out of production. Such grants could also be used for USDA programs that require a state match, such as the Conservation Reserve Enhancement Program, which provides fifteen-year rental payments and management support to steward nonirrigated lands.

Pooling Resources and Incentivizing Landowner Decisions

People will need to be strategic to make the dollars count. Pooling funds from several sources will often be necessary to cover both upfront investments and ongoing stewardship. Aligning funds with planning goals will also be important to encourage farmers to direct their land conversion decisions toward the best locations, with the most suitable array of stewardship practices. A voluntary, incentive-based approach will discourage piecemeal land fallowing while leaving the ultimate decisions to farmers.

Many growers are likely to be more interested in participating if they can maintain their groundwater allocation to use on other lands they farm, in addition to their surface water allocations.

Technical Support

Landowners and other stakeholders also need technical help to implement land stewardship strategies. Because there is still much to learn about the best ways to manage resources for multiple benefits, this support needs to include piloting and testing, such as cost-effective approaches to restore habitat for San Joaquin Desert wildlife (see chapter 3), grazing techniques that generate desired habitat conditions (see chapters 2 and 4), and water-efficient approaches to maintain soil health. Third-party "honest brokers," entities such as Resource Conservation Districts that can provide scientific and engineering expertise and identify common ground among landowners, regulators, and local governments, can be especially valuable.

Looking Forward

Effectively addressing water stress and land use changes in the San Joaquin Valley offers opportunities to put lands coming out of production to good use and ease the transitions that are coming as the SGMA is implemented. Multibenefit approaches can be targeted to yield enhanced groundwater recharge, improved air and water quality, healthier soils, new recreational opportunities, additional flood protection, improved habitat, and new revenue streams for private landowners engaging in conservation-oriented management. But adopting such approaches will require valley stakeholders to engage in much broader and more comprehensive planning for management of the region's lands than ever before. Here are a few takeaways for approaching this effort:

- Decision making about how best to manage the coming changes will be done at many levels, ranging from individual farms and irrigation districts to GSAs and county governments. Creating practical pathways for improved communication and coordination will be essential.
- Determining how best to achieve coordinated fallowing and multiple benefits will require a significant upfront investment in trust building. A regional planning exercise to review the possibilities—along with the risks of inaction—and seek broad consensus on best practices for managing idle lands could be a useful early step.
- Creating targeted approaches to address key issues is one way to break down what might seem to be a daunting planning effort. For example, focusing on multibenefit approaches for recharging groundwater and managing floods could offer a starting point for broader planning around water supply augmentation under SGMA.
- Finding opportunities to pilot new approaches, such as voluntary land retirement in strategic areas, and then build on early successes is another way to grow confidence in these processes.
- Various kinds of support, such as planning expertise, outreach, facilitation, and funding, are needed to advance planning and piloting efforts, involving broad stakeholder engagement. Beyond financial help, state and federal support for regulatory flexibility will be needed to create the large-scale multibenefit projects that arise.

References

Gennet, Sasha, Jeanette Howard, Jeff Langholz, Kathryn Andrews, Mark Reynolds, and Scott Morrison. 2013. "Farm practices for food safety: an emerging threat to floodplain and riparian ecosystems." *Frontiers in Ecology and the Environment* 11, no. 5: 236–42. doi.org /10.1890/120243

Hanak, Ellen. 2010. "Show me the water plan: urban water management plans and California's water supply adequacy laws." *Golden Gate University Environmental Law Journal* 4, no. 1.

Hanak, Ellen, Alvar Escriva-Bou, Brian Gray, Sarge Green, Thomas Harter, Jelena Jezdimirovic, Jay Lund, Josué Medellín-Azuara, Peter Moyle, and Nathaniel Seavy. 2019. *Water and the Future of the San Joaquin Valley*. San Francisco: Public Policy Institute of California.

Hanak, Ellen, Brian Gray, Jay Lund, David Mitchell, Caitrin Chappelle, Andrew Fahlund, Katrina Jessoe, Josué Medellín-Azuara, Dean Misczynski, James Nachbaur, and Robyn Suddeth. 2014. *Paying for Water in California*. San Francisco: Public Policy Institute of California.

Hanak, Ellen, Jelena Jezdimirovic, Alvar Escriva-Bou, and Andrew Ayres. 2020. "A review of groundwater sustainability plans in the San Joaquin Valley." Public comments to the California Department of Water Resources. May 15.

Hanak, Ellen, Jelena Jezdimirovic, Sarge Green, and Alvar Escriva-Bou. 2018. *Replenishing Groundwater in the San Joaquin Valley*. San Francisco: Public Policy Institute of California.

Huber, Patrick, Steven Greco, and James Thorne. 2010. "Spatial scale effects on conservation network design: trade-offs and omissions in regional versus local scale planning." *Landscape Ecology* 25, no. 5: 683–95.

Jezdimirovic, Jelena, and Ellen Hanak. 2019. *Leveraging USDA Programs to Promote Groundwater Sustainability in the San Joaquin Valley*. Technical Appendix F to *Water and the Future of the San Joaquin Valley*. San Francisco: Public Policy Institute of California.

Kelsey, Rodd, Abby Hart, Scott Butterfield, and Dan Vink. 2018. "Groundwater sustainability in the San Joaquin Valley: multiple benefits if agricultural lands are retired and restored strategically." *California Agriculture* 72, no. 3: 151–54.

Mount, Jeffrey, Brian Gray, Karrigan Bork, James Cloern, Frank Davis, Ted Grantham, Letitia Grenier, Jennifer Harder, Yusuke Kuwayama, Peter Moyle, Mark Schwartz, Alison Whipple, and Sarah Yarnell. 2019. *A Path Forward for California's Freshwater Ecosystems*. San Francisco: Public Policy Institute of California.

Opperman, J. J., P. B. Moyle, E. W. Larsen, J. L. Florsheim, and A. D. Manfree. 2017. *Floodplains: Processes, Ecosystems, and Services in Temperate Regions*. Berkeley: University of California Press.

Phillips, Scott, and Brian Cypher. 2015. *Solar Energy Development and Endangered Upland Species of the San Joaquin Valley: Identification of Conflict Zones.* Prepared for the California Department of Fish and Wildlife. CSU Stanislaus Endangered Species Recovery Program.

Pottinger, Lori. 2018. "A bottom-up approach to groundwater sustainability." *PPIC Blog.* February 28.

Rosenzweig, Michael. 2003. *Win–Win Ecology: How the Earth's Species Can Survive in the Midst of Human Enterprise.* Oxford: Oxford University Press.

Sustainable Conservation. 2018. *Sustainable Conservation's Essential Guide for Expedited Restoration Permitting.* San Francisco: Sustainable Conservation.

Wu, Grace C., Emily Leslie, Douglas Allen, Oluwafemi Sawyerr, D. Richard Cameron, Erica Brand, Brian Cohen, Marcela Ochoa, and Arne Olson. 2019. *Power of Place: Land Conservation and Clean Energy Pathways for California.* Arlington, Va.: The Nature Conservancy.

Chapter 12

Learning from Case Studies to Encourage Landowner Participation in Rewilding the San Joaquin Valley

Abigail K. Hart

T WO YEARS AGO, AS OUR TEAM AT The Nature Conservancy was beginning to explore the potential for restoring retired farmland in the San Joaquin Valley, we conducted a series of interviews with landowners and farmers across the valley. In a simple double-wide that operated as the farm office, a lone structure in a seemingly unending sea of trees, we sat across from a man whose family had farmed in the valley for several generations. Although he was a large landowner with a successful farming operation, managing and farming land had become increasingly challenging for his family. So, the year before, the family had decided to sell the farm. As we talked, the farmer reflected, "I don't think anyone expected the valley to look like this," he said looking out over the expanse of trees. "If we could do it all over again, maybe we wouldn't farm the valley wall to wall. You know, when you drive up through the Sacramento Valley, the farms are mixed in with natural areas. It's kind of peaceful and beautiful. If we could do it all over again, maybe we should have put more thought into it and planned. . . . Maybe the San Joaquin would have looked more like the Sacramento Valley. But things are going to change, and we need a vision. We need a vision that shows people the potential for what the San Joaquin could look like, something that inspires people."

We are at a critical moment in which water scarcity, regulatory pressures on agriculture, and climate change are causing a major transition in land use in the San Joaquin Valley. For some landowners this will mean making decisions that permanently change the trajectory of their businesses, their farms, and even their families. The challenge for rewilding the San Joaquin Valley will be to cast a vision that includes and inspires local landowners, helps them navigate through uncertainty, and engages them as willing partners in restoration.

The discussion about habitat, particularly in California's Central Valley, often pits farmers against conservationists. Although habitat loss has been linked to agricultural expansion, as the interview brought to light, current land use may have more to do with a lack of planning and misaligned incentives than with landowners' lack of appreciation for habitat and natural areas. In fact, private landowners, including farmers and ranchers, have been the protagonists in large-scale conservation efforts in the United States and around the world. In such cases, however, landowners have not acted alone. Rather, they have been supported by robust partnerships with conservation organizations and government agencies, as well as financial and regulatory incentives that made change possible.

The Power of Partnerships

The following cases provide a few examples of how partnerships have enabled large-scale conservation efforts and demonstrate some of the possibilities and constraints we might face in bringing a vision for restoring habitat in the San Joaquin Valley to life.

The sage-grouse has become the emblem of a hallmark large-scale conservation program. Two sage-grouse species historically inhabited 240,000 square miles of sagebrush habitat that includes parts of eleven states in the western United States and two Canadian provinces. These charismatic birds represent a larger community of more than 350 species that now have access to less than half of their historic habitat. Over time, parts of this extensive landscape of sagebrush, native grasses, and wildflowers were plowed under for grain production and fenced off for cattle ranching. Fragmentation and encroachment of invasive species diminished bird habitat, and in turn, sage-grouse populations plummeted by an estimated 69 to 99 percent of their historic numbers. Spurred by warnings that the sage-grouse would become a listed species under the Endangered Species Act (ESA), a diverse consortium of stakeholders—including ranchers, public agencies, and environmental groups—mobilized to collaboratively create plans and take management actions that would protect remaining sage-grouse populations and the broader sagebrush ecosystem. Since the mid-2000s, new partnerships have been essential to the protection of sage-grouse species and the conservation of sagebrush habitat.

Importantly, the broader partnership has not taken a one-size-fits-all approach to partnerships. Because of the vast extent of sagebrush habitat and the number of overlapping jurisdictions, state-level agencies decided to establish Local Working Groups (LWGs) to incorporate local knowledge, expertise, and priorities into sage-grouse conservation. These groups include local staff of federal and state wildlife agencies, local nonprofit organizations, and local landowners. By 2010, more than fifty LWGs had been established across the West. In the region that spans the California–Nevada border, the LWG was able to combine the conservation planning expertise and institutional memory of government staff with the local knowledge of private landowners. The LWG, composed primarily of local staff and landowners, needed additional scientific expertise and official authorization to implement the conservation activities identified in the plan. So the LWG coordinated with two other committees that were formed to support sagebrush conservation: a Technical Advisory Committee and an Executive Oversight Committee. These committees provided the scientific analysis and underpinning for the conservation plan from sage-grouse experts and facilitated interagency coordination to grant authority to execute the plan and supporting projects, respectively. The committees also provided an avenue for landowner knowledge and local needs to shape state and federal programs that could provide financial incentives to private landowners for participating in conservation projects. According to members of the LWG in the bi-state region, these partnerships helped all stakeholders develop a shared vision for sagebrush conservation. Along the way private landowners learned more about the needs of the sage-grouse and other sagebrush species, while agency representatives became more aware of the ways in which private landowners would be affected by the listing of the greater sage-grouse under the Endangered Species Act (Duvall et al. 2017).

Although each working group of this broader coalition tailored their work and plans to local needs, an important lesson has been that these partnerships between government agencies, nonprofit organizations, and private landowners shared a few common characteristics: They prioritized voluntary participation of local landowners, they used science to drive management decisions, and local stakeholders were given the authority to implement locally crafted management plans and actions (Belton and Jackson-Smith 2010). All these ingredients are also going to be important for crafting solutions to meeting groundwater sustainability and finding the best ways to include rewilding as part of the solution in the San Joaquin Valley.

In eastern Montana, The Nature Conservancy is part of a different type of partnership, the Matador Grassbank, with applicable lessons for the future of the San Joaquin Valley. The Nature Conservancy purchased the 60,000-acre Matador Ranch in 2000 with the goal of protecting an important piece of the prairie where greater sage-grouse and other species can persist. Although large, this ranch is only a fraction of the habitat needed to support a wide-ranging species such as the greater sage-grouse. The survival of sage-grouse and a number of other species in this region, such as prairie dogs, black-footed ferrets, and burrowing owls, depends on ranchers keeping their rangelands intact. But drought and market variability have put pressure on ranchers to "bust sod" and convert rangeland into row crop agriculture. The pressure has been especially strong in drought years, when ranchers need access to affordable forage for cattle and it is often in very short supply. Recognizing this need, The Nature Conservancy developed a grassbank on Matador Ranch that provides ranchers across the landscape with below-market-cost grazing leases in exchange for the rancher's commitment to manage their own ranch according to grassbank principles. The core of these commitments is to maintain ranches as working grasslands and not convert rangelands to row crops. And in addition to this commitment, ranchers have the option to implement other conservation actions on their home ranches, such as weed management or protection of sage-grouse leks and prairie dog colonies, to further lower the grazing rental rates on the Matador Ranch. After ten years, the network of lands protected by the grassbank is more than 200,000 acres strong and serves as a testing ground for new conservation methods. Ranchers have changed how they fence, putting white clips on the wires to prevent the sage-grouse from colliding with them and placing the bottom wires at 18 inches so that the pronghorn antelope can scoot underneath as they migrate across the prairie. Rather than being built on long-term legal agreements, the grassbank is held together by annual, voluntary commitments from local ranches that continue to keep this landscape intact (Ginn 2013; McMillion 2013).

These stories are just two good examples from other contexts. There are also valuable models of collaboration from other chapters in this book that have advanced and continue to support habitat restoration in the San Joaquin Valley. For example, the public agency partnerships that tested restoration on retired lands at Atwell Island provide important lessons about not only how to do restoration in this challenging landscape but also how to bring public resources to bear on ambitious restoration projects (see chapter 3). The Kern Water Bank (see chapter 11) is perhaps the valley's best example of collaboration between public agencies, the farming community, water districts, and investors to bring about massive land and water use change to remake parts of the valley with multiple benefits (see figure 11-2). Finally, the work of The Wildlands Conservancy (see chapter 14) with local communities to engage youth in dual education and restoration programs is a compelling example of how to meaningfully include communities in the process so that they have a say and, ultimately, a stake in the outcome. All these models of collaboration have important lessons for us as we embark on what will be the largest transformation of this landscape since the early twentieth century. They succeeded because they created value for each of the parties involved. The partnerships served as a foundation for understanding stakeholders' interests. From there, the partners could tap into incentive programs that aligned with those interests and the desired conservation outcomes.

Regulatory and Financial Incentives

Although many farmers and ranchers may be interested in creating benefits for wildlife, they will face legal and financial barriers. Conservation can be an expensive endeavor, both in the direct costs of restoring and maintaining habitat and in the opportunity cost of other potential land uses that generate revenue for businesses and families. Providing appropriate incentives will be essential for enabling landowners to willingly participate in restoration at a significant scale.

In the California context, a complex set of regulations govern agriculture, restoration, and endangered species protection. Complying with regulations can be quite costly. Therefore, streamlining or reducing the burden of regulatory compliance and helping landowners cover the cost of implementing restoration activities are the two key ways in which private landowners can be incentivized to participate in large-scale restoration. At the national scale, the Natural Resources Conservation Service (NRCS) offers cost share programs for private landowners to implement conservation activities on their farms. Most of their programs are best suited to the kinds of practices that diversify the landscape described in chapter 10, but they can also be used for larger-scale restoration efforts on fallowed lands. These NRCS programs provide the largest investments in conservation of any national programs. On the regulatory side, the U.S. Fish and Wildlife Service has facilitated habitat creation on private lands through safe harbor agreements. These agreements assure private landowners that they will not be penalized for accidentally harming endangered species while implementing activities designed to support the species' recovery. In addition, over the past two decades a number of programs have emerged that are unique to California and help incentivize conservation on private lands. Here we highlight examples from two such programs: a Voluntary Local Program (VLP) between the California Department of Fish and Wildlife (CDFW) and dairy farmers in the San Joaquin Valley, and the Regional Conservation Investment Strategy (RCIS) framework and emerging RCIS programs in the San Joaquin Valley.

Protecting Landowners from Regulatory Risks: The Tricolored Blackbird Voluntary Local Program

Historically, tricolored blackbirds lived throughout California's Central Valley, nesting and foraging in the extensive wetlands that covered large areas of the valley floor. This species is unique to California, occurring nowhere else. Over time, as dairies moved from southern California up into the San Joaquin Valley and wetlands were lost to agriculture and other land uses, tricolored blackbirds began nesting in grain fields as the only available habitat, particularly triticale fields used to provide feed for dairies (figure 12-1). Scientists estimate that today more than 50 percent of all tricolored blackbirds

Figure 12-1. In absence of wetland habitat, tricolored blackbirds build their nests in grain fields, like this nest in a triticale field on a dairy in the southern San Joaquin Valley. Not only are these nests difficult to spot, but the timing of tricolored blackbird nesting and fledging of blackbird chicks puts them at risk of being mowed when grain fields are harvested. (Photo by Jesse Bahm)

nest on agricultural fields. According to accounts from the 1930s, a single colony of tricoloreds may once have consisted of 300,000 birds. Nearly a century later, the entire remaining population of tricolored blackbirds comprises only 300,000 individuals. In addition to wetland loss, two other pressures led to the decline of the species: harvesting schedules for triticale fields that coincided with the birds' nesting season and, more recently, conversion of grain fields used by the birds to orchard crops such as pistachios and almonds.

As populations of tricolored blackbirds declined and rumors spread that the bird could be listed as endangered by the state of California, tensions mounted between dairy farmers and wildlife agencies. When a colony nested in a field, a state biologist would approach the landowners directly, notifying them that they could not mow the field. On a few occasions, farmers were paid silage buyouts for unharvested fields or for delaying harvest, but more often farmers felt that they were bearing the cost of protecting a colony of birds that would appear on their fields seemingly out of nowhere. At the peak of the drought in 2014, the conflict reached a climax. When a California Department of Fish and Wildlife biologist went to monitor a colony of 40,000 birds on a dairy in Madera County, the farmer threatened to mow his field unless he was paid full value for his crop.

It was clear that the existing strategy of biologists approaching landowners was not leading to positive outcomes for the birds or the farmers. An unlikely partnership formed between Western United Dairies, the California Farm Bureau, DairyCares, Sustainable Conservation, and the Audubon Society to change how farmers were approached about colonies on their farms. Together they came up with a process in which biologists informed representatives from the California Farm Bureau and DairyCares about the presence of colonies. Then a farmer would be contacted by a trusted partner with options for protecting the colony on their farm, combining compensation for crops left unharvested with regulatory coverage for agricultural activities around the prescribed buffer from the colony. In 2015 the tricolored blackbird was emergency listed by the state of California as a threatened species, solidifying legal protections for the birds. With new legal protections in place, the partners approached the CDFW about farmers' options for regulatory assurances in carrying out the program they put in place. Because farmers were not actively creating habitat for the birds, a safe harbor agreement program did not seem like the right fit. So the CDFW recommended an option established in 1995 called the Voluntary Local Program. This option would provide farmers ongoing assurances against penalties for incidentally harming tricolored blackbirds while participating in the partners' program to protect nesting colonies. To participate, landowners must sign a cooperative agreement with CDFW to protect existing colonies during routine agricultural activities, such as harvesting. The tricolored blackbird VLP is only the third VLP in California, and its success is still being measured. Every three years, the partners survey the tricolored population. In 2017 the survey counted 178,000 birds, up from 140,000 counted in 2014. The partners are hoping the 2020 survey will indicate that the VLP is continuing to benefit tricolored blackbird populations through an effective partnership model.

In terms of the partnership, it took several years of building trust with each partner assuming the best intent on the part of others. The conservation organizations learned to respect the dairy farmers' care for their cows and their obligation to provide an income for their families, and the dairy farmers learned to appreciate the uniqueness of the tricolored blackbird and the need to protect their last remaining nesting habitat. This program provides an example of how conservation organizations and agencies involved in rewilding can collaborate with farmers and agricultural associations to shape a VLP or safe harbor that would provide regulatory assurances to landowners participating in endangered species conservation through a valley-wide rewilding effort.

Mitigating the Impacts of Future Development: Regional Conservation Investment Strategies

In 2017, California Assembly Bill 2087 was passed, creating the RCIS program. This program aims to create higher-quality conservation outcomes by providing a framework for planning and investing in habitat creation, protection, and restoration. It has three main components: regional conservation assessment, a regional conservation investment strategy, and mitigation credit agreements. This program provides a policy structure that helps align mitigation for development, conservation investments, and other local activities with regional conservation objectives, with the added benefit of incorporating regional, stakeholder-driven planning. There are several RCIS pilot programs in the state that are designed to address demand for habitat mitigation and conservation at a landscape scale. The creation of Mitigation Credit Agreements (MCAs) within an RCIS can enable advanced mitigation before an impact, allowing mitigation to be located strategically and planned further in advance. The RCIS program is still new, with pilots across the state. No MCAs yet exist, but the hope is that the flexibility of MCAs will make it easier for individual landowners to generate mitigation credits and be compensated for creating environmental benefits.

Recently, the state lifted the cap on the number of pilot RCIS programs in the interest of seeing the RCIS address new conservation opportunities. In February 2020, California's Wildlife Conservation Board awarded funding to the East Kaweah Groundwater Sustainability Agency (GSA) to develop the first RCIS in the San Joaquin Valley and the first to address groundwater management concerns. East Kaweah GSA is working with other key stakeholders in the region, including city and county land use planners, conservation groups, and other groundwater agencies, to develop the conservation investment plan. By coordinating at a regional scale, this process will provide the three GSAs in the Kaweah Subbasin a forum to assess the potential for and implement multibenefit projects on former agricultural lands to reduce groundwater pumping demand while creating other benefits for the community. For example, the RCIS may ultimately outline which areas of the basin are best suited for low-impact solar development, habitat corridors, groundwater recharge, and flood management. By doing so, the RCIS will help direct funding toward projects aligned with these landscape-scale objectives. The RCIS steering committee, composed of representatives of local stakeholder groups, will determine what is included in the plan, giving local stakeholders an opportunity to create a solution set of their own while tapping into science and expertise of nongovernment organization and agency partners, like the spatial planning illustrated in chapter 9.

Environmental Defense Fund, a nongovernment organization dedicated to supporting landowners in creating environmental benefits while ensuring the continued success of agricultural communities, helped East Kaweah and its partners navigate the RCIS application process and understand the conservation opportunities. One participant they interviewed noted that "farmers are a strong, creative group who understand the importance of being stewards of our natural resources. This RCIS process will provide us with new tools—and dollars—to create a more resilient water supply and vibrant community. It might mean farmers do things a little differently than past generations in order to create new opportunities for future generations." As the RCIS develops, it will be fertile ground for new partnerships and projects that support the recovery of San Joaquin desert species. Because mitigation is required for all major development projects, mitigation credits are currently underdeveloped but a promising mechanism to support landowners in paying to create habitat for endangered species. The RCIS provides a planning structure in which we can incorporate our priorities and vision for rewilding in order to tap into mitigation funding.

Reimagining Federal Incentive Programs to Restore San Joaquin Desert Habitat

A few parts of the San Joaquin Valley are facing particularly strong pressure to reduce the demand for pumping groundwater by retiring irrigated farmland. One of those areas is the southwestern corner of Tulare County, where many landowners do not have surface water contracts. In 2017, one of the irrigation districts in the region, Pixley Irrigation District (Pixley ID), reached out to The Nature Conservancy and Audubon to explore how converting some irrigated farmland into habitat could ease the transition to a smaller agricultural footprint. Together, Pixley ID, The Nature Conservancy, and Audubon began exploring the U.S. Department of Agriculture (USDA) Small Watershed Program (PL 83-566), a pro-

Figure 12-2. The dry channel of Deer Creek near Pixley, California is straddled by a pistachio orchard and open lands. (Photo by Lara Weatherly/The Nature Conservancy)

gram historically used to help private landowners plan, design, and implement small water infrastructure projects. However, in this case the partners worked with the California NRCS to reimagine how this program could be applied in the context of groundwater sustainability in the Lower Deer Creek Watershed (figure 12-2).

In the first stage, the partners are preparing a watershed plan that identifies poor-quality agricultural land that has the highest potential to be restored to upland and wetland habitats. Where there is overlap, the plan identifies areas for wildlife-friendly recharge basins and restored upland habitat. The plan will take the partners' vision from concept stage to a fully permitted set of projects throughout the watershed that will be eligible for federal financial assistance. The plan is providing partners with a vision that will help Pixley ID meet its goal to transition approximately 20,000 acres of irrigated farmland into other land uses while creating habitat that will significantly benefit San Joaquin Desert species. With the plan in place, partners will be able to tap other sources of funding and can leverage this federal funding to be used on permitted projects that provide clear benefits to nature and agriculture.

Apart from the unconventional use of this USDA program, the project partners are choosing to prepare the plan as a team. Although the process moves a little more slowly than if Pixley ID had hired a single expert to complete the plan, preparing the plan as a team is allowing the partners to learn about each other's concerns, develop a collective vision for the watershed, and demonstrate how new types of partnerships can support the path to groundwater sustainability. These partners and others are also working to create the Tule Basin Land and Water Conservation Trust, which will serve as an important, perhaps essential way to access information and technical and financial assistance to support the transition and as the final landowner or manager on lands that have been restored. Landowners are hoping that the land trust will function as a "storefront" where they can go to understand what conservation activities have value, what grant programs might be available to support habitat creation on retired farmlands, and what options they have for selling conservation easements or portions of their property that they dedicate to habitat. The watershed plan will serve as a springboard for the land trust and other local stakeholders to incorporate rewilding into local Groundwater Sustainability Plans and will encourage other investments in rewilding as restoration and recharge projects are implemented.

Applying These Lessons to Engaging Private Landowners in Rewilding Efforts

Rewilding offers undisputed benefits for wildlife in the San Joaquin Valley, but achieving our vision for rewilding at scale will require that rewilding provide concrete benefits for private landowners. Although the primary challenge that landowners and growers face in rebalancing their land and water use is an economic one, conservation organizations and wildlife agencies can provide a variety of benefits, from risk mitigation to technical expertise, that will help them navigate this transition. At the start of this chapter, we identified the need to engage landowners in a way that includes and inspires them, helps them to navigate through uncertainty, and engages them as willing partners in restoration. This chapter includes several examples that we could replicate in rewilding efforts to strengthen landowner engagement.

First, taking time to build trust, whether between conservation organizations and ranchers or between conservation organizations and dairy farmers, establishes relationships that prove to be critical to decades of partnership and significant conservation benefits. Taking time to develop a plan together in a way that clarifies each party's interests, as in the Lower Deer Creek Watershed, ensures that each partner can communicate in a way that recognizes the values that matter to another partner. Once trust is built and there is an understanding that conservation organizations are willing to share in the risks private landowners face, they may be more willing to share information openly, expose vulnerabilities in their operations or business plans, and explore creative solutions.

Uncertainty is one of the primary risks that private landowners are looking to mitigate in order to confidently invest in conservation actions. Conservation partners can support landowners in mitigating uncertainty by providing foundational science, ongoing technical assistance, and advocacy for rewilding activities in exchange for regulatory assurances, such as safe harbor agreements or VLPs. Sharing costs through state and federal financial assistance programs and mitigation programs, such as those highlighted in the cases above, is another way to mitigate the risks private landowners incur when implementing habitat restoration projects.

Finally, all cases depended on the voluntary participation of landowners, and in some cases they were led by landowners. Coercion will not lead to long-term success. It behooves conservation organizations to invest early in learning what specific values rewilding projects can provide to private landowners, demonstrating success on the ground, and offering our sincere financial and intellectual support in exploring solutions.

The cases here and in chapter 11 also provide examples of specific federal and state programs that may offer pathways for implementing rewilding at scale in partnership with private landowners. No one public or private program will fit the entire landscape. The local context, in terms of both policy and culture, will determine which programs are best suited for a given set of landowners. Whether we are implementing tried-and-true conservation programs, repurposing underused programs for rewilding purposes, or testing new programs specifically designed to support rewilding in the San Joaquin Valley, there are many options for engaging landowners.

In the science of negotiation, there is a distinction between having common interests, in which both parties want the same outcome, and complementary interests, in which the parties' interests are different but compatible. In the case of rewilding, we are fortunate to have complementary interests with private landowners; habitat restoration can help landowners defray the cost of achieving groundwater sustainability. However, to get the most out of this opportunity, conservation organizations will need to better understand how to present rewilding to private landowners in a way that makes the benefits to them clear. This chapter outlines examples of how existing partnerships in California and beyond developed a shared vision with landowners in which there is room for thriving ecosystems and a vibrant agricultural economy. Now it is up to us to start putting these principles to work for rewilding the San Joaquin Valley.

References

Belton, Lorien R., and Douglas Jackson-Smith. 2010. "Factors influencing success among collaborative sage-grouse management groups in the western United States." *Environmental Conservation* 37, no. 3: 250–60.

Duvall, Alison L., Alexander L. Metcalf, and Peter S. Coates. 2017. "Conserving the greater sage-grouse: a social-ecological systems case study from the California–Nevada region." *Rangeland Ecology & Management* 70, no. 1: 129–40.

Ginn, William J. 2013. *Investing in Nature: Case Studies of Land Conservation in Collaboration with Business.* Washington, D.C.: Island Press.

McMillion, Scott. 2013. "Ranching rebooted: at Montana's Matador Ranch, what's good for the prairie is good for its people." *Nature Conservancy* November/December: 34–43.

Chapter 13

Economics of Rewilding the San Joaquin Valley: Benefits, Costs, and Early Adoption

Andrew B. Ayres

SIGNIFICANT LAND USE TRANSITIONS can affect not only local but also regional and, indeed, global stakeholders. The San Joaquin Valley stands before just such a transition: An agricultural landscape of global importance, and the economic activities and daily life based on it, must make way for alternative land uses as implementation of the Sustainable Groundwater Management Act (SGMA) unfolds. These local land management decisions will ideally maintain broad-based economic benefits for valley residents while also reflecting local, regional, and global priorities, such as air quality, habitat, and climate change mitigation.

At the local level, air quality in cities and counties in the valley regularly ranks among the worst in the United States. Wind erosion of open land results in fugitive dust (particulate matter) emissions and contributes to air pollution in the valley. As discussed in chapters 9 and 11, the SGMA is anticipated to result in between 200,000 and 500,000 acres of retired farmland as reduced water access renders some lands uneconomical to keep in production. As a result, despite recent trends toward air quality improvement over the past two decades, there is a concern that poor management of retired farmlands could contribute to a renewed decline in air quality. At the regional scale, restoring habitat on retired farmlands presents an opportunity to manage air pollution while delivering additional benefits that are valued by stakeholders throughout California. How land transitions are managed could also deliver greenhouse gas mitigation benefits by either increasing stored carbon or avoiding its release. Local, regional, and global stakeholders, including local public agencies, environmental groups, and utilities, may be willing to pay for some of these benefits and thereby lessen the economic impact of this major land use transition. However, effectively addressing these decision-making challenges at all scales will require coordinating stakeholders in a way that overcomes fragmentation, delivers meaningful economic signals about potential benefits, and does so in a way that is tractable for landowners facing uncertainty on several fronts.

Linking people across these scales to influence land management is not easy, but successful international and California examples of how to do it exist. At the global scale, firms facing pressure to reduce greenhouse gas emissions have engaged in initiatives to generate emission mitigation credits by paying locals to halt deforestation in countries where there is intense pressure to convert forests to other land uses. In Kenya, for example, leasing contracts with landholders—coupled with aid to facilitate employment opportunities—have not only reduced forest loss and helped mitigate climate change but also stemmed illegal hunting activities (Boucher et al. 2014). Another story from California highlights how beneficiaries have organized to support forest management that protects the headwaters of major rivers flowing out of the Sierra Nevada mountains as part of an effort to reduce wildfire risk. Leaders of the Yuba Water Agency observed the damage to flood control and hydropower infrastructure owned by the neighboring Placer County Water Agency resulting from the 2017 floods that followed major wildfires in the upper watershed. Sediment and large debris, more easily mobilized after the fires, clogged reservoirs and halted hydropower generation; lost energy production and costly repairs led to millions of dollars in damages. Mitigating this risk became a priority for Yuba's management, and a privately organized "forest resilience bond" emerged as a solution (Koren 2018). The water agency will pay more than $1 million to improve upstream land management, primarily through forest thinning and meadow restoration, and thereby benefit regional stakeholders by protecting power generation and reducing flood risk.

As stakeholders in the San Joaquin Valley seek to minimize the cost of this transition and coordinate to deliver a new suite of benefits, they will need to consider what tools, including new land uses, an effective transition plan might include. The case for including rewilding is strong. Rewilding has the advantage of providing a suite of benefits at once: reducing dust generation, increasing soil carbon storage, and facilitating, where sensible, contiguous habitat provision. However, to achieve the best outcome, the benefits provided by rewilding must be weighed against its costs, which include not only the cost of restoration itself but, importantly, the opportunity cost of forgone alternative land uses. This chapter will explore connections between groups of potential beneficiaries with individual landowners and will lay out some of the costs borne, benefits gained, and risks faced in rewilding parts of the San Joaquin Valley.

Where and how farmlands are fallowed or retired and how those lands are managed have important implications for local, regional, and global stakeholders. First, the chapter takes a closer look at the costs to local communities of not managing retired farmlands that could emit dust. Then, it explores how fallowed or retired lands could simultaneously leave benefits for global stakeholders on the table by failing to retain soil carbon stocks. Finally, it looks at the benefits and costs of rewilding itself, by exploring first the benefits to regional stakeholders through the creation of habitat and recreational opportunities and then the costs of restoration and protection, as well as the opportunity cost of dedicating land to habitat.

Benefits, Avoided Costs, and Their Uncertainty

The costs of an uncoordinated approach to farmland fallowing and retirement are easy to imagine: a fragmented landscape with individual unmanaged parcels interspersed among those remaining in production, where the negative effects on others are not considered. Fallowed or retired farmlands can generate dust, pests, weeds, and perhaps fire risk for neighbors when unmanaged. They also do not maintain soil carbon stocks. Although the worst-case scenario may be an unlikely outcome, considering the cost of a failure to coordinate and manage fallowed or retired land helps demonstrate the value of developing the institutions, rules, and partnerships that will enhance the benefits of alternative land uses.

Currently, dust control plans are not required for fallowed or retired lands, yet wind erosion of soil is a potential source of air pollution that could negatively affect residents throughout the valley. Fallowed or retired farmlands may generate airborne particulate matter of various sizes, including less than 10 microns in diameter (PM_{10}) and 2.5 microns in diameter ($PM_{2.5}$). Inhaling these particulates has near-term effects on respiratory health. Additionally, studies point to links between particulate matter (especially $PM_{2.5}$) concentrations and reduced test scores among children and reduced labor force participation among adults (Fan and Grainger 2019; Gilraine 2020). Moreover, a large body of evidence accumulated over several decades reveals that particulate matter exposure during development can have long-term negative effects on educational attainment and earnings (Currie et al. 2014). These costs are borne by valley residents every day. Respiratory problems are common, children study and play while exposed to some of the poorest air quality in the United States, and anyone working outdoors, particularly in agriculture, is subject to increased health risks and lowered productivity as a result. Therefore, the benefits of reducing dust emissions from fallowed land are not simply a matter of clearing the air but rather may prove important in maintaining viable living and working conditions in the valley.

Looking at one of California's other major agricultural regions, we see evidence that residents are willing to pay to avoid exposure to poor air quality. A recent study from California's Imperial and Riverside Counties assessed home sale prices near the Salton Sea (Singh et al. 2018). They estimated that, on average, a household was willing to pay $1,349 (in 2019 dollars) to live in an area with 1 percent lower mean annual PM concentration. Several important factors vary in the San Joaquin case, including income, overall PM concentration levels, and the composition of PM_{10} versus $PM_{2.5}$ in the air. Nonetheless, it does illustrate how costly additional dust emissions from fallowed land may be, should they substantially affect air quality in the valley.

The size of a landowner's holdings also affects the costs and benefits of different land management decisions. As individual landholdings become smaller and the landscape of landholdings more fragmented, the portion of the costs resulting from dust emissions (or pests or weeds) that accrue to the landowner from any given square foot of land decreases. Accordingly, incentives to manage and reduce such emissions decrease. Drawing a lesson from history, during the Dust Bowl of the 1930s, small farms systematically cultivated land more intensively and invested less in erosion control than larger farms, unintentionally worsening conditions at a regional scale (Hansen and Libecap 2004). There are almost 20,000 irrigated farms in the San Joaquin Valley, and they range in size from less than 10 acres to several thousand. Table 13-1 lists average irrigated farm size by county, the total amount of agricultural land with irrigation, and the proportion of small operations. In most counties, average farm size is well below the

Table 13-1. Irrigated Farm Sizes in the San Joaquin Valley

County	Average Size of Irrigated Farm (Acres)	Total Land in Farms with Irrigation (Acres)	Proportion of Irrigated Operations under 500 Acres	Proportion of Irrigated Operations under 180 Acres
Kern[a]	1,232	1,324,492	0.63	0.43
Kings	699	571,609	0.70	0.57
Madera	503	496,221	0.67	0.54
Merced	380	751,269	0.74	0.61
Fresno	316	1,291,051	0.74	0.62
Tulare	269	945,987	0.78	0.67
San Joaquin	229	680,057	0.78	0.68
Stanislaus	187	604,940	0.82	0.71

Note: Data from 2017 USDA Census of Agriculture.
[a]Includes portions of eastern Kern outside the San Joaquin Valley.

U.S. average (757 acres for farms with irrigation). It may prove to be the case that as SGMA spurs fallowing and retirement, managing small, interspersed parcels will become difficult and onerous for landowners, particularly in areas where average farm sizes are small. Alternatively, a coordinated approach to SGMA implementation between groundwater sustainability agencies (GSAs) and counties could help incentivize consolidation of fallowed and retired farmlands into larger, contiguous areas that provide more sensible opportunities for restoration projects.

Moving from the local to the global, another salient cost of leaving fallowed and retired farmlands unmanaged is the potential loss of soil carbon storage. Research is still under way to understand exactly how much carbon land managed as grasslands and shrublands could store (see chapter 9). Rewilding benefits would include preventing the loss of soil carbon from tillage and erosion, as well as any active sequestration of carbon in grasses and shrubs. With this knowledge, the carbon storage benefits could then be valued. Although such calculations are complicated by uncertainty, researchers have aimed to evaluate the cost of carbon emissions by calculating the social cost of carbon. The social cost of carbon, equal to the economic value of damages incurred by the global community from 1 ton of carbon dioxide emissions, is estimated to lie between $10 and $200 (Nordhaus 2017; Rennert and Kingdon 2019; Tol 2007). Note that this does not include local impacts to air quality or other unpriced spillovers that result from activities generating CO_2.

The global community may be willing and able to pay for carbon offset credits. One option would be through California's own cap-and-trade system for carbon emissions. Additionally, there may be potential to fund restoration with state revenues from this same program's permit auctions. However, there is substantial uncertainty related to the amount of carbon sequestered in upland habitat. Resolving this uncertainty may pave the way for changes to California's cap-and-trade program or new opportunities at the global level to provide incentives for rewilding.

Other benefits of rewilding derive from the resulting habitat itself. People value habitat for a host of reasons: for recreational opportunities, for the aesthetic value that landscapes provide, and for the support that functional habitat provides native plants and animals. These values represent a variety of ecosystem services, including what economists call the existence value of the ecosystem, or what one would be willing to pay to ensure its continued existence even absent recreational opportunities or other tangible benefits.

Habitat in the San Joaquin Valley is no exception. A 2007 effort summarized a series of studies that estimated California households would be willing to pay, on average, $5.47 per year to restore 1,000 acres of marginal San Joaquin wetland habitat (in 2019 dollars) (Schwabe and Baerenklau 2007). Summed across all California households, this exceeds $60,000 per acre. Although the focus of this book concerns dry upland habitat rather than wetland, this work provides evidence that habitat provision in the valley can provide significant benefit to the regional population. A better understanding of these ecosystem service values could help underpin funding to support rewilding, which could flow through various programs, including the federal and state programs identified in chapters 11 and 12.

The Costs of Restoration and Encouraging Early Rewilding

The previous section paints a picture of how rewilding can deliver benefits to stakeholders at several scales. However, any effort to undertake this rewilding will also face specific costs associated with restoration activities themselves, including not only land but also fixed and variable inputs needed to alter the landscape. Estimating restoration costs is difficult and depends on the objectives of the restoration effort, as we saw in chapter 3, yet doing so is necessary for planning cost-effective restoration with limited budgets. In the case of San Joaquin Desert grassland and shrubland habitat, retired farmland can serve as a valuable input for restoration, but more work is needed to understand the costs of a full transition from intensive use to rewilded habitat. Seeds for native vegetation are expensive and difficult to acquire in large quantities from commercial seed distributors (see chapters 2, 3, and 5), and acquiring them from the landscape is likely to prove costly and unreliable (Borders et al. 2011). As a result, the cost of seeding lands will not be trivial. Depending on the scale and speed of rewilding, it may be valuable to understand the price at which local seed growers and distributors would consider maintaining such seed stocks. Managing weedy nonnative grasses, fire risk, and fencing also affects operations and maintenance costs and may require more or less attention depending on proximity to neighbors.

Finally, the cost of protecting or acquiring fallowed or retired farmland cannot be overlooked, because land is likely to represent a substantial portion of project cost, whether for a purchase or conservation easement acquisition. The expected value of land in the San Joaquin Valley is likely to undergo many shifts as SGMA implementation proceeds. Appraisers have already documented declines in land value in areas that depend primarily on groundwater (Gatzman et al. 2018). Although a portion of this decline is probably linked to a clear understanding that water will certainly become scarcer for users in these areas, these declines also relate to uncertainty over viable future land uses and the extent of pumping cutbacks. As SGMA implementation proceeds, a clearer understanding will emerge of how heavily GSAs will rely on augmenting water supplies rather than reducing demand for water and whether stakeholders can effectively integrate planning processes across GSA and county boundaries. As discussed in chapter 11, initiatives designed to protect farmland acreage, such as the Williamson Act and prime farmland designations, may need to be relaxed to make strategic consolidation of habitat and water resources possible.

In the face of this uncertainty, it is worth remembering that farmers always face numerous risks (e.g., yield variation, crop price variation, input price variation) and are adept at mitigating them. In particular, although they have played a small role in the San Joaquin Valley, compensated conservation payment programs have helped manage farm risk across the United States (Wallander et al. 2013). There may be opportunities for landowners and conservation groups with rewilding aspirations to benefit mutually from getting started early, before SGMA's 2040 deadlines arrive and water use cutbacks become mandatory.

From a conservation perspective, habitat for endangered species is always welcome earlier, but the benefits that stakeholders derive from rewilded farmland are likely to depend on a stock that is built up over time. For example, ecosystem function does not recover immediately after land is retired and restored; it may take years for these benefits to materialize (Lortie et al. 2018). Likewise, sequestering soil carbon requires that soils retain carbon stocks, and this delivers benefits only as long as that stock remains intact. Temporary restoration of San Joaquin Desert habitat will not deliver full ecosystem or carbon benefits. As a result, if it is important to have established stocks of habitat or carbon by some future date—for example, if a core of rewilded habitat helps support more successful species introduction on additional land that comes out of production in 2040—getting started early is advantageous even from an economic perspective. It also means that long-term commitments are needed to retain the value of these early investments.

To be successful, easements and other management arrangements will need to be robust as conditions change over time. On one hand, farmers do not know what alternative land uses may prove economical in the future; by agreeing to a long-term easement on their land, they may forgo an option to transition the land to a more productive and profitable use later. Abdicating the right to do so may be costly and require additional compensation, for example, where future solar energy development is possible (see chapter 11). On the other hand, SGMA uncertainty looms as well. It remains unclear in many basins exactly how much demand reduction will be necessary, when it will become necessary, and how the responsibility for cutting back will be apportioned. Landowners may want to hedge the risk of uncertain future land values. If a landowner waits too long, lands that can no longer be irrigated may have no alternative uses, and land sale prices or conservation payments will decline further. By enrolling marginally productive farmland in an easement today, the landowner can ensure a higher return than might result in a future where SGMA requires substantial demand reduction. In fact, a landowner averse to risk may even accept a conservation payment below the current rental rate of the farmland under irrigation in exchange for the certainty of income over many years or a few decades.

Even farmlands that do not end up permanently retired may become more likely to benefit from conservation easements. The San Joaquin Valley faces some of the highest drought risk in the country (Wallander et al. 2013). This risk is likely to increase in a warming climate. Historically, drought (and associated reduced surface water availability) was buffered by pulling from and depleting groundwater stocks; the immediate cost incurred was merely that of pumping. Now, effective implementation of SGMA will see drought-time water access become more difficult, because of either higher prices or rationing. As a result, it is possible that some marginal farmlands will be profitable to irrigate under wet conditions but not during drought or that reduced watering during successive droughts will exhaust soil moisture and threaten yields. Farmers in other parts of the United States have reached for conservation easement programs, especially the Conservation Reserve Program, as a tool not only to ensure consistent income but also to improve drought preparedness. Although farmland fallowed intermittently to deliver these kinds of benefits would not become rewilded, it could nonetheless complement permanently retired farmlands to provide a suite of benefits to local stakeholders.

Conclusions

Rewilding retired farmland in the San Joaquin Valley presents an opportunity to reduce costs to neighbors from fallowed land (primarily dust and weeds), enhance recreational opportunities and local amenities, and create additional climate change mitigation options. However, the success of rewilding efforts will depend on designing the correct rules, institutions, and incentives.

It also depends on better understanding several key factors that could make or break the economics of rewilding. For example, accessing carbon mitigation payments will require reliable calculations of how much additional carbon can be stored in rewilded farmland landscapes. A robust method for quantifying these benefits will help justify offset investments and advocate for additional restoration grants. Similarly, the availability and cost of native seeds will determine, to some degree, the feasibility of rewilding at scale. In addition, government funds to incentivize rewilding, such as from the Natural Resources Conservation Service, can play a pivotal role if they are available, particularly when there is a streamlined process for landowners to access these incentives. Finally, landowners currently face great uncertainty over SGMA implementation. A number of decisions, including the extent to which groundwater recharge can address overdraft and whether groundwater pumping allocations can be reallocated through markets, will have important implications for how much and which land comes out of production, and subsequently for how costly it will be to acquire land of high conservation value.

Rewilding may also support SGMA implementation in the San Joaquin Valley by reducing conflict between water user interest groups. Such competing interests have stymied attempts at groundwater management in the past (Ayres et al. 2018). How the benefits of groundwater management and costs of implementation may vary by geography and water user group is important. The proliferation of GSAs in the San Joaquin Valley suggests a high level of fragmentation in bargaining positions. Offering promising alternative land uses that can reduce landowner losses—and perhaps conflict—is paramount.

Furthermore, counties, GSAs, cities, and other stakeholder groups may be reluctant to embrace coordinated and integrated solutions to implement the SGMA if they think doing so would disadvantage them. Concerns include anticipated loss of county revenue due to a reduction in property taxes from devalued fallowed or retired farmlands and, importantly, localized losses in employment opportunities. In many San Joaquin Valley cities, agriculture is the predominant source of employment. Rewilding can provide some relief for landowners, but it must be coupled with sensible approaches to transition not just land but also labor to be successful.

This chapter concerns itself with the economics of rewilding the San Joaquin Valley, but similar transitions may arise elsewhere in the world over the coming decades. Globally, groundwater withdrawals are depleting major aquifers, in some places at alarming rates (Aeschbach-Hertig and Gleeson 2012). As climate change threatens supply reliability and the value of scarce water resources increases, efforts to reform management and end unlimited pumping will intensify, perhaps opening doors for rewilding in other areas facing major land use transitions. Identifying beneficiaries, articulating benefits and costs, and describing the key uncertainties will be necessary to make space for rewilding as these processes unfold.

References

Aeschbach-Hertig, Werner, and Tom Gleeson. 2012. "Regional strategies for the accelerating global problem of groundwater depletion." *Nature Geoscience* 5: 853–61. https://doi.org/10.1038/ngeo1617

Ayres, Andrew B., Eric C. Edwards, and Gary D. Libecap. 2018. "How transaction costs obstruct collective action: the case of California's groundwater." *Journal of Environmental Economics and Management* 91: 46–65. https://doi.org/10.1016/j.jeem.2018.07.001

Borders, Brianna D., Brian L. Cypher, Nur P. Ritter, and Patrick A. Kelly. 2011. "The challenge of locating seed sources for restoration in the San Joaquin Valley, California." *Natural Areas Journal* 31, no. 2: 190–99. https://doi .org/10.3375/043.031.0213

Boucher, Doug, Pipa Elias, Jordan Faires, and Sharon Smith. 2014. *Deforestation Success Stories: Tropical Nations Where Forest Protection and Reforestation Policies Have Worked* (p. 51). Cambridge, Mass.: Union of Concerned Scientists.

Currie, Janet, Joshua S. Graff Zivin, Jamie Mullins, and Matthew J. Neidell. 2014. "What do we know about short- and long-term effects of early-life exposure to pollution?" *Annual Review of Resource Economics* 6, no. 1: 217–47.

Fan, Mingxuan, and Corbett Grainger. 2019. "The impact of air pollution on labor supply in China." Working paper.

Gatzman, Janie, Tiffany Holmes, Liz McAfee, and Suzie Roget. 2018. *2018 Trends in Agricultural Land and Lease Values.* Glendale, Colo.: American Society of Farm Managers and Rural Appraisers.

Gilraine, Michael. 2020. *Air Filters, Pollution and Student Achievement.* Providence, R.I.: Annenberg Institute at Brown University.

Hansen, Zeynep K., and Gary D. Libecap. 2004. "Small farms, externalities, and the Dust Bowl of the 1930s." *Journal of Political Economy* 112, no. 3: 665–94.

Koren, James R. 2018. "Start-up Blue Forest secures funding for first privately financed forest fire bond." *Los Angeles Times*. https://www.latimes.com/business/la-fi-fire-bond-20181101-story.html

Lortie, Christopher J., A. Filazzola, R. Kelsey, Abigail K. Hart, and H. S. Butterfield. 2018. "Better late than never: a synthesis of strategic land retirement and restoration in California." *Ecosphere* 9, no. 8: e02367.

Nordhaus, William D. 2017. "Revisiting the social cost of carbon." *Proceedings of the National Academy of Sciences* 114, no. 7: 1518–23.

Rennert, Kevin, and Cora Kingdon. 2019. "Social cost of carbon 101." *Resources for the Future*.

Schwabe, Kurt, and Kenneth A. Baerenklau. 2007. *A Preliminary Investigation of the Potential Non-Market Benefits Provided by the Salton Sea.* [Final Report]. Glendale, Calif.: K2 Economics.

Singh, Amrita, Jean-Daniel Saphores, and Tim Bruckner. 2018. "A spatial hedonic analysis of the housing market around a large, failing desert lake: the case of the Salton Sea in California." *Journal of Environmental Planning and Management* 61, no. 14: 2549–69.

Tol, Richard S. J. 2007. *The Social Cost of Carbon: Trends, Outliers and Catastrophes* (FNU-144; Working Papers). Hamburg, Germany: Research Unit Sustainability and Global Change, Hamburg University. https://ideas.repec.org/p/sgc/wpaper/144.html

Wallander, Steven, Marcel Aillery, Daniel Hellerstein, and Michael Hand. 2013. *The Role of Conservation Programs in Drought Risk Adaptation* (Economic Research Report ERR-148). Washington, D.C.: Economic Research Service of the U.S. Department of Agriculture.

Chapter 14

Using Environmental Education and Community-Based Programs to Rewild Habitat

Landon Peppel, Brooke Wainwright, Melissa Dabulamanzi, and Daisy Carrillo

KERN COUNTY, AT THE SOUTHERN END of the San Joaquin Valley, has a rich ecological, geophysical, cultural, and social fabric that sets it apart as a unique region in California. Its ecological diversity, which represents many of the most sensitive species in California, is juxtaposed with its role as the top oil-producing and agricultural county in the state. The region is the point of convergence of five distinct ecoregions—the Transverse Range, the Coast Range, the Sierra Nevada, the western Mojave Desert, and the San Joaquin Valley—and the homeland of several Native American tribes.

Yet despite having abundant resources, many families in Kern County experience hardship; one in three households with children falls below the federal poverty level. Environmental justice issues such as poor air quality, loss of habitat, water quality concerns, and socioeconomic barriers affect many residents. The farmworker communities that support this agricultural powerhouse, which consist largely of people who identify as Hispanic or Latino, often are underserved and lack access to the natural world, furthering a disconnection that makes it difficult to address issues of environmental justice.

Yet in this context, The Wildlands Conservancy has an inspiring history of fostering community participation in rewilding. It recognizes nature as a birthright and strives to bring it to all citizens by creating preserves in disadvantaged areas where community members can access free education programs, trails, campsites, and public facilities. Through its programs, it reveals how the interest and involvement of San Joaquin Valley communities will need to be at the heart of any successful rewilding movement.

At the southern end of Kern County, bordered by farmland and farmworker communities, you will find The Wildlands Conservancy's 93,000-acre Wind Wolves Preserve (see figure 3-1). Each year Wind Wolves Preserve hosts nearly 10,000 school children from surrounding communities and about 60,000 total visitors. The preserve serves as a social hub where knowledge, experience, and a sense of place can develop. Its staff have integrated this philosophy into habitat restoration programs that bring together education, experience, and hands-on involvement. Each year, volunteers place thousands of native shrubs on the landscape by hand, a few acres at a time, making a small but certain contribution to rewilding.

This chapter uses Wind Wolves Preserve as a model for integrating outdoor education, community involvement, financial partnerships, and regional ecological goals to generate outcomes in all of those areas.

Wind Wolves Preserve

With elevation ranging from approximately 600 feet on the valley floor to more than 6,000 feet at its southern border with Los Padres National Forest, Wind Wolves Preserve contains various habitats including grassland, saltbush scrub, riparian corridors, wetlands, oak woodlands, and pinyon–juniper forests. Multiple listed species call the preserve home, including the San Joaquin kit fox, blunt-nosed leopard lizard, and Bakersfield cactus.

Wind Wolves Preserve offers free outdoor access every day of the week, throughout the year, except major holidays. Visitors are welcome to explore trails, practice photography, picnic, camp, and take in the stunning biodiversity of the preserve, all at no cost. Most visitors are Kern County residents, although the preserve regularly attracts people from all over California, the United States, and beyond. The preserve also offers free weekend programs, including educational hikes, nature crafts, and volunteer days, which consist of a variety of land stewardship activities. Volunteers assist with invasive species removal and native seed collection, plant seedlings in the on-site nursery, and plant mature nursery stock in the field to improve or restore ecological function in degraded areas. Volunteers receive an overview of the natural history of the preserve and the need for habitat restoration and are encouraged to ask questions and learn more about their native landscape.

Beyond regular volunteering, the preserve hosts several interns annually through its Land Steward Internship Program. A multiyear academic learning agreement with local institutions allows students from nearby colleges to earn academic credit after completing a minimum hourly requirement. Interns work alongside preserve rangers performing trail maintenance, biological monitoring, and habitat restoration projects, as well as occasionally leading outdoor education programs. Most interns have little or no prior knowledge of local plants and wildlife or experience with land stewardship but leave their internship with a greater understanding of the habitats that surround their communities and the importance of protecting and restoring them.

On top of educating and engaging visitors, the Wind Wolves Preserve provides award-winning, free outdoor education to local schools throughout Kern County. The curriculum follows next-generation science standards and emphasizes the natural history themes that are specific to the preserve and Kern County, such as Chumash,

Yokut, and Kitanemuk history. All programs are hosted entirely outdoors on the preserve's trails with hands-on activities led by naturalists. The program has longstanding impact, as nearly 200,000 local school children have participated in this program since 1998.

A large piece of the educational content provided to students and visitors is the restoration of the landscape. A few years ago, preserve staff began to brainstorm ways to get the community involved and become passionate about restoring native habitats at their local nature preserve, and to fund projects while doing so. Engaging volunteers in the restoration process supports a local cultural moment for biodiversity and magnifies the impact to the land as more hands are putting plants into the ground, pulling weeds, and collecting seeds.

Embracing Diversity

Providing outdoor opportunities for underserved populations is a top priority for Wind Wolves Preserve. Underserved populations include low-income, racial minorities, non–English speakers or English language learners, and people with disabilities. More than half of all children in the San Joaquin Valley are Latino, and the region is likely to become increasingly racially diverse as the population grows to 7.4 million by 2060 (Hartzog et al. 2006). Language is one of the many barriers that residents of underserved communities face. Because a significant proportion of the people who visit the preserve come from Spanish-speaking backgrounds, most of the signage, website content, and social media posts are in both English and Spanish, and many weekend programs are conducted by bilingual staff. Maintaining cultural traditions, including language, allows community members to be not only more engaged in social programs but also be more proactive in their community. A study of Native American students found that they performed better on the California Achievement Test after integrating curriculum with hands-on outdoor education activities compared with a solely traditional textbook-based classroom setting (Zwick and Miller 1996). Not only is there a tremendous need in the San Joaquin Valley to serve ethnic minorities and non–English speakers, but honoring their experiences and broadening inclusivity in program planning has a ripple effect of positive benefits throughout the community.

One program designed for low-income and Spanish-speaking visitors is called Nature's Niños. The program serves migrant and farmworker families, English language learners, and members of economically disadvantaged communities throughout Kern County. One of the goals of the program is to introduce participants to their first camping experience. Wind Wolves Preserve and its partners (e.g., Lamont Migrant Program) aim to remove common barriers to camping by providing transportation, food, and camping equipment, as well as bilingual nature programming for a free, multiday camping experience.

Children in the Nature's Niños program receive a journal and get to participate in activities such as night hikes, award ceremonies, reptile presentations, and a service learning activity. The service learning activity consists of taking field notes in English or Spanish or drawing out natural observations. Children learn to look closely at the thorns of a mesquite tree, to smell the refreshing scent of blue elderberry flowers, to stop and listen for a coyote, and to watch a hummingbird pollinate a yellow flower–laden bladderpod. After making observations and learning details about local native plants, participants work alongside preserve rangers and naturalists in a land stewardship activity. Depending on the season, participants plant seedlings in containers in the preserve nursery (figure 14-1) or take seedlings and plant them directly in the field. Some groups get to take multiple camping trips a year through this program, and returning participants are able to revisit their plants during future visits and educate their family and friends (figure 14-2). This creates lasting memories for families and facilitates and fosters environmental stewardship.

Through this program children and families feel at home and safe in nature by becoming familiar with the preserve, thus allevi-

Figure 14-1. Participants in the Nature's Niños program fill containers with soil in the nursery, with instruction from the bilingual preserve staff. Native seeds, such as California buckwheat, bladderpod, and desert milkweed, were planted in these containers and later planted in the field. (Photo by The Wildlands Conservancy)

ating the barrier of unfamiliarity and encouraging them to return. Preserve staff are able to show visitors that nature is for all people and that they can visit the preserve at any time to take part in any number of programs, to camp with loaner equipment, hike, picnic, chat with staff, or check on their plants. Finally, by covering all costs, the preserve and its partners remove the financial burden of an outdoor experience.

Partnerships

As mentioned in chapter 12, partnerships are essential to the success of a project, be it a new education program or a large-scale rewilding project. Partners offer funding, expertise, marketing, community connections, and guidance for the projects in which they invest. Partners of the preserve span corporate, government,

Figure 14-2. Nature's Niños participants learn about pollinator plants, such as rubber rabbitbrush. (Photo by The Wildlands Conservancy)

and community entities. Collaboration with and support from these groups are critical for the preserve to achieve its many large-scale goals, including restoring watersheds, enhancing or restoring habitat for state and federally listed species, and providing programs and accessibility to a community in need.

An example of rewilding in partnership is the restoration of Bakersfield cactus (see chapter 7), an endangered and endemic species in Kern County. After a lightning-ignited fire swept through the Pleito Hills Bakersfield cactus population on the preserve in 2011, The Wildlands Conservancy acquired a permit from the California Department of Fish and Wildlife to collect and restore cactus pads at the Pleito Hills site and four new sites on the preserve. After self-funding cactus restoration from 2012 to 2017, Wind Wolves Preserve began working with the U.S. Fish and Wildlife Service's Partners for Fish and Wildlife Program. Through the program, the preserve was able to cover the cost of materials for pad collection and propagation, maintenance, and monitoring. The project relies on community volunteers, such as college students, local biologists, and interns. The link to the cactus's namesake, Bakersfield, the largest city in Kern County (see figure 3-1), brings a sense of place and identity to participants. Second, going home with a fingertip full of glochids (hairlike spines) that readily attach to the well-intentioned volunteers' hands is hard for them to forget. For many this is their first experience with an endangered species.

Cactus rewilding at Wind Wolves Preserve has been highly successful, with up to 1,500 plants added to the population annually. Volunteers can collect nearly all the pads needed for annual propagation in a single volunteer day, and planting takes two or three volunteers to complete (see figure 7-1).

Besides planting Bakersfield cactus, the preserve has conducted habitat restoration for threatened and endangered species at other sites. At Pleitito Creek, volunteers, interns, and students planted native rye grasses and stinging nettle, after the removal of invasive perennial pepperweed, to benefit the threatened tricolored blackbird. At Santiago Creek, nonnative tamarisk was removed, with the help of the local Kern Service and Conservation Corps, and native riparian shrubs and trees were restored to support populations of endangered species such as least Bell's vireo and southwest willow flycatchers. The restorations of Pleitito Creek and Santiago Creek are financially supported by an array of state and federal grants from the U.S. Department of Agriculture National Resources Conservation Service, the U.S. Fish and Wildlife Service Partners for Fish and Wildlife Program, and the California Wildlife Conservation Board.

Financial Stability

Chapter 13 highlighted the significant cost of rewilding. The ability to develop and maintain community-led restoration projects at Wind Wolves Preserve is made possible through financial planning and fundraising. Preserves have limited staff, so funding opportunities are chosen wisely to reduce time spent on projects that do not have grant funding. The preserve often focuses fundraising on existing strengths and tested programs, such as Nature's Niños, because funding for new and experimental programs is much harder to acquire.

Wind Wolves Preserve has been able to access many of the state and federal programs mentioned in chapters 11 and 12. These programs have provided the largest pool of funding for the preserve's rewilding projects and include California Proposition 68–Parks, Environment, and Water Bond; the California Wildlife Conservation Board's Habitat Enhancement and Restoration Program; and various federal programs. To put these sorts of funding programs to use for rewilding projects, applicants need to have the skills and expertise to administer large public grants. For small organizations that want to use these funds, cash flow can also be a challenge. Many government grant programs provide payment after achieving certain benchmarks, meaning that funds are spent first, and a task is completed (i.e., nonnative species removal) before receiving financial reimbursement.

Small organizations and community-led efforts would benefit from grant funding that provides a cash advance so that grant funds can be put directly to work on the project.

Volunteers benefit the preserve, but successful volunteer-driven restoration projects need consistent management and make up a large component of regular operations at Wind Wolves Preserve. The preserve relies on social media marketing and flyers to recruit volunteers, word of mouth, and family and friends to participate in volunteer days. Over time, the preserve has experienced a significant increase in volunteer hours, which at one point surpassed 5,000 annual hours—nearly a $150,000 value.

Outcomes for Habitat and the Community

Rewilding a landscape has the potential to generate multiple benefits for society. Often the primary focus of an initiative is on overall ecosystem health and biodiversity, with the goal of directly benefiting the organisms inhabiting the project site. However, as chapter 13 pointed out, the benefits of rewilding that spill over into social outcomes and environmental services are also critically important.

Protecting existing habitats and restoring others creates invaluable benefits: replenishing groundwater basins, filtering air pollution, improving wildlife corridors, promoting outdoor recreation, and supporting healthier communities. In addition, we know that spending time outdoors has a positive impact on health and well-being. Access to nature improves psychological health. Residents who participate in restoring native habitats to the San Joaquin Valley develop a connection with their local environment, leading to a cascade effect of engagement and participation in their communities. The preserve recognizes that promoting personal experience and creating a need to care for the environment are essential in developing a community's sense of stewardship. When the connection is developed early in childhood, children grow to become environmentally conscious adults.

Greater impact occurs when projects are long term and involve multiple participation opportunities for attendees, such as the Wind Wolves Preserve's programs that engage students in several stages of a restoration project (e.g., seed collection, nursery work, and field planting). These lessons translate to the public school system's objective to deepen students' knowledge of science, technology, engineering, and mathematics (STEM) subjects while incorporating a service learning component supported by preserve staff. Interns and long-term volunteers gain valuable knowledge and hands-on experience right before entering the workforce.

Multigenerational change can occur when families volunteer together. Children learn the importance of giving back and being involved in their local community, especially with their family members beside them. At Wind Wolves Preserve, children learn about San Joaquin Valley habitat and actively help restore it. This knowledge and legacy will be passed down to their children and grandchildren, creating generations of change through activism and involvement.

Conclusions

Part of the success of rewilding the San Joaquin Valley will depend on careful consideration of how to include San Joaquin Valley communities in planning and carrying out restoration. Many Kern County residents face significant barriers to accessing nature and therefore may not understand what they stand to gain from restoration of the valley's diverse and sensitive habitats. Yet the case of Wind Wolves Preserve highlights how children and adults in underserved communities can get to know and then grow to love the natural communities that surround them. For many, Wind Wolves Preserve becomes their first and most frequently visited outdoor experience. Preserve projects such as Nature's Niños, Bakersfield cactus restoration, and riparian habitat restoration for tricolored blackbirds demonstrate this success and the lasting impact that an integrated vision for rewilding can have.

Conducting community-led rewilding comes with challenges. Generating community engagement, from an initial small group of volunteers to large sustained volunteer programs, takes diligence and careful management. Once established, community engagement takes a significant amount of time to sustain through ongoing programs and community outreach. Not all organizations are equipped to do this level of engagement, and so as new organizations form or local stakeholders look to broaden community engagement in rewilding, Wind Wolves Preserve offers these recommendations:

- Build and rely on personal relationships with local partners and government agencies.
- Cater to the needs of diverse and underserved populations.
- Engage your audience with meaningful experiences.
- Develop restoration projects founded in science.
- Get creative in your approach and do not be afraid to fail.
- Learn to tell the story of your work to fund and build on successes.

Expanding rewilding efforts from cases such as this to a sustained, coordinated valley-wide effort will take significant time and resources. However, community engagement will be essential for lasting stewardship of habitat created or restored. Also, the experiences these communities gain will enrich their own lives and reinforce their commitment to the landscape. Integrating multiple strategies offers a pathway to create sustained community engagement that leads to lasting outcomes for nature.

References
Hartzog, Cassie, Carolyn Abrams, Nancy Erbstein, Jonathan K. London, and Sara Watterson. 2016. *California's San Joaquin Valley: A Region and Its Children under Stress*. Report commissioned by Sierra Health Foundation and conducted by the UC Davis Center for Regional Change.

Zwik, Thomas T., and Kenneth W. Miller. 1996. "A comparison of integrated outdoor education activities and traditional science learning with American Indian students." *Journal of American Indian Education* 35, no. 2: 1–9.

Part IV

A Rewilding Vision

Chapter 15

A Vision for Rewilding the San Joaquin Valley

H. Scott Butterfield, T. Rodd Kelsey, and Abigail K. Hart

THE VISION WE ARE LAYING OUT in this book is simultaneously urgently needed and a grand experiment for the San Joaquin Valley. Drinking water wells going dry, land sinking, air quality among the worst in the nation, and the highest concentration of threatened and endangered species in the continental United States—these are symptoms of a larger problem. We have treated the San Joaquin Valley as a landscape with unlimited capacity, pushing it to its limits and threatening the livelihoods of the people who live and work here while producing much of the food for others in the United States and globally. It is at this tipping point that we see more clearly what nature has to offer in striking a new balance that can work for both people and nature. As we put forth a vision for restoration of San Joaquin Valley habitats, we are also putting forth a vision for restoring the health of San Joaquin Valley communities and the long-term viability of San Joaquin Valley agriculture. Achieving this vision will not be easy and will take time and patience as creative new solutions are tested and new partnerships forged. We will need to inspire local communities to be involved. It will be expensive, and there will undoubtedly be resistance to such change.

So Why Do It? Why Put Forth a Vision for Rewilding the San Joaquin Valley?

The authors of this book have fallen in love with places such as the Carrizo Plain, Wind Wolves Preserve, and Panoche Valley. When you see a giant kangaroo rat bounce around a landscape for the first time, watch a blunt-nosed leopard lizard on two legs proudly display its coloring in the hot summer sun, catch a glimpse of kit fox cubs freshly emerging from their den, or come down over the Temblor Mountains into the Carrizo Plain and see a wildflower superbloom surrounding the sparkling Soda Lake, it is hard not to be moved by the beauty of these places. We are driven to make sure places such as this are protected so that the plants and animals that depend on them can thrive. We are also driven to strike a balance that ensures that the people of the San Joaquin Valley thrive. We believe that rewilding portions of the San Joaquin Valley will be a vital ingredient in a more balanced future and that by recreating new places such as the Carrizo Plain closer to where people live and work, it will also provide communities an opportunity to fall in love with them while reaping the benefits they can provide. Rewilding is not just a nature endeavor but a people one too.

This kind of transition will be hard and expensive, and it will take time. Although there is optimism among some, there is even greater fear about what this will mean for agriculture and communities in the valley. So this work and the partnerships needed to see it through will require building the trust needed to work creatively and collaboratively for many years. We need to begin now, using the lessons, tools, and insights from this book to build a common vision for the valley and its future. This book has laid out many different lessons learned and considerations—from the San Joaquin

Valley and more broadly across deserts and dryland ecosystems globally—that must be addressed when thinking about the future of the San Joaquin Valley in the age of the Sustainable Groundwater Management Act (SGMA).

Where We Do Rewilding Matters

Despite the need for planning at a regional scale to achieve the right balance, local implementation of rewilding as one part of the solution will never be one-size-fits-all. There will be many local solutions that work for specific communities but with each informed by and adding to the best regional outcomes. All these solutions can be developed as parts of a whole by building deliberately from the remaining foundations of native habitat already present in the valley, from the Wind Wolves Preserve, Carrizo Plain, and Kern Water Bank in the southern part of the valley to the Panoche Valley and the Grasslands Management Area in its more northern stretches. Success will inevitably mean connecting these building blocks, learning from what has worked at each of these places, and finding ways to reproduce their success in new places with new partners.

Also, the SGMA will drive land use change whether rewilding is embraced or not. Large tracts of agricultural land will be fallowed, some temporarily and some permanently. Uncoordinated and unplanned, this fallowing will largely occur in small, disconnected units forming a checkerboard across the valley. But we know that location and configuration matter a lot. Strategically consolidating and repurposing only a fraction of these fallowed lands into larger, less fragmented habitat blocks could meet the needs of dozens of threatened and endangered species while minimizing human impacts and even producing other benefits. And finally, we have the opportunity to integrate rewilding with other aspects of the bigger solution by incorporating other land uses and needs, engaging the community, and addressing the socioeconomic impacts honestly and directly.

What Is Already There Matters

Selecting the best places to rewild is only the beginning. Once we know where to get the most out of restoration, we need to apply the best lessons and tools in executing the restoration: learning from the deep past in the seedbanks, the records of original explorers and settlers, and our own attempts at restoration. The basic principles we have learned suggest we need to first do something about the soils, whether our approach is more passive and allows nature to reclaim these areas with minimal human input or more active, with humans involved in every step of restoring the natural communities. Ecological principles, restoration theory, and basic agricultural practices all teach us that we need to make sure we have good, healthy, productive soils. Without good soils, we will have a hard time growing anything, whether it is native shrubs or pistachios. Retired agricultural lands in the San Joaquin Valley have been farmed for more than 150 years. The cumulative effects of intensive agricultural management and irrigation, such as soils contaminated by salt and toxic minerals or compacted and unnaturally level fields, need to be remediated and reversed. There are many ways to do this, including creating variations in topography (as we see in more natural landscapes shaped by native animals and plants growing over time) by moving soil and creating mounds and by adding soil nutrients and remediating toxic mineral conditions, if they exist.

Next, no restoration project, however big or small, will ever be successful in the San Joaquin Valley if it does not address nonnative weedy grasses. They provide those famous California golden hills in the spring and summer, but they also create a management headache for farmers and habitat managers. They harbor insect populations that can be detrimental to neighboring crops and increase fire risk. If allowed to, they dominate the landscape, choking out native species and threatening the success of restoration efforts. Unfortunately, nonnative weedy grasses have become naturalized; in other words, they have been around long enough and cover enough ground that they are here to stay. These nonnative grasses dominate, even in "pristine" natural places such as the Carrizo Plain.

Despite these challenges, we have the tools to reduce the cover of nonnative weedy grasses, increasing space for native plants and animals. Science tells us this is possible, and there are many examples across California where this is done successfully each year. Cattle grazing and prescribed fires are cost-effective tools where they can be used, opening the door for grazing as an alternative form of agricultural use. Also, native animals that will recolonize restored landscapes, such as kangaroo rats, ground squirrels, and pocket gophers, can help graze down these grass species each year. By using these tools effectively, we can ensure that native plants and animals thrive, reduce the threat of wildfire, and reduce the pressure of weeds and detrimental insects on adjoining farmlands.

In some cases, maybe most, the active part of restoration could be done at this point, having laid the foundations for natural processes of species dispersal and recolonization to take care of the rest. This will be most likely where the newly restored land, now with healthy soils and a long-term plan to manage nonnative weedy grasses, is connected to land that is already occupied by San Joaquin Valley plant and animal species. Allowing the natural colonization and evolution of these communities to take place will require a lot of patience but may be less expensive in the long run. Where this happens close to human communities that can begin to enjoy these spaces for recreation and appreciate their impact on cleaner water and air, it will also provide the opportunity for people to watch, learn, and rejoice in how nature can repair itself.

Taking a More Active Role in Restoration

Setting the stage with healthy soils and minimal management to let nature take its course will not be enough in many locations. We will want or need to take a more active role and make a greater investment in restoration in parts of the landscape, deliberately reintroducing plants and animals to kickstart the system and reestablish a natural community. More intensive restoration may ultimately be necessary for recovering healthy, diverse natural communities and ecological function. More active restoration will be a process of setting the stage, reintroducing the key actors, and giving them a helping hand until they are fully established and self-sustaining.

A key lesson has been that the types of plants planted first matter a lot. Plant species play important ecological roles beyond their individual contributions to plant diversity. Some plant species, such as ephedra and saltbush shrubs, serve foundational roles, affecting the types of plants that grow around them and providing habitat, shade, and cover from predators for animals, such as the blunt-nosed leopard lizard. They may even serve as a buffer against future changes in climate. In these ways, similar to how the first plant colonizers of new volcanic islands such as Hawaii set the trajectory for whole island plant and animal communities, the plants selected for initial planting will set the trajectory of the entire San Joaquin Valley community. They may even determine success or failure.

Which plants to select must be informed by both the role they play in the community and the local site conditions and the genetic sources of the seeds used. Most plant and even some animal species have very specific preferences about the types of soils they grow on. For example, native plant species that prefer sandy or crumbly soils will not thrive on the former lakebeds of the valley, with heavy clay soils where wetlands once dominated. Any plant palette we choose needs to be driven by the soils that are present and our objectives for the site. Also, the success of newly reintroduced plants will be driven not only by the external conditions such as soil type but also by the internal capacity of the plants selected. Plants, even more than animals, become adapted to local conditions. In other words, they genetically evolve the traits that make them most adapted to the physical conditions of specific sites. Thus, to preserve natural genetic diversity within species and maximize the potential for success, restorationists often focus on collecting seeds from local sources for restoration projects. Selecting local seed stock increases the certainty that those individuals will be well suited to the environment in which they will grow. Having the necessary stockpile of local seed sources for rewilding will thus require a renewed commitment to and investment in developing native greenhouses from Bakersfield to Fresno and from the Carrizo Plain to the Panoche Valley. Seeds can be collected across public protected spaces where these species are thriving. This is already happening at small scales, but it will need to happen at much larger scales. These greenhouses could also benefit local communities by providing jobs, supporting local communities, and allowing them to feel ownership in the rewilding of the landscapes around them. In the end, such an effort and the building of a restoration economy will not be cheap, but it will ensure greater success of the restoration projects themselves, thus securing a higher return on the investment made by agencies, communities, and landowners.

Direct reintroduction for more intensive restoration will not necessarily be limited to plants. In some cases, successful rewilding may also require that we physically reintroduce focal wildlife species to new sites. In fact, as with foundational plants, some animal species play an outsized role in helping structure and sustain the whole community. We talked earlier about the role that kangaroo rats, pocket gophers, and ground squirrels can play in rewilded valley landscapes. These species create important structure for native plant and animal species both aboveground, through grazing the nonnative grasses and churning the soils, and belowground, through burrow creation. Burrows are vital in these landscapes because many of the native animals spend large portions of their day and year underground in what is a very hot and dry landscape. Deliberately reintroducing threatened or endangered species, such as the giant kangaroo rat, will be challenging for many reasons, both practically and legally. Nevertheless, it may be necessary in some cases. However, to restore ecosystem function, some more common species can also serve a similar role in returning this function back to the landscape much more quickly and efficiently. For example, the much more common California ground squirrel and its burrowing activity can play a vital role in engineering the landscape to benefit many other species. In such cases, this does not mean we would not attempt to reintroduce protected species. However, reintroductions (to places where species used to live) or assisted migrations (to places where they did not live but probably can and will live in the future) are far more complicated legally and socially. Thus, finding ways to facilitate their own abilities to recolonize restored lands will be an important option.

Regardless of the species, successful reintroductions and assisted migrations will require that we use all the tools in our restoration toolbox—from spatial modeling to genetic analysis to remote sensing—to determine where these species have lived in the past, where they can live now, and where they might thrive in the future in a changing climate. We will also need to make sure habitat areas, new and old, are connected. Ultimately, true recovery of these communities, and especially the wild species that depend on moving over larger areas, will depend on their ability to disperse to new, suitable areas over time. Thus, it is our responsibility to make sure they can move across both natural and agricultural areas in the landscape. This will make for more genetically robust, self-sustaining populations with the best chance of surviving climate change. Movement will depend on strategically restoring corridors of natural habitat between larger patches of native landscape. Also, wildlife movement can be greatly increased by softening portions of agricultural landscapes with natural or seminatural habitat into portions of productive farmland, such as along the edges of farms, in less productive corners, or near infrastructure and outbuildings. These seminatural features that increase the natural diversity of farms and nearby natural areas can also benefit farmers by providing ecosystem services, such as pollination and insect pest control. But farmers may understandably be concerned about inviting the natural world onto their farms, for fear of unintended consequences such as having endangered species occur in what are actively farmed areas. Thus, it will be vital that permitting agencies work closely with the farming community to provide assurances, through safe harbor agreements or other options, that reduce legal risk. Similarly, natural habitat can also serve as a reservoir of pest species, such as leafhoppers, that damage nearby crops. To engage in rewilding, farmers want and need support in managing the negative spillover effects of having habitat nearby. This will require deeper collaboration between permitting agencies, conservation organizations, and farmers to implement existing approaches or develop new ones to mitigate these risks of rewilding.

Planning for a Different Future

In the places where we devote more resources—time, money, and partnerships—to rewilding, an important consideration will be whether we put back species and community types that have a good chance of living there now versus in the future, especially when existing information suggests these are mutually exclusive because the climate is expected to change conditions dramatically. Although there remains significant uncertainty, we have, with greater confidence than ever before, the ability to use spatial modeling and genetic analysis to project where, across an agricultural landscape, native species that have not lived there for more than 150 years will be able to survive 50, 100, or even more than 200 years into the future. But how should we manage the trade-offs between which species can survive now versus in the future? Site- and regional-based goals and objectives will drive these decisions. If we project that the valley will be hotter, do we introduce species that are genetically predisposed to survive in hotter climates? It seems so. As the San Joaquin Valley's climate looks increasingly like the Mojave Desert's and the San Joaquin Desert inevitably expands its footprint northward, we need to consider how the long-term health and survival of species will be best served within this rapidly changing landscape.

Softening the Blow to Farmers

As one farmer put it, "This [rewilding] only works if it pencils out for the farmers of the San Joaquin Valley." It is clear the economic impact of rewilding will play an important role in driving where and what areas are restored. Habitat hubs are one answer to the question of where we can optimize habitat restoration, species recovery, and groundwater sustainability while limiting the impacts to the agricultural economy. These hubs are places that are likely to be fallowed because of lack of surface water and reduced access to groundwater but that are also potentially good habitat for native plant and animal species if restored. The good news is that these hubs show that we can meet our habitat goals without displacing farmers from areas that are likely to be sustainable well into the future. We recognize that the habitat hubs are not the only places where rewilding could work. However, to be most successful and to limit the negative impacts to the agricultural community, any efforts will need to include basic conservation planning principles, such as aggregating retired and restored pieces to make habitat blocks as big as possible and locating these pieces close to existing habitat areas. The checkerboard approach to fallowing, which we saw during the most recent California drought, benefits neither farmers nor native species.

Ultimately, the social impact of rewilding matters as well and will influence how successful rewilding is for both nature and people in the valley. To be truly successful, newly rewilded areas will need to inspire and support local valley communities, because these will be the people who use and manage them well into the future. These will be the people who can ultimately tell stories about what the valley used to look like before rewilding and drive the policies that will be needed to support this vision over the long term.

Funding Rewilding in the San Joaquin Valley

Active restoration is expensive. Public money for restoration exists but is hard to get and may be even harder to get in the more challenging economic times after the COVID-19 pandemic. So, although federal and state funding will undoubtedly be part of paying for rewilding, it cannot be the only solution. What is the role of private funding? There is large private wealth in California and across the San Joaquin Valley. There may be philanthropic landowners willing to donate agricultural lands that are no longer farmable to support restoration projects that improve water and air quality or provide recreational opportunities to local communities. There may also be private funders outside the valley, inspired by a rewilding vision, who will want to support some of the first demonstration projects. However, these sorts of funding mechanisms are unlikely to support rewilding at the scale we have described in this book. To do that, we need land use policies that generate consistent funding—potentially tied to clean water and air initiatives—and the development of compatible land uses that generate income while helping to fund restoration. One of these land uses will be solar energy. The state of California continues to lead the country in solar energy development and has committed to have all electricity produced by renewable sources by 2050. The San Joaquin Valley has been identified as one of the key regions in the state for solar energy development. Our rewilding vision could harness this interest to develop partnerships between private landowners (who own lands no longer able to be farmed in the SGMA era), local and regional governments (who are concerned about and depend on tax revenues from agricultural land uses), agencies of the state of California (who control transmission line development), permitting agencies, and solar companies. These partnerships would allow us to more efficiently design solar energy projects on portions of land that can no longer be sustainably used for farming but that have been identified as being important for rewilding and species recovery. For example, a portion of the funds generated from solar energy development would go to the farmer, to offset losses to farm income, another portion to habitat creation, and finally a portion to local counties to support the tax base, a win–win–win opportunity.

New Partnerships and New Examples about Engaging Local Communities to Effect Change

One of the most impactful parts of this book is the diversity of partners who came together from the nonprofit, government, private, and academic sectors to share their expertise in, experiences with, and hopes for the San Joaquin Valley. But we know that no matter how great the collaborative engine was for this book, implementing this vision requires new and much more diverse partnerships. We will need to forge partnerships with the agricultural sector, water and irrigation districts, the newly formed groundwater sustainability agencies, legislators and elected officials, funding agencies, and philanthropists. Most importantly, the people who live and work and have cultural roots in this landscape need to be core partners. It is also important that local stakeholders are inspired by this vision and that they help create it and own it. This vision must be embraced in ways that connect it to local, regional, and statewide policy and to long-term funding efforts that are committed to make the valley sustainable and a place with clean air and water and healthy communities. Importantly, this vision itself will evolve over time as more is learned. Therefore, the partnerships that support it will need to evolve as well. In closing, we want to highlight two examples from the book that illustrate how some of these partnerships may be developed: the Nature's Niños program at the Wind Wolves Preserve and the Kern Water Bank.

Nature's Niños focuses on bringing back native species, such as the Bakersfield cactus, to the Wind Wolves Preserve. It is important work because we need more hands to put plants in the ground, to collect seeds, to grow those seeds into plants, and to nurture those plants as they grow. But a coequal goal, and crucial for the long-term success of rewilding projects, is bringing local community members, often from disadvantaged communities, to the preserve (and to others like them in the future) so that they can be inspired by nature. As they watch the cactus that they planted grow into a towering adult, they may have "ah-ha" moments, experiences that build a local connection to the native plant and animal species around them. It is the appreciation of these special nature values that will cultivate the advocacy and leadership that are needed to make nature conservation an explicit part of a sustainable, healthy future in the valley.

Rewilding the San Joaquin Valley will necessitate projects that come in all shapes and sizes. Habitat creation does not pay for itself. And in some cases, farmers may not see habitat creation—at least initially—as compatible with their goals and objectives. That is why multibenefit projects that contribute to groundwater sustainability and local recreation while paying for restoration can be ideal. The Kern Water Bank is an example of that model. At almost 20,000 acres, the Kern Water Bank is massive, and duplicating it elsewhere in the valley may be as challenging as creating another 300,000-acre Carrizo Plain. But the Kern Water Bank demonstrates how landowners, through groundwater recharge, water storage, and conservation banking, can create water security in the valley while funding and creating high-quality habitat. Groundwater recharge is a popular topic in the valley right now. Demonstrating how to develop recharge projects in ways that allow for habitat creation, water storage (and long-term water security), and income generation is key to the success of our rewilding vision.

Conclusions

We write this book at a time of great economic uncertainty, a time of upheaval in our society, a time when the climate is changing and forcing us to think about how we make the right decisions for current and future generations so that they can live healthy, sustainable lives. In times like this, it is hard to be optimistic. And yet the public response to the COVID-19 pandemic and public demonstrations in response to racial injustice prove that we are capable of collective action at a scale we might have previously thought impossible. It inspires us to be optimistic about the future of the San Joaquin Valley. We strive to make this vision a reality because not doing so would mean letting go of this once-in-a-lifetime opportunity. We have a water crisis in the valley that will intensify as the population grows and the climate becomes warmer. We have a public health crisis in the valley that could intensify as more agricultural land is fallowed and more dust is created. We have a nature crisis in the valley that will probably get worse with urbanization and climate change. Yet the valley supports one of the world's largest agricultural economies, made up of farms big and small, operated by multigenerational families with long legacies in the valley who do not want to give up on that legacy and their role in feeding the world. We know rewilding portions of the valley will lead to great habitat gains for plant and animal species. But rewilding cannot just be about nature. Achieving the vision presented in this book will require that people's needs be met as well. The beauty of this vision is that, if it is planned for and executed in generous and collaborative partnerships across the region, ultimately the lives of people in the San Joaquin Valley will be lifted up on balance, rather than diminished. That is especially true for the disadvantaged communities who benefit least and suffer most from the challenges this region faces. Rewilding in the San Joaquin Valley will succeed only if it also leads to more sustainable agriculture, cleaner water and air, healthier human populations, and greater connections between the local populations that live and work in the valley and the diversity of plants and animals that make up the natural landscapes that surround them.

Contributors

Andrew B. Ayres

Andrew Ayres is a research fellow at the Public Policy Institute of California. He holds a PhD in environmental and natural resource economics from a joint program between the Bren School of Environmental Science and Management and the Department of Economics at UC Santa Barbara.

William Tim Bean

William Tim Bean is an assistant professor of biology at Cal Poly–San Luis Obispo. His research focuses on the spatial ecology and conservation of vertebrates.

Benjamin P. Bryant

Ben Bryant is currently a nonresident research collaborator with Water in the West at Stanford University, where he was previously a research scholar, also holding a courtesy affiliation with the Natural Capital Project. He specializes in modeling for decision support at the intersection of environment and economic development. He holds a BS in mathematics from Harvey Mudd College and a PhD in policy analysis from the Pardee RAND Graduate School.

Jennifer Buck-Diaz

Jennifer Buck-Diaz is a vegetation ecologist and botanist with the California Native Plant Society Vegetation Program, where she surveys, classifies, and maps vegetation across California. She earned both a BS and an MS in plant biology from the University of California, Davis.

H. Scott Butterfield

Scott Butterfield is a senior scientist for The Nature Conservancy, where he is the lead scientist for the Strategic Restoration Strategy and program lead for the Managing Partnership at the Carrizo Plain National Monument. Scott holds a PhD from Michigan State University.

Daisy Carrillo

Daisy Carrillo is the assistant preserve manager at Wind Wolves Preserve, the largest privately owned nature preserve on the West Coast. Her work has focused on habitat restoration and environmental education. She holds a BS in biology from the University of California, Los Angeles and a GIS certificate from California State University, Bakersfield.

Mitchell Coleman

Mitchell Coleman is a research botanist and land manager working with the Tejon Ranch Conservancy. He holds a BS in environmental biology from Westmont College and an MS in biology from California State University, Bakersfield and is currently a PhD student at the University of California, Riverside.

Brian L. Cypher

Brian Cypher is a research ecologist with the California State University–Stanislaus Endangered Species Recovery Program. He has been working on the ecology and conservation of rare species and their habitats in the San Joaquin Desert since 1990.

Ellen A. Cypher

Ellen Cypher has been involved in conservation, research, and recovery efforts for endangered plants and animals in the Central Valley and southern Sierra Nevada foothills since she joined the California State University–Stanislaus Endangered Species Recovery Program in 1992.

MELISSA DABULAMANZI

Melissa Dabulamanzi is the manager of Wind Wolves Preserve and has many years of experience in outdoor education. She holds a BS in ecology, behavior, and evolution and a minor in marine biology from the University of California, San Diego.

ALESSANDRO FILAZZOLA

Alessandro Filazzola is a postdoctoral fellow at the University of Alberta and has a PhD in community ecology. He is a community ecologist and data scientist who explores broad questions on our natural systems by using advanced quantitative methods.

SASHA GENNET

Sasha Gennet earned her undergraduate degree from Yale University and her MS and a PhD from the University of California, Berkeley in the Department of Environmental Science, Policy, and Management. She has worked in the private, public, and non-profit sectors on natural resource management, science policy, and agricultural research and conservation, and since 2008 she has been at The Nature Conservancy, where she currently directs the North America program on grazing land conservation and beef sustainability.

DAVID J. GERMANO

David Germano is a professor emeritus of biology at California State University, Bakersfield. He continues to actively conduct research to understand the life history traits and conservation concerns of reptiles and small mammals, especially turtles, lizards, and rodents.

BRIAN GRAY

Brian Gray is a senior fellow at the Public Policy Institute of California (PPIC) Water Policy Center and professor emeritus at the University of California, Hastings College of the Law in San Francisco.

He has published numerous articles on environmental and water resource law and coauthored numerous PPIC reports, including *Water and the Future of the San Joaquin Valley.*

ELLEN HANAK

Ellen Hanak is director of the Public Policy Institute of California (PPIC) Water Policy Center and vice president and a senior fellow at the PPIC, where she holds the Ellen Hanak Chair in Water Policy. She has authored dozens of reports, articles, and books on water policy, including many focused on the San Joaquin Valley, and was lead author of *Water and the Future of the San Joaquin Valley.*

ABIGAIL K. HART

Abigail Hart is a project director in The Nature Conservancy's California Water Program. Her work and research focus on stakeholder engagement and collaborative management of working landscapes.

JELENA JEZDIMIROVIC

Jelena Jezdimirovic is a research associate at the Public Policy Institute of California Water Policy Center. Her research interests include water marketing, water finance, and groundwater management. She is a coauthor of *Water and the Future of the San Joaquin Valley.*

T. RODD KELSEY

T. Rodd Kelsey is associate director of the Water Program at The Nature Conservancy California. He helps lead the conservancy's strategy focused on developing and expanding water management solutions to meet nature's and people's needs.

CLAIRE KREMEN

Claire Kremen is the President's Excellence Chair in Biodiversity and a professor in the Institute for Resources, Environment and Sustainability and the Department of Zoology at the University of British Columbia. Her current research and conservation work focus on identifying management practices at the farm and landscape scale that restore and regenerate biodiversity and ecosystem services in farming landscapes.

KENNETH D. LAIR

Kenneth Lair is a restoration ecologist and revegetation science practitioner through his consulting practice as Lair Restoration Consulting and formerly as lead restoration ecologist for the U.S. Department of the Interior Bureau of Reclamation and U.S. Department of Agriculture Natural Resource Conservation Service over a thirty-one-year federal career. He conducts revegetation research and practical field studies in disturbed land reclamation, in cooperation with federal agencies and conservation districts throughout California.

STEPHEN LAYMON

Stephen Laymon is a wildlife biologist for the Bureau of Land Management and was project manager at the Atwell Island Project for ten years. He designed and directed the habitat restoration activities on the 8,000-acre project.

CHRISTOPHER J. LORTIE

Christopher Lortie is a professor of ecology at York University in Canada and a senior research fellow at the National Center for Ecological Analysis and Synthesis, Santa Barbara, California. He has a PhD in community ecology. Chris is an integrative scientist with expertise in community theory, applied ecology, and quantitative methods.

MARJORIE D. MATOCQ

Marjorie Matocq's research program is focused on the population and evolutionary genetics of mammals across western landscapes. She is a foundation professor in the Department of Natural Resources and Environmental Science and the Program in Ecology, Evolution, and Conservation Biology at the University of Nevada, Reno.

María Florencia Miguel

Florencia Miguel is a postdoctoral fellow at the Argentine Dryland Research Institute of CONICET and has a PhD in biological sciences. She is a community ecologist who uses field work, statistical tools, and network ecology to evaluate ecological questions.

Peter Moyle

Peter Moyle is distinguished professor emeritus in the Department of Wildlife, Fish and Conservation Biology and associate director of the Center for Watershed Sciences, University of California, Davis. He has long research experience in restoration ecology, has authored or coauthored more than 275 peer-reviewed publications, and was a coauthor of Public Policy Institute of California's *Water and the Future of the San Joaquin Valley*.

Ryan E. O'Dell

Ryan O'Dell has been a natural resource specialist with the Bureau of Land Management Central Coast Field Office for thirteen years. His research includes a focus on endangered plant species recovery (including *Monolopia congdonii*) and San Joaquin Desert flora.

Landon Peppel

Landon Peppel is a resource conservation director at The Wildlands Conservancy, a California-based nonprofit that owns and operates nature preserves statewide. Previously, he was the preserve manager at Wind Wolves Preserve, a 93,000-acre nature preserve in the southern San Joaquin Valley from 2013 to 2019.

Scott Phillips

Scott Phillips is the GIS manager for the California State University–Stanislaus Endangered Species Recovery Program and a geography instructor at Clovis Community College.

Laura Prugh

Laura Prugh is an associate professor of quantitative wildlife sciences at the University of Washington. Her research focuses on the population and community dynamics of mammals.

Jonathan Q. Richmond

Jonathan Richmond is a wildlife geneticist working for the U.S. Geological Survey. His research emphasizes the use of genetic data to inform conservation efforts for a variety of reptiles, amphibians, and native freshwater fish in western North America, northern Baja California, and Pacific Islands.

Lawrence R. Saslaw

Larry Saslaw is a research technician with the California State University–Stanislaus Endangered Species Recovery Program. He is a retired wildlife biologist from the Bureau of Land Management. He has worked on San Joaquin Desert wildlife and ecosystems since 1985, now as an independent consultant.

Joseph A. Stewart

Joseph Stewart is a postdoctoral researcher at the University of California, Davis. His research focuses on ecological restoration, conservation, and climate adaptation in plants and animals.

Erin N. Tennant

Erin Tennant is an environmental scientist for the California Department of Fish and Wildlife. Her research interests include conservation of rare species and the ecology of the San Joaquin Desert.

Adrian L. Vogl

Adrian Vogl is a lead scientist with the Natural Capital Project at Stanford University. She specializes in spatial assessment of ecosystem services for sustainable land use planning. She earned a BA in cultural anthropology from the University of Arizona and a PhD in aquatic resources from Texas State University–San Marcos.

Brooke Wainwright

Brooke Wainwright is currently a master's degree candidate at the University of New Mexico investigating plant community change at the germination level. She holds a BS in field biology from Cal Poly, San Luis Obispo and is a former ranger at Wind Wolves Preserve.

Dustin A. Wood

Dustin Wood is a geneticist with the U.S. Geological Survey. His research activities span varied themes within the realm of conservation genetics and genomics, where he seeks to understand how historical and contemporary landscape and environmental change affect populations and shape evolutionary potential.

Index